Meeting the Standards in Secondary Science

A Guide to the ITT NC

Edited by Lynn D. Newton

Routledge
Taylor & Francis Group

LONDON AND NEW YORK

First published 2005 by Routledge
2 Park Square, Milton Park, Abingdon, Oxon OX14 4RN

Simultaneously published in the USA and Canada
by Routledge
270 Madison Ave, New York, NY 10016

Routledge is an imprint of the Taylor & Francis Group

Typeset in Bembo by Keystroke, Jacaranda Lodge, Wolverhampton
Printed and bound in Great Britain by Bell and Bain Ltd, Glasgow

British Library Cataloguing in Publication Data
A catalogue record for this book is available from the British Library.

Library of Congress Cataloging in Publication Data
Meeting the standards in secondary science: a guide to the ITT NC / edited by
Lynn D. Newton. – 1st ed.
  p. cm.
Includes bibliographical references and index.
(pbk. : alk. Paper)
1. Science-Study and teaching (Secondary). I. Newton, Lynn D., 1953 –
Q181.M396 2005
507'.1'2–dc22   2004022281

ISBN 0–415–23091–8

Meeting the Standards in Secondary Science

All students training to be teachers must demonstrate certain levels of skill and knowledge before attaining Qualified Teacher Status. The standards are very specific and this useful book addresses all the skills related to secondary science teaching, as well as some more general issues, that teachers will be required to demonstrate on qualification. Chapters include:

- Pupils' learning in science education;
- Progression in science education;
- The KS3 science strategy;
- Key skills in secondary science;
- ICT and secondary science;
- Career development and moving on.

Written in a clear and accessible style this is an essential read for anyone training to be a secondary science teacher and will be a useful resource for teacher educators and teacher mentors.

Lynn D. Newton is currently Director of Initial Teacher Training at the University of Durham.

Meeting the Standards Series

Series Editor:
Lynn D. Newton, School of Education, University of Durham, Leazes Road, Durham, DH1 1TA

Meeting the Standards in Primary English
Eve English and John Williamson (editors)

Meeting the Standards in Primary Mathematics
Tony Brown

Meeting the Standards in Primary Science
Lynn D. Newton

Meeting the Standards in Primary ICT
Steve Higgins and Nick Packard

Meeting the Standards in Secondary English
Frank Hardman, John Williamson, Mike Fleming and David Stevens

Meeting the Standards in Secondary Science
Lynn D. Newton (editor)

Meeting the Standards in Secondary ICT
Steve Kennewell

Contents

Illustrations

FIGURES

TABLES

Contributors

Sue Betts was for a long time a teacher of science in schools on Tyneside. She is now a part-time lecturer in science education at the University of Newcastle upon Tyne School of Education. Although trained as a chemist, she has developed an interest in the effective use of ICT, and carried out research for her Ph.D. into the use of ICT in secondary school science.

Alan Brennan is a biologist with an interest in freshwater ecology, the focus of his Ph.D. studies. He taught in London before moving to the North East where he taught science in a number of secondary schools in the region. He has recently moved from his post of head of department in a large comprehensive school to take on the role of science coordinator for the Redcar and Cleveland City Learning Centre in Eston, Middlesborough.

Judith Dobson has taught in all phases of education and moved from teaching in a middle school in Northumberland into the advisory service for Northumberland LEA as an advisory teacher for science and technology. She now works as a part-time lecturer in science education across primary, middle school and secondary level courses at the University of Newcastle upon Tyne School of Education.

Ahmed Hussain began his career as a university researcher, carrying out genetics-based research on plants. He later became a biology teacher in a large comprehensive school in Durham LEA. He is now a lecturer in secondary PGCE science at the University of Durham School of Education and is also involved in the work of the regional Science Learning Centre based in Durham.

Marion Jones is a lecturer in science education in the University of Durham, with responsibility for the Secondary PGCE science programme. She was previously head of science in a large comprehensive school in the North East of England. Her research interests include the Cognitive Acceleration through Science (CASE) project, which she introduced into secondary schools in one local LEA during a secondment as an advisory teacher.

Douglas Newton was a physics teacher for many years and Director of Science in a large comprehensive school before moving to the University of Newcastle upon Tyne where he is Professor of Science Education. He is also a Professorial Fellow at Durham University. He writes and researches widely on many issues in science education and teaching and learning, and is particularly interested in teaching for understanding.

Lynn D. Newton taught in schools and worked as an advisory teacher for science in Durham LEA before moving into initial teacher training. She worked initially at Newcastle University and is now at the University of Durham School of Education, where she is Director of Initial Teacher Training. She lectures, researches and writes on science education and is particularly interested in questioning in science (the focus of her Ph.D.) and effective communication in science more broadly.

Ros Roberts is a lecturer in science education and teaches biology and scientific evidence modules to undergraduate primary education students and to non-science specialists at the University of Durham School of Education. She is also course leader for the Masters' Degree Programme. Prior to that, she was based in Bristol, and taught biology in 11–18 comprehensive schools, FE colleges and university as well as PGCE science. Her research interests include the teaching of biological investigations, curriculum development in biology and environmental education, and Sc1 and concepts of evidence.

Frank Sambell is an ex-adviser for science for Northumberland LEA and part-time lecturer in science education at the University of Newcastle upon Tyne School of Education. Prior to that, he taught chemistry for many years in secondary schools.

Series Editor's Preface

This book has been prepared for students training to be secondary school science teachers who face the challenge of meeting the many requirements specified in the government's Circular 02/02, *Qualifying to Teach: Professional Standards for Qualified Teacher Status* (DfES/TTA, 2002a). The book forms part of a series of publications that sets out to guide trainees on initial teacher training programmes, both primary and secondary, through the complex package of subject requirements they will be expected to meet before they can be awarded Qualified Teacher Status.

Why is there a need for such a series? Teaching has always been a demanding profession, requiring of its members enthusiasm, dedication and commitment. In addition, it is common sense that teachers need to know not only what they teach but also how to teach it most effectively. Current trends in education highlight the raising of standards (particularly in the areas of literacy and numeracy), the use of new technologies across the curriculum and the development of key skills for lifelong learning. These run alongside the requirements of the National Curriculum, the National Strategies, PSHE and citizenship work, National Curriculum Assessment Tests (NCATs), interim tasks, GCSE examinations, new post-16 examination structures, BTEC qualifications. . . . The list seems endless. Such demands increase the pressure on teachers generally and trainee teachers in particular.

At the primary school level, since the introduction of the National Curriculum there is an even greater emphasis now than ever before on teachers' own subject knowledge and their ability to apply that knowledge in the classroom. Trainees have to become Jacks and Jills of all trades – developing the competence and confidence to plan, manage, monitor and assess all areas of the National Curriculum plus religious education. The increasing complexity of the primary curriculum and ever more demanding societal expectations make it very difficult for trainees and their mentors (be they tutors in the training institutions or teachers in schools) to cover everything that is necessary in what feels like a very short space of time. Four of the books in this series are aimed specifically at the trainee primary teacher and those who are helping to train them:

- *Meeting the Standards in . . . Primary English*
- *Meeting the Standards in . . . Primary Mathematics*
- *Meeting the Standards in . . . Primary Science*
- *Meeting the Standards in . . . Primary Information and Communications Technology*

For those training to be secondary school teachers, the pressures are just as great. They will probably bring with them knowledge and expertise in their specialist subject, taken to degree level at least. However, content studied to degree level in universities is unlikely to match closely the needs of the National Curriculum. A degree in medieval English, applied mathematics or biochemistry will not be sufficient in itself to enable a secondary trainee to walk into a classroom of 13- or 16-year-olds and teach English, mathematics or science. Each subject at school level is likely to be broader. For example, science must include physics, chemistry, biology, astronomy, and aspects of geology. In addition, there is the subject application – the 'how to teach it' dimension. Furthermore, secondary school teachers are often expected to be able to offer more than one subject and also to use ICT across the curriculum as well as ICT being a subject in its own right. Thus four of the books are aimed specifically at the secondary level:

- *Meeting the Standards in . . . Secondary English*
- *Meeting the Standards in . . . Secondary Mathematics*
- *Meeting the Standards in . . . Secondary Science*
- *Meeting the Standards in . . . Secondary Information and Communications Technology*

All the books deal with the specific issues that underpin the relevant TTA requirements identified in Circular 02/02. The very nature of the subject areas covered and the teaching phases focused upon mean that each book will, of necessity, be presented in different ways. However, each will cover the relevant areas of:

- subject knowledge – an overview of what to teach, and the key ideas underpinning the relevant subject knowledge that the trainees need to know and understand in order to interpret the National Curriculum requirements for that subject;
- subject application – an overview of how to interpret the subject knowledge so as to design appropriate learning experiences for school pupils, how to organise and manage those experiences and how to monitor progress within them.

The former is not presented in the form of a textbook. There are plenty of good-quality GCSE and A level textbooks on the market for those who feel the need to acquire that level of knowledge. Rather, the key subject knowledge is related to identifying what is needed for the trainee to take the National Curriculum for the subject and translate it into a meaningful package for teaching and learning. In most of the books in the series, the latter is structured in such a way as to identify the generic skills of planning, organising, managing, monitoring and assessing teaching and learning. The content is related to the specific requirements of Circular 02/02. The trainee's continuing professional development needs are also considered.

The purpose of the series is to give practical guidance and support to trainee teachers, in particular focusing on what to do and how to do it. Throughout each book there are suggested tasks and activities that can be completed in the training institution, in school or independently at home. They serve to elicit and support the trainee's development of the skills, knowledge and understanding needed to become an effective teacher.

Professor Lynn D. Newton
University of Durham
July 2004

1 Welcome to Your Teaching Career

LYNN D. NEWTON

Teaching is without doubt the most important profession; without teaching there would be no other professions. It is also the most rewarding. What role in society can be more crucial than that which shapes children's lives and prepares them for adulthood?

Teaching: A Guide to Becoming a Teacher (TTA, 1998, p. 1)

So, you have decided to become a secondary school teacher of science. You will no doubt have heard many stories about teaching as a profession. Some will have been positive, encouraging, even stimulating. Others will have been somewhat negative. But you are still here, on the doorstep of a rewarding and worthwhile career. Without doubt teaching *is* a demanding and challenging profession. No two days are the same. Your students are never the same. The curriculum seldom stays the same for very long. But these are all part of the challenge ahead of you. Teaching as a career requires dedication, commitment, imagination and no small amount of energy. Yet, despite this, when things go well, when you feel your efforts to help these students learn have been successful, you will feel wonderful. Welcome to teaching!

RECENT DEVELOPMENTS IN SECONDARY TEACHING

As with most things, the teaching profession is constantly buffeted by the winds of change. In particular, the past decade or so has been a time great change for all involved in the compulsory phases of education. At the heart of this change has been the Education Reform Act (ERA) of 1988. The Act brought about a number of far-reaching developments, the most significant of which was the creation of a National Curriculum and its related requirements for monitoring and assessment.

The curriculum thought to be appropriate for students of school age inevitably changes over time in response to social and political pressures, as different skills, competencies and areas of knowledge are valued. Although there have always been guidelines from professional bodies (such as teachers' unions), local authorities, examination boards and even official government publications, until 1988 teachers generally had freedom to decide for themselves *what* to teach and *how* to teach. Different approaches to curriculum planning and delivery have proved influential at different times. In England and Wales, the Education Reform Act provided for schools a formal curriculum policy and identified what was deemed essential for all students between the ages of 5 and 16. What the ERA did, from 1989 on, was to prescribe the *what*, the content in the form of a progressive curriculum. It did not specify *how* schools were to interpret and implement this curriculum policy, although guidance was given. Initially, this was in the form of various National Curriculum Council documents (see e.g. NCC, 1989). Later, various non-statutory Schemes of Work were provided (see e.g. QCA, 1996). Most recently, the various National Strategy Documents have been introduced (see e.g. KS3 Strategy for Science, DfES, 2002).

A series of reports have been published over the past two decades that have impacted on the teaching of science in secondary schools, largely arising from ongoing concerns about the quality and provision of science at this level. Probably the most influential was *Science 5–16: A Statement of Policy* (DES, 1985). Although produced long before the first version of the National Curriculum Order for Science (DES, 1990), it was prophetic in its vision. It paved the way for science to be a compulsory subject from 5 to 16 years of age, and identified the nature of the science curriculum necessary to meet the needs of modern society. It also identified ten criteria for good practice in science education which all teachers should meet, as relevant today as they were when they were first stated nearly twenty years ago.

1   *Breadth*: All students should experience a broad science curriculum, learning about science as a product, a body of knowledge, and about science as a process, a way of thinking and working. Opportunities and experiences provided by you as their teacher must support the students' development of mental and physical skills for investigation and experimentation as well as the acquisition of knowledge and the construction of understanding of living things, materials, forces, energy, and the Earth and its place in space.

2   *Balance*: All students should study science throughout their time at school, and the programme you devise for them should reflect a balance in the major components of science and also make provision for all students to have access to these components. The National Curriculum Order of Science selects *Life Processes and Living Things* [Sc2], *Materials and their Properties* [Sc3] and *Physical Processes* [Sc4] to represent the major components of biology, chemistry and physics. The Order also defines the skills and processes to be developed and practised in *Scientific Enquiry* [Sc1]. Each should be given a fair and reasonable representation in the science curriculum offered.

3   *Continuity*: If what has been achieved at each stage is not to be lost or devalued, it is necessary to establish links between the stages to ensure continuity. Most schools have structures in place to aid transition from one phase (or Key Stage) of education to the next. Structures are often concerned with reducing students'

worries about transition, but that alone does not bring about continuity in science experiences.

4   *Progression*: There are two ways in which the word *progression* may be used. First, it can refer to the course or programme of study for science, whether planned for a group, such as a single class, or for a whole year group or Key Stage. This kind of progression generally relates to the long-term planning goals. The second use of the term describes progression in experiences planned for individuals in order to support them in achieving their potential in science. This type of progression is more closely related to the short-term, specific learning or behavioural objectives or targets planned at the lesson level. The two are obviously related, although not interchangeable. Schemes of work or programmes of study in science, planned for the whole year group or Key Stage, should support increasing levels of skill, knowledge and understanding in science by individual students. This is generally what is thought of as progression.

5   *Relevance*: One aim of science education is to prepare students for life in an increasingly scientific and technological society. Students need to appreciate that science is a human activity which satisfies needs. The kinds of need which come to mind most readily are those that are associated with the application of scientific knowledge through technology. Students should be made aware that this involves difficult decisions which may have consequences that are beneficial, benign or detrimental. At the same time, science teachers must not neglect the other needs that science satisfies, personal needs such as satisfying curiosity and the need to understand the biophysical world. This is what makes it relevant, but the relevance may not always be made explicit by teachers.

6   *Differentiation*: This is a complex process that means different things to different teachers. In essence, the intellectual and practical demands made in science teaching should be suited to the abilities of students. Their prior experiences and abilities should be taken into account when planning new experiences. In the extreme, differentiation could involve a totally separate science education for some students. More commonly, it involves streaming or grouping by ability within a year group or class. In a more general sense, almost anything can be differentiated – the tasks and activities, the targets and outcomes, the resources to be used, and the nature of the support from or interaction with you as the teacher.

7   *Equal opportunities*: As a teacher of science, you need to plan and teach your subject so that every student in all of your classes has equal access to the range of experiences offered and can make progress in line with his or her potential, regardless of sex, race or ability.

8   *Links across the curriculum*: Science pervades all aspects of our lives and lends itself well to integrated experiences, whenever possible, crossing traditional subject boundaries and using a wide range of skills. One way to make the relevance of science more explicit is to take opportunities to link science experiences to other areas of experience and break down the compartmentalisation of subjects.

9   *Teaching methods and approaches*: Science involves the acquisition of mental and physical skills as well as procedural and conceptual knowledge and understanding.

It should be taught in ways that will enable both to develop. It is important that you recognise that there are many different teaching styles and ways of working to meet children's learning needs.

10   *Assessment*: As a teacher, you will be constantly judging what your students do in science. In the first instance, this is likely to be based on general impressions. An experienced teacher will quickly sense when things are going well or otherwise. However, there are times when such subjective judgements are insufficient and more objective evidence will need to be collected through the process of assessment. You will need to think about the purposes of the assessment. Why do you need the information? You will need to consider the methods that will collect this information most appropriately. Finally, you will need to consider how you will use the evidence. Internal and external requirements will also be influential in this process.

This preoccupation with progression in students' learning throughout the period of compulsory schooling and in all subjects resulted in the development of the idea of an official curriculum for England, Wales and Northern Ireland. Many other countries already had national curricula, so the idea was not new and there were models to draw upon. The focus of the National Curriculum is a 'core curriculum' of English, mathematics, science, and information and communications technology (ICT). This core is supported by a framework of 'foundation' subjects: art and design, design and technology, geography, history, modern foreign languages, music and physical education. In some Welsh-speaking areas of Wales, Welsh is included as a core subject, and in other areas as a foundation subject.

The National Curriculum Order for Science (DES, 1990) was generally, if cautiously, welcomed by science teachers. Initially grossly overloaded, with twenty-one separate attainment targets, the National Curriculum has undergone a sequence of judicial prunings to reduce the burden. The most recent revision was in 1999, when the content was further reorganised into four Programmes of Study. This has generated a slimmed-down document (DfEE/QCA, 1999b) which addresses some of the criticisms and concerns of teachers, and was accompanied by a promise that teachers would have a sustained period of calm.

THE STANDARDS DEBATE

Parallel to the changing perspectives on curriculum has been an increasing emphasis on standards. There has, in essence, been a shift in perspective from *equality in education* (as reflected in the post-war legislation of the late 1940s through to the 1970s) to the *quality of education*, the bandwagon of the 1980s and 1990s.

The term 'standard' is emotive and value-laden. According to the *Oxford English Dictionary*, among other descriptors of a standard, it is a weight or measure to which others conform or by which the accuracy of others is judged and also a degree of excellence required for a particular purpose. Both of these definitions sit well with the educational use of the term, where it translates as acceptable levels of performance by schools and teachers in the eyes of the public and the politicians.

Over the past decade, the media have reported numerous incidents of falling standards and the failure of the educational system to live up to the degree of excellence required for the purpose of educating our young in preparation for future citizenship. We teachers have, purportedly, been measured and found lacking. It was this, in part, which was a major force behind the introduction of the National Curriculum.

In 1989, when the National Curriculum was introduced, the Department for Education and Science claimed:

> There is every reason for optimism that in providing a sound, sufficiently detailed framework over the next decade, the National Curriculum will give children and teachers much needed help in achieving higher standards.
>
> (DES, 1989, p. 2)

One of the major thrusts underpinning changes over the past decade or so has been the question of how we measure and judge the outcomes of the teaching and learning enterprise. To produce the appropriately educated citizens of the future, schools of the present must not only achieve universal literacy and numeracy but must be measurably and accountably seen to be doing so, hence the introduction of league tables as performance indicators. David Blunkett, Secretary of State for Education and Employment, stated:

> Poor standards of literacy and numeracy are unacceptable. If our growing economic success is to be maintained we must get the basics right for everyone. Countries will only keep investing here at record levels if they see that the workforce is up to the job.
>
> (DfEE, 1997, p. 2)

While the economic arguments are strong, we need to balance the needs of the economy with the needs of the student. Few teachers are likely to disagree with the need to get the 'basics' right. After all, literacy and numeracy skills underpin much that we do with students in science and in the other areas of the curriculum. However, the increased focus on the 'basics' should not be at the expense of these other areas of experience such as science. Students should have access to a broad and balanced curriculum if they are to develop as broad-minded, balanced individuals.

All schools are now ranked each year on the basis of their students' performances in the standardised national tests and external examinations. While the performances of individual students are conveyed only to their parents, the school's collective results are discussed with school governors and also given to the local education authority (LEA). The latter then informs the DfES, which publishes the national figures on a school/ LEA basis. This gives parents the opportunity to compare, judge and choose schools within the LEA in which they live. The figures indicate, for each school within the LEA, the percentage above and below the expected level – in other words, the schools that are or are not meeting the standard. This results in inevitable conclusions as to whether standards are rising or falling. Such crude measures as Standard Assessment Tasks (SATs) for comparing attainment have been widely criticised, notably by education researchers such as Fitz-Gibbon (1996) who criticised the fact that such measures ignore the 'value added elements' – the factors which influence teaching and learning, such as the catchment area of the school, the proportion of students for whom English is an additional language and the quality and quantity of educational enrichment a child receives in the home.

There are also targets for Initial Teacher Training (ITT) to redress the perceived inadequacies in existing course provision. These centre on a National Curriculum for Initial Teacher Training which prescribes the skills, knowledge and understanding which all trainees must achieve before they can be awarded Qualified Teacher Status (QTS). It follows, therefore, that as a trainee for the teaching profession you must be equipped to deal with these contradictory and sometimes conflicting situations as well as meeting all the required standards. So how will you be prepared for this?

ROUTES INTO A CAREER IN TEACHING

To begin, let us first consider the routes into teaching open to anyone wanting to pursue teaching as a career. Teaching is now an all-graduate profession, although this has not always been the case. Prior to the 1970s it was possible to become a teacher by gaining a teaching certificate from a college of higher education. However, in the late 1960s and early 1970s, following a sequence of government reports, the routes were narrowed to ensure graduate status for all newly qualified teachers.

For many teachers in the United Kingdom this has usually been via an undergraduate pathway, reading for a degree at a university (or a college affiliated to a university) which resulted in the award of Bachelor of Education (B.Ed.) with QTS. Such a route has usually taken at least three and sometimes four years. More recently, such degrees have become more linked to subject specialisms, and some universities offer Bachelor of Arts in Education (BA(Ed.)) with QTS and Bachelor of Science in Education (B.Sc. (Ed.)) with QTS. Many other teachers choose to gain their degrees from a university first, and then train to teach through the postgraduate route. This usually takes one year, at the end of which the trainee is awarded a Postgraduate Certificate in Education (PGCE) with QTS. In all cases, the degree or postgraduate certificate is awarded by the training institution but the QTS is awarded by the Department for Education and Skills (DfES) as a consequence of successful completion of the course and on the recommendation of the training institution.

Which ever route is followed, there are rigorous government requirements which must be met both by the institutions providing the training and the trainees following the training programme before QTS can be awarded. In the 1970s and early 1980s, teacher training institutions were given guidelines produced by a group called the Council for the Accreditation of Teacher Education (CATE) . The guidelines identified key requirements which all ITT providers should meet to be judged effective in training teachers. Alongside the CATE criteria were systems of monitoring the quality of programmes.

During the late 1980s and early 1990s, there were a number of government documents which have moved ITT in the direction of partnership with schools. This has involved school staff taking greater responsibility for the support and assessment of students on placement and a transfer of funds (either as money or as in-service provision) to the schools in payment for this increased responsibility. Along with this responsibility in schools, staff have become increasingly involved in the selection and interviewing of prospective students, the planning and delivery of the courses and the overall quality assurance process.

More legislation culminated in the establishment of the Teacher Training Agency (TTA), a government body which, as its name suggests, now has control over the nature and funding of ITT courses. This legislation is crucially important to you as a trainee teacher, since the associated documentation defines the framework of your preparation for and induction into the teaching profession. So how will the legislation affect you?

REQUIREMENTS ON COURSES OF INITIAL TEACHER TRAINING

In 1997, a government circular (DfEE, Circular 10/97) introduced the idea of a centrally prescribed curriculum for Initial Teacher Training to parallel that already being used in schools (DfEE, 1997). This was to be a major development in the training of teachers. In the circular there was an emphasis on the development of your professionalism as a teacher. This implies:

> more than meeting a series of discrete standards. It is necessary to consider the standards as a whole to appreciate the creativity, commitment, energy and enthusiasm which teaching demands, and the intellectual and managerial skills required of the effective professional.
>
> (DfEE, 1997, p. 2)

At the heart of this is the idea of raising standards. Circular number 10/97 had specified:

1   the Standards which *all* trainees must meet for the award of QTS;
2   the Initial Teacher Training curricula for English and mathematics;
3   the requirements of teacher training institutions providing courses of Initial Teacher Training.

Subsumed under the first set of criteria were groups of standards relating to the personal subject knowledge of the trainee, criteria related to his or her abilities to apply the skills, knowledge and understanding to the teaching and learning situation, and criteria related to the planning, management and assessment of learning and behaviour.

In April 1998, the DfEE issued Circular number 4/98, *Teaching: High Status, High Standards*, in which the Secretary of State's criteria were revised and extended. As well as generic standards for the award of QTS, the new document specified separate national curricula for initial teacher training in English, mathematics and science at both primary and secondary levels, and a national curriculum for the use of information and communications technology in subject teaching to be taught to all trainees, regardless of phase focus. The fundamental aim of this new National Curriculum for ITT was to:

equip all new teachers with the knowledge, understanding and skills needed to play their part in raising student performance across the education system.

(DfEE, 1998, p. 3)

With uncanny parallels to the evolution of the schools' National Curriculum documents, Circular 4/98 proved to be an unwieldy document to handle, with hundreds of standards to be covered. A major revision occurred in 2001, resulting in yet another government circular to be operationalised by initial teacher trainers in autumn 2002. Circular 02/02, *Qualifying to Teach: Professional Standards for Qualified Teacher Status* (DfES/ TTA, 2002a), reverts to generic standards and lists the requirements in terms of:

1   Professional values and attitudes
2   Knowledge and understanding
3   Teaching – 3.1 Planning
                3.2 Monitoring and assessment
                3.3 Teaching and class management.

While Circular 02/02 identifies the statutory criteria to be met for the award of QTS, permeating these generic standards is the teacher's knowledge and understanding of relevant subject knowledge and subject application. This is further emphasised in the Teacher Training Agency's accompanying *Handbook*, which contains non-statutory guidance to supplement the *Standards for the Award of Qualified Teacher Status* (QTS) *and the Requirements for the Provision of Initial Teacher Training* (ITT) (DfES/TTA, 2002b). This is designed as a reference document and resource which sets out in greater detail the range of skills and knowledge relevant to each of the Standards, and covers pedagogical and subject knowledge and skills. Of particular relevance to you as a secondary science teacher is exemplification of the expected knowledge, understanding and skills relevant to:

- subject knowledge in science;
- the National Strategy for Key Stage 3;
- what should be expected in science of the Key Stages either side of your main focus (i.e. Key Stage 2 and post-16 provision);
- the expanding and flexible provision for 14–19-year-olds;
- understanding and practical application of the standards expected of students nationally and locally;
- the principles and practice of entitlement and inclusion for all students;
- core pedagogical skills (e.g. planning and teaching to clear objectives; setting students targets; interactive teaching; differentiation; assessment for learning; class organisation and management; behaviour management; and support for students with different educational needs).

So how does this affect you as a student teacher? In essence, it means that you must 'meet the standards' before you can be awarded QTS. One of the major tasks facing you as an entrant to the teaching profession is that of wading through dozens of standards and statements relating to your skills, knowledge and understanding. As a trainee, you must show that you have met these standards by the end of your training programme so as to be eligible for the award of QTS. Courses in universities, other higher education institutions and school-based programmes are all designed to help you to do so but the onus is likely to be on you to provide the evidence to show how you have met the requirements. This book, *Meeting the Standards in Secondary Science*, is designed to help you with this task, focusing on those skills and competences you will need to acquire to show that you have met the requirements for secondary science.

There is more to teaching science than simply having a good knowledge and understanding of the subject as it is often taught in universities. One of the major tasks ahead of you is to develop your knowledge of the whole range that is covered by the science component of the National Curriculum. This involves an appreciation of the nature of science and the development of scientific ideas over time. You will also need a knowledge of the full spectrum of 'broad and balanced science' – biology, chemistry, physics, geology and astronomy – so as to be able to teach not only single-subject science but also combined or double-award science programmes. Those of you coming to your training via a B.Sc. plus PGCE route may be familiar with some of these components but few will be prepared for all of them. Furthermore, you will need the ability to transform what you know and understand about science into worthwhile teaching and learning experiences for your students. You need to develop your pedagogical skills, knowledge and understanding. This is as important as your knowledge and understanding of the National Curriculum Order for Science. The latter provides you with a framework of *what* to teach in science. It does not tell you *how* to teach it – how to plan, organise, manage and assess the learning of the thirty or so students in class, each with varied and changing needs. This is left to your own professionalism. This book is designed to help you to make a start on this task.

AUDITS AND DEVELOPMENT OF SCIENCE SUBJECT KNOWLEDGE

Very few students on Initial Teacher Training programmes begin their courses with all the knowledge they will need to teach science effectively and often arrive with some apprehensions about teaching particular aspects of the subject. The ITT National Curriculum for secondary trainees states that all trainees need to be aware of the strengths and weaknesses in their own subject knowledge, to analyse it against the students' National Curriculum and examination syllabuses, and to be aware of gaps they will need to fill during training. It is likely that at an early stage in the course you will be asked to audit your subject knowledge against the Standards and identify strengths and areas for development.

There are different approaches to subject audits. At worse, they can take the form of a quiz which simply poses questions about decontextualised, isolated bits of knowledge and which embodies all the worst aspects of assessment in science (see Chapter 13). On the other hand, an audit that simply asks you to state whether or not your own knowledge of specific aspects of science is adequate may be unhelpful because it does not give guidance or means of determining what counts as 'adequate'. A balance between these two extremes is needed. It is important not to think of a subject audit as a 'one-off' exercise but as a focus for your own development throughout the course and during your teaching career. There are a number of possible approaches to an audit of your subject knowledge that you can use independently or collectively to achieve this desired objective of personal professional development. They are presented in the tasks below.

Rank ordering your science specialism

This approach represents a positive starting point because it asks you to think initially about the strengths in science that you bring to the course before concentrating on areas for development.

Task 1.1

1 Make a list of all the broad areas of science (e.g. physics, biochemistry, molecular biology, genetics).
2 Place these broad areas in rank order in terms of your own level of subject knowledge confidence. (*This task is not straightforward, since you may have specialised in geophysics but feel less confident with biophysics.*)
3 Use notes to record any specific observations about areas of strengths or areas for development.

These strengths need not be related only to your first degree, but may derive from other interests or professional or life experiences. They also serve to highlight the priority areas that need attention even though you may not, at the start of your training, have a real feel for the type of subject knowledge that is required. Members of a course can use the areas of science with which they feel most confident in order to provide support for others in a spirit of mutual support and collaboration. Having identified the areas of science with which you feel least confident, the *TTA Handbook* of support may then be used for a more detailed view of what is needed.

Self-audit related to the standards

The second approach asks you to audit your own level of subject knowledge confidence against the QTS Standards of Circular 02/02, particularly Section 2: Knowledge and understanding. It has the advantage of bringing together knowledge and the effective teaching of secondary science which we term 'pedagogical subject knowledge'.

> **Task 1.2**
>
> 1 Read through the Standards listed in Circular 02/02 and highlight all those that refer explicitly to subject knowledge.
> 2 Audit your own level of confidence against these highlighted Standards, identifying your 'comfort level' in terms of the gaps in your knowledge or skills.
> 3 Cross-reference your audit with the National Curriculum for Science at Key Stage 3 and Key Stage 4.
> 4 Set targets for your development and discuss these with relevant course tutors and subject mentors to determine how best to address the gaps identified (e.g. *supported self-study, observations, teaching specific topics*).

Audit through focused questions

The final approach to subject audits is more robust because it is less subjective, relying as it does not on self-assessment but on your responses to a set of test questions. You will need to purchase or borrow from the library the audit and self-study guide, *Science for Secondary Teachers* (Letts, 2002) and work through the sets of questions. The advantages of such an approach are that it is objective, and provides feedback and explanations on each set of questions as you work through them and advice on improving your subject knowledge. The danger is that, read in isolation, the questions can give the impression that subject knowledge is merely a matter of knowing facts.

Whatever method of audit is used on your own course, it is up to you to make the best use of the outcome by using it as a focus for your own development both during your training and in your teaching.

OVERVIEW OF THIS BOOK

As suggested above, very few students on ITT programmes begin their courses with all the knowledge they will need to teach science effectively. Nor are you likely to have expertise in the teaching and learning process, although you will all have experienced it in some shape or form. While such experience and expertise does vary from person to person, you all have one thing in common – *potential*. You have successfully cleared the hurdles of the application form and the interview and have been offered a place on an Initial Teacher Training course. Your tutors have decided that you have the necessary personal qualities which indicate that you are capable of acquiring the skills, knowledge and understanding needed to become an effective teacher. In other words, you have shown evidence that you have the *potential* to meet the Standards.

This book is designed to help you to do this, but it is only a part of the picture. It will be most useful to you if you read it in conjunction with the other experiences offered to you on your training programme. These will range from the theoretical to the practical in the following way.

- *Directed reading*: reading might be handouts related to lectures, books and articles for assignments or professional newspapers and magazines simply to broaden your own professional base;
- *Taught sessions*: these could take the form of formal lectures, informal practical workshops or combinations of either, whether in schools or in the institution;
- *Talks/discussions*: again, these could be held in school or in the institution and can range from formal structured seminars with a group to more informal one-to-one discussion, usually with the aim of integrating theory and practice;
- *Tutorial advice*: one-to-one sessions with a tutor, mentor or teacher to plan for and reflect upon your practical experiences;
- *Observations*: opportunities to watch your mentor or other experienced teachers at work in their classrooms;
- *Restricted experience*: opportunities to try out, under the guidance of your mentor or other teachers, limited teaching activities with a small group of students, perhaps building up to a whole class session;
- *Teaching practice*: a block placement where you take responsibility for the planning, teaching and assessment of classes of students, under the guidance of your school mentor and tutor and usually within defined parameters.

What is important about all of these experiences is the amount of effort you put into them. No one else can do the work for you. Your tutors, your mentors in school and other teachers can all offer you advice, guidance and even criticism, but how you respond is up to you. This, once again, is a reflection of your professionalism.

The book is written with the aim of giving you a general introduction to teaching science in secondary schools. Each chapter has clear headings and subheadings, so you can relate them not only to the QTS Standards but also to your institution's training programme for science and to the experiences you have in school. Throughout, whenever appropriate, there is reference to recent research into topics and issues in science education, directed tasks to help you consolidate your ideas and suggestions for further reading.

SUGGESTIONS FOR FURTHER READING

If you would like to explore further some of the issues touched upon in this introduction, the following books should be of interest to you.

Bennett, J. (2003) *Teaching and Learning Science: A Guide to Recent Research and its Applications*, London: Continuum Books
Bennett argues that teaching and research would both benefit from being brought closer together. She does this by synthesising relevant research findings in science education for the professional practitioner, highlighting the implications.

Hodson, D. (1998) *Teaching and Learning Science: Towards a Personalized Approach*, Buckingham: Open University Press.
Derek Hodson provides the reader with an interesting blend of the philosophy of science, cognitive psychology and motivation theory to extend the debate on contemporary science education.

Wallace, J. and Louden, W. (eds) (2002) *Dilemmas of Science Teaching*, London: Routledge Falmer.

The editors bring together in one volume sixteen contemporary issues in science education that are of relevance to any teacher of science. Each issue begins with a real case study provided by a classroom teacher. The issues raised in the case study are then discussed by academics and researchers in the field, who place the everyday classroom dilemma within a wider theoretical context.

2 What is Science? Why Science Education?

AHMED HUSSAIN

INTRODUCTION

Science has greatly influenced the evolution of society, and will profoundly affect its future development (Rotblat, 1999). Therefore, before we discuss the nature of the science education that constitutes a significant portion of the school curriculum, we need to consider the nature of science and the relationship between science and society. A brief history of secondary school science education will be provided as a context for the arguments for the inclusion of science within the National Curriculum.

WHAT IS SCIENCE?

It is generally believed that the word *science* originated from the Latin word *scientia* meaning *knowledge*. However, the contemporary view of science is ambiguous, often provoking different notions and criteria with which to classify disciplines as sciences (Ratcliffe, 1998). A common interpretation of science is that of a discipline by which an understanding is developed by employing a unique system of investigation and observation of the living, material, physical and technological components of the environment (Feynman, 1998). A dichotomy between the scientific knowledge and scientific practice frequently exists. The body of knowledge of which science is composed was gained by employing a philosophy comprising careful and rigorous observation, experimentation and deduction in order to produce a reliable explanation of phenomena. Karl Popper (1935) described scientific method as a 'rigorous experimental testing of ideas or hypotheses'. Professional scientists create new knowledge or use existing knowledge to create new materials or techniques for routine tests (Black, 1993). Their findings then go through a process of communication and checking before being accepted by the scientific community. A discipline must employ the above philosophies before general acceptance as a science.

A scientific revolution occurred during the sixteenth and seventeenth centuries resulting in a surge of scientific advancement (Hall, 1954). For example, Francis Bacon (1605) denounced previous approaches to scientific study and proposed a system of observation and experimentation to provide more influential and effective understanding of phenomena (Hall, 1954). Total reliance on rigorous observation and experimentation within science is, however, a comparatively recent phenomenon, although not all the work carried out prior to this must be dismissed (e.g. the work of Isaac Newton (1687)). During the eighteenth century, science developed at an enormous rate due to the widespread employment of contemporary philosophies, although the discipline was yet to be termed science and was instead referred to as *natural philosophy*. This discipline encompassed the full range of scientific fields and was carried out in the most part by well-educated, affluent members of society as a pastime. As the understanding and development within fields of natural, physical and material phenomena expanded, the discipline of natural philosophy needed recategorising. This resulted in the fields of science, which generally exist today, namely biology, chemistry and physics. Due to the adoption of rigorous scientific techniques, knowledge within the sciences increased dramatically, including the works of such eminent scientists as Mendeleyev (1869), Darwin (1859) and Mendel (1865), providing a sound foundation for the extensive scientific knowledge that exists today. Indeed, science has diversified to such an extent that it is difficult to discern which disciplines are true sciences. Discoveries in the early twentieth century were greatly facilitated by the advancement of technology; moreover, technology plays such an important role in contemporary science that it is difficult to separate them.

Feynman (1998) proposed that contemporary science consists of three concepts: first, a special method for attempting to understand phenomena; second, a body of knowledge arising from study, and third, new capabilities available due to the understanding gained from rigorous experimentation. The third aspect proposed that science possesses a technological appliance. Indeed, often within society it is the application of science that influences its development, most prominently in the fields of medicine and food production. It may be argued that the technological advances resulting from scientific knowledge are an empowerment of society by science and thus school curricula should focus on using science for public welfare and benefit (DeHart Hurd, 2002). The relationship between science and technology is often ambiguous since many contemporary fields of science are based largely upon technology (e.g. biotechnology (Ratcliffe, 1998)). Nevertheless, science has provided the understanding and capacity for technological advances.

To obtain a reliable model of natural and material phenomena, rigorous standards of systematic experimentation and observation are necessary. Furthermore, data must be presented in a salient and logical order pertaining to a hypothesis. However, such an approach to scientific study need not be without imagination or creativity (Black, 1993); indeed, proposing models on the basis of sound scientific understanding or extrapolation of existing data may still be recognised as scientifically acceptable. It is the methods of scientific study that are most frequently misunderstood by society. The thorough and objective approach adopted by scientists may be viewed as being cold, calculated and impenetrable. Often, it is the philosophy of scientific method that becomes interchangeable with science *per se*, with scientific research often accepted as fact or taken as proven despite the fact that research may result in only accepted theories. Indeed, Carr *et al.* (1994) reported that even science teachers frequently perceive scientific knowledge as an unproblematic means of providing truths, often believing textbooks as fact.

SCIENCE EDUCATION

The word *education* originates from the Latin word *educere* meaning to draw out, which concurs with the view of science teachers as facilitators of learning. Layton (1973) postulated that science education evolved in the early nineteenth century and consisted of two opposing views: first, that it should encapsulate everyday practices and the observation of artefacts; and second, it should be academic in nature in order to promote future scientists. The second viewpoint prevailed (Black, 1993); thus the formal style of traditional science education was established which involved learning many definitions, derivation and bland experiments on foregone conclusions, a practice maintained until the 1950s and 1960s. Subsequent reforms, stimulated by two events – the inferior scientific technology of the USA in the space race with Russia engendered a desire for better-educated students (McCormack, 1992) and the dissatisfaction of British teachers with science in schools (Black, 1993) – greatly influenced science education. These reforms, first, maintained the emphasis on preparing students for science by introducing a mechanistic and abstract curriculum. Second, epitomised by the Nuffield Foundation Project correlated with the introduction of the comprehensive school system in the UK, educational reforms introduced a change in teaching method with greater emphasis on practical work. But the failing streaming system and maintenance of an academic-centred curriculum resulted in growing dissatisfaction in science. Consequently, in the 1980s, reforms aimed to introduce a broader and more balanced science curriculum (SSRC, 1987). These changes were designed to make science accessible and meaningful to all students, even acknowledging the typical decline in enthusiasm for science observed in the transition from primary to secondary schools. The reforms to science education during the 1980s introduced the importance of scientific processes and skills, encouraging students to co-ordinate their own investigations and introduced relevance such as environmental issues.

The relationship between science and society greatly influences science education. It is unlikely, therefore, that science education will remain stable due to changes in scientific understanding (Dunne, 1998). In addition, more relevant pedagogy may arise or changes in the expectations of science education within society may affect the nature of science education (Black, 1993).

Perhaps the best means of introducing the topic of science education is to discuss its purpose and why it commands a high priority within the National Curriculum. Science education is compulsory and thus must be fully justified as being valuable, especially as under a quarter of students will study any science at a higher level and fewer still will be employed within a scientific field (Ratcliffe, 1998). The increasing involvement of science within the private, social and political spheres of society is often overlooked. Since the National Curriculum may provide a student's only exposure to science, this experience is vital if the student is to fully participate in society. The National Curriculum views science as an essential capability for an educated person and emphasises the importance for scientific literacy (NCC, 1993).

The term *scientific literacy* involves the capacity to seek out explanations of phenomena in accordance with an understanding of the methods used to test and evaluate scientific claims (Ponchaud, 1998). Driver *et al.* (1996) described a scientifically literate student as possessing knowledge and understanding of fundamental scientific concepts, having an awareness that scientific endeavours are human activities laden with values and exhibiting an appreciation of the process involved in scientific reasoning. Moreover, a scientifically literate citizen must comprehend the relationship between science and the economy, democracy and culture (Millar, 1996). It is imperative that scientific literacy enables a student to distinguish evidence, understand probabilities and evaluate statements or claims (Hurd, 1998). Furthermore, an understanding of science is necessary in a technological society, since it allows participation in social issues and encourages cultural development. Society demands knowledge of the function of medicines, electronic devices, effects of chemicals and drugs, nutritional value of foods, ecology of different habitats and the ethics of transplant surgery and genetics; all important values for citizenship. Science education is necessary to alter the many incorrect scientific preconceptions developed by children prior to arriving at secondary school (Wittrock, 1994).

It is indisputable that science is one of mankind's greatest achievements (Black, 1993). Therefore, it is necessary that the students whom we teach appreciate significant scientific advances and philosophies. Millar (1993) suggests that public understanding of science also comprises science as an institution.

Cross-curricular links that are developed in science education further validate its inclusion as a statutory subject within the National Curriculum. The separate disciplines within science possess differing philosophies. For example, those of biology frequently overlap with topics in social sciences (Black, 1993). Understanding scientific method provides transferable skills for an array of subjects (e.g. geography, English and mathematics (Fensham *et al.*, 1994)).

For science education to be effective, it must be accessible to all regardless of ability (Black, 1993). It is vitally important that the relevance of science education is introduced to students in a manner that inspires enthusiasm and enjoyment with the aim of providing a confident understanding of the topics studied. The science curriculum may be divided into six distinct components:

1   understanding key scientific concepts;
2   using scientific methods;
3   appreciating the contribution science makes to society;
4   science's contribution to personal development;
5   appreciating the powerful but provisional nature of scientific knowledge;
6   giving students access to careers in science and technology.

(NCC, 1989)

These components of science education are deemed important economically because there is a relationship between the level of public understanding and national wealth (Millar, 1996).

The present science curriculum attempts to relate science to the everyday lives of students. Teaching science in context by linking it to technology and society may promote relevance and stem the loss of interest (McGrath, 1993); however, there is a paradox that conceptual knowledge of science is necessary for an applied approach to science teaching. Relating science education to industry or technology may enable students to identify that their products are created from scientific knowledge (Millar, 1993). Such changes have been incorporated into curricula (QCA, 1999) with the aim of making science applicable to the varying levels of ability within each class (Reiss, 1998). The moral and social implications of science may also be taught in the context of relevance, aiming to inspire objective personal views on topics such as pollution.

Science education must contribute to personal and intellectual development (Ratcliffe, 1998). Providing your students with a basis for logical explanations may invoke confidence in their scientific ability and empower students with the capacity to make explanations. Moreover, encouraging initiative, decision-making and group work is suggested to facilitate future employment (White and Gunstone, 1989). Therefore, it is essential that students understand the nature of science as comprising not only conceptual knowledge but also observational, measurement and fair-testing skills facilitating the construction of accurate hypotheses. Encouraging your students to employ a scientific philosophy within society may promote a sceptical and questioning approach to experiences encountered, a favourable attribute in a society which is often exposed to the hard-sell mentality.

Science education is most successful when based on constructivist ideologies, providing a framework of knowledge and understanding whereby students interpret their experiences, build on existing ideas and apply them to new experiences. Baird (1986) suggested that a metacognitive approach to science education increases scientific understanding relative to passive approaches. Practical and field work is central to the principle of constructivist teaching, since it provokes motivation and curiosity (Black, 1993); moreover, scientific knowledge develops with contact to events culminating in the identification of patterns and construction of hypotheses (Kant, 1983; Driver et al., 2000). By coupling conceptual understanding and procedural skills such as interpreting data, hypothesising and data analysis, students may be given a platform of true scientific understanding. Thomas and Durant (1987) reported that some conceptual knowledge is required for a utilitarian understanding of science.

Therefore, science education may be considered to comprise two main facets: substantive and procedural, with substantive science comprising the underpinning structure of the subject while procedural science involves the notions pertaining to the collection, understanding and evaluation of scientific evidence (Gott and Duggan, 1998). Both theoretical and practical experiences are crucial in science education.

Students must be able to access, synthesise, codify and interpret the scientific information that increasingly pervades society, into civic and personal contexts (DeHart Hurd, 2002). Boujaoude (2002) claimed that within a democracy, citizens must appreciate science so that informed decisions may be made on a social, environmental and cultural level. Conversely, Shamos (1995) suggested that scientific literacy is a myth, as students rarely retain and use the knowledge gained through education.

The National Curriculum explicitly portrays its aims as promoting the development of scientifically literate students in an attempt to produce a scientifically literate society

(NCC, 1993). To achieve this, a comprehensive curriculum is prescribed. The curriculum comprises four sections, three dictating content pertaining to the main fields of scientific endeavour, while the remaining section defines the procedural aspects of science (Sc1). The scientific content of the National Curriculum comprises the main concepts associated with the physical, biological and material sciences. Sc1 involves studying scientific enquiry by considering ideas and evidence in science and developing investigative skills (QCA, 1999). The National Curriculum stipulates that students should be given an opportunity to appreciate how scientific ideas are presented and evaluated, different interpretations of evidence, the impact of values on science, and to consider the power and limitations of science.

The notion that future citizens will employ an evaluative approach to interpreting scientific issues raised within society is central to the ethos of scientific literacy (Jenkins, 1997). Therefore, it is imperative that students are capable of effectively interpreting evidence if they are to be deemed as being scientifically literate (Ratcliffe, 1999). The National Curriculum places a strong emphasis on evidence in terms of obtaining, analysing and evaluating, yet no attempt has been made to define the notion of evidence (Gott and Duggan, 1998).

Roberts (2001) described a need to improve student ability to 'think scientifically', and considered the need to explicitly teach the main concepts comprising procedural science; such as analysis and evaluation of evidence. The National Curriculum has developed the Sc1 component to try and invoke scientific thinking, while other initiatives have included CASE and Somerset Thinking Skills (Blagg et al., 1988; Jones and Gott, 1998). When CASE has been used to enhance the delivery of the National Curriculum, higher levels of Sc1 reasoning and superior GCSE results have been attained (Jones and Gott, 1998), thus illustrating the importance of both substantive and procedural understanding in science (Gott et al., 1999).

Holman (1986) proposed that we are all born scientists since we possess an inherent curiosity about the world around us; some people retain this curiosity, while others lose it, possibly because science education is too esoteric and removed from everyday life. Indeed, Claxton (1991) provides a damning report on science education, suggesting that the present system is failing, mostly due to the retained elite curriculum catering for able students as opposed to the masses, leaving the slogan of 'science for all' rather empty. However, the National Curriculum attempts to provide a breadth of scientific knowledge, which may be a weakness sacrificing depth. Future amendments to the science curriculum must address the lower proportion of girls who study science to a higher level. Indeed, in a study investigating teachers' views on the future of science education, Leach (2002) noted that the structure of the National Curriculum is not considered to prepare students to construct informed viewpoints about scientific issues. Moreover, the curriculum was considered to be remote, irrelevant and overcrowded, and thus limited time for developing student ability to evaluate and interpret scientific issues exists (Leach, 2002).

Science education is generally perceived by society as beneficial; however, the public understanding of science is lower than expected. Is a scientifically literate society attainable? It certainly appears easier to criticise science education than to improve it. The most apparent area for change within the current science curriculum is that it still only provides science for the few over a hundred years since this problem was identified.

CONCLUSION

Science is a unique discipline comprising three main facets: a methodology for obtaining rigorous data on phenomena, a body of knowledge ascertained by scientific methods, and new technologies generated from scientific knowledge. As a discipline, science has profoundly influenced contemporary societies, and thus demands significant attention within the National Curriculum. The inclusion of science within school curricula is justified by the need for students to appreciate the main principles of scientific knowledge, to understand scientific method for obtaining and analysing data and to acquire an awareness of the cultural significance of science within society. By developing an appreciation for the nature of science and the major principles that comprise scientific knowledge, students will exhibit the skills needed to interpret information with scientific content within society and thus act as effective citizens. Moreover, the skills developed through the study of science are applicable across the curriculum. Therefore, science education should provide students with a broad and balanced review of the main principles of scientific knowledge and opportunities to effectively develop an appreciation of scientific methods. Many educational reforms have intended to facilitate these aims, although the success of the current curriculum has been questioned. Nevertheless, science will remain a major component within school curricula.

Task 2.1

Without spending too much time thinking about it, write a brief statement of your immediate conceptions on what science is and what scientists do. Subsequently, compare your own views with the accepted views on the nature of science and the conduct of professional scientists. Repeat the first part again to review and revise any misconceptions on the nature of science and to enable you to embark upon science education with a more accurate perception of science.

Task 2.2

Make a list of a range of occupations and then categorise them into science and non-science disciplines. Consider the criteria you adopted in order to classify the occupations and relate these to your views on the nature of science.

Task 2.3

Collect a range of media articles on science. Review them and prepare an account of how science is perceived and reported upon within society. Use the discourse from studying media articles to reflect on the influence of science upon society.

SUGGESTIONS FOR FURTHER READING

If you would like to explore further some of the issues touched upon in this chapter, the following should be of interest to you.

Feynman, R. P. (1998) *The Meaning of It All*. Penguin Books, London
This collection of notes from lectures delivered by Richard Feynman addresses the questions of the nature and value of science and the relationship between science and religion.

Fortey, R. (1997) *Life: An Unauthorised Biography*. HarperCollins, London
Richard Fortey eloquently describes the history of the Earth and the evolution of the biological systems that now cover its surface. This book provides an elegant insight into how science can elucidate the complex, yet intricate, story of life on Earth.

Chalmers, A. (1999) *What is This Thing Called Science?* Open University Press, Buckingham
This is the third edition of an introductory textbook describing the philosophy of science. Alan Chalmers expressively introduces contemporary ideas pertaining to the nature of science.

3 Evidence – The Real Issues Behind Science 1

MARION JONES AND ROS ROBERTS

INTRODUCTION

One of the greatest changes to secondary science teaching came about with the introduction of the National Curriculum in 1989 (NCC, 1989). Within the National Curriculum Order for Science were two Attainment Targets (ATs): *Exploration of Science* (AT1) and *The Nature of Science* (AT17). Never before had teachers been required to teach 'the procedures of scientific exploration and investigation' and 'the ways in which scientific ideas change through time' (NCC, 1989). The revision in 1991 reduced the total number of Attainment Targets to four, with the above two included in the new Programme of Study 'Scientific Investigation' (now commonly referred to as Sc1) where it was stated:

> students should develop the intellectual and practical skills which will allow them to explore and investigate the world of science and develop a fuller understanding of scientific phenomena, the nature of the theories explaining these and the procedures of scientific investigation.
>
> (DES, 1991)

In 1995, Sc1 became *Experimental and Investigative Science* through which students were taught about experimental and investigative methods with the focus on obtaining and evaluating evidence. There was little mention of the nature of science, although it was covered in the generic issues (commonly referred to as Sc0).

In 1999, the National Curriculum (DfEE/QCA, 1999b) saw an adjustment to the language once again, with four Programmes of Study:

- Sc1 – *Scientific enquiry*;
- Sc2 – *Life processes and living things*;
- Sc3 – *Materials and their properties*;
- Sc4 – *Physical processes*.

The Programmes of Study set out what students should be taught at each Key Stage, the skills to be developed, knowledge to be acquired and understanding to be constructed. Attainment Targets (ATs) still exist, paralleling the Programmes of Study. They set out the expected standards of students' performance. It is left to staff in schools to decide how they organise their school curriculum to include all aspects of the Programmes of Study.

SCIENCE AND SCIENTIFIC ENQUIRY

Science involves more than just knowing the scientific facts about the world in which we live. It is an active mental and physical process through which we solve problems by gathering evidence and making sense of data to extend our understanding and explanations. This is what Wynn and Wiggins (1997) call the road to discovery. Nor, according to Wynn and Wiggins, does thinking and working like a scientist 'require incredibly precise, highly sophisticated, other-worldly logic' (p. 2).

In science, ideas which explain what we see in the world around us are not merely discussed and either rejected or accepted. Scientists try to put the ideas to the test and make judgements based on evidence. This procedure is a key feature of scientific investigation, and underpins thinking and working methodically in science.

Some people argue that there is no such thing as *the* scientific method. They suggest that scientific problem solving and discovery is just too complex to be described by any single, recipe-like method or procedure, carried out in a logical and systematic way. It is undoubtedly true that scientists are all different and have their unique ways of thinking and working. There are, however, some common elements to the ideas they use to evaluate evidence, which can be identified on reflection. It is these common elements which have given rise to the *concepts of evidence* (Gott and Duggan, 1995) which will be discussed below.

If you look in any book on teaching science, you will come across descriptions of methods and procedures which may be used to put ideas to the test as we try to explain events in the world around us. They are usually in the form of flow diagrams, showing a sequence of stages or actions, and the suggestion is that they have certain features in common:

1   Something is noticed or *observed*.
2   A tentative *hypothesis* is created to explain what is observed.
3   The hypothesis is used to make a *prediction* about the event.
4   An *experiment* is carried out to test the prediction.
5   A *conclusion* is reached as to whether or not the hypothesis is valid.
6   If not, then a *re-test* is carried out to check a revised hypothesis.

It is important to emphasise that it is *a* method and not *the* method, since it must, of necessity, be flexible. Not all of these stages will be carried out by all scientists when solving practical problems. However, this is a model of science as a way of working that has been adopted by Sc1.

The procedure (or 'method') is often shown as a cyclical one, since testing ideas and collecting evidence does not always lead to an acceptable or clear-cut solution. Sometimes more questions are raised for investigation or new phenomena are noticed. According to Wynn and Wiggins (1997, pp. 107–8),

> Observation and experimentation are the 'facts' upon which scientific hypotheses are based. Although observation precedes hypothesis formation and experimentation follows prediction, when a hypothesis needs to be recycled, the experiments are included as observations leading to the recycled hypothesis.

CLARIFYING THE TERMINOLOGY

The view is taken here that practical science, ultimately, is about solving problems, be they to create new knowledge, to answer empirical questions, or to make something, or to make that something work. Gott and Mashiter (1991) proposed a model for problem-solving in science that has been modified by Roberts (2004), shown in Figure 3.1. The diagram presents a pared-down model of the content-based demands of science. It is intended, quite deliberately, to act as a skeleton for development and *not* as an all-encompassing model.

In this model, solving a problem in science requires a synthesis of two sets of understandings, each with its own knowledge base: a *substantive understanding* (such as the concept of a force or the theory of natural selection) and an understanding of the ideas required to interpret and analyse evidence – a *procedural understanding*. The mental processing involved in putting the ideas together in the scientist's head may vary according to the context of the problem. For instance, sometimes the problem being solved is so similar to previous problems that familiarity with the ideas and approach used means that there is minimal decision making required and, in effect, the scientist is following a 'protocol'. In solving completely novel problems, the solution may have to be designed from scratch, drawing on skills, substantive ideas and procedural ideas in a far more complex way. In many situations past experience enables the scientist to select and adapt previously conducted protocols which seem to be intermediate in these other extremes.

If you look in books to do with teaching science you will find that some authors refer to skills, others to processes and some to process skills. The terms are very often used rather loosely, in an interchangeable and confusing way. In this model, the term *skills* is restricted to activities that can be improved with practice (such as setting up apparatus, drawing a table or graph, or reading an instrument). The model emphasises the ideas that are required to interpret and analyse evidence which we would argue need to be taught rather than just picked up with practice.

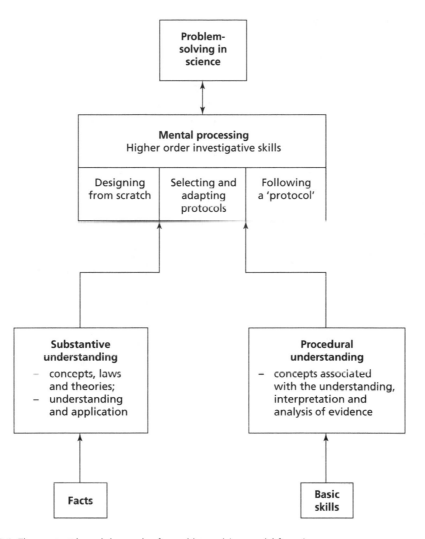

Figure 3.1 The content-based demands of a problem-solving model for science

EVIDENCE IN SCIENCE

> Understanding evidence is a central part of science and of informed decision-making in everyday life. As technology advances and more 'critical thinkers' are required, science education has a duty to enable students to examine the quality of scientific evidence.
>
> (Gott and Duggan, 1998, p. 98)

Understanding evidence has been emphasised in the National Curriculum for Science. Yet one of the major difficulties in experimental and investigative work in science is planning an investigation which will yield worthwhile evidence. This is probably because,

as Gott and Duggan comment, there has been no attempt to define what exactly constitutes an understanding of evidence. They suggest that there are two aspects of evidence
to be considered. First, there is an understanding of the *quality* of the evidence to be
considered. Second, there are factors which influence making decisions *about* evidence
to be taken into account.

Evidence can take a variety of forms, from descriptive notes (which rely on subjective
observations, guesses and estimates) to tabulated data (which rely on standardised measures
and formats). How valid and reliable the evidence is, and how acceptable it will be to
others in the scientific community, will depend upon the care, control and accuracy
used in collecting the evidence. Validity refers to the extent to which you can answer
'Yes' to the question, *Is the evidence really answering the question I think it is answering?*
Reliability relates to the extent to which you feel sure you can answer 'Yes' to such
questions as, *Is the data to be trusted? If I do it again, will I get similar results?*

To this end, carefully planned procedures (which include controlling variables and
fair testing), the use of appropriate measuring instruments both to observe and gather data,
and the use of standardised units for recording results, can all help with the process of
obtaining evidence.

How the evidence is recorded and presented is also important. Skills in the use of
recording sheets, designing suitable tables for recording data, and constructing graphs
and charts (perhaps with the help of a computer package) are all relevant. They enable
patterns and trends to be seen more easily when the evidence is being considered. As
much time should be spent considering evidence and explaining the findings as in
collecting it, since this is the essential precursor to reaching a conclusion. The aim is to
demonstrate whether or not the evidence answers the question posed.

CONCEPTS OF EVIDENCE

Within Sc1, the latest version of the National Curriculum for Science reintroduces the
'ideas and evidence in science' strand. This includes a consideration of:

1a   how scientific ideas should be presented, evaluated and disseminated;
1b   how scientific controversies can arise from different ways of interpreting
     empirical evidence;
1c   ways in which scientific work may be affected by the contexts in which it takes
     place, and how these contexts may affect whether or not ideas are accepted;
1d   the power and limitations of science.

(Taken from DfEE/QCA, 1999b, p. 46)

Underpinning all of these considerations are the concepts of evidence.

Task 3.1	Look at this statement 2h from Sc1:

'Make sufficient relevant observations and measurements to reduce error and obtain reliable evidence.'

What does this mean to you? How many is sufficient? What is a relevant observation? What does error mean? How can you reduce it? What is reliable evidence? Have you ever been explicitly taught any of this?

The above exercise may have shown you just how much there is to understand about the issues involved in Sc1. The important point to realise from this exercise is that just as in the key areas of biology (Sc2), chemistry (Sc3) and physics (Sc4), there are key, underlying concepts involved with this Programme of Study that need to be identified, understood by you as the teacher and then explicitly taught to your students. These underpinning concepts have been termed *concepts of evidence* (Gott and Duggan, 1995). A summary of these concepts is given in Table 3.1[1] and some are introduced and discussed briefly below.

Table 3.1 The concepts associated with evidence (design – variables and values, fair test and the sample size)

Variable identification: independent and dependent variables which define the experiment. Variables have values which may be words (categoric) or numbers (continuous)

Fair test: control variables and the 'control experiment' in biology

Sampling and sample size: its effects on the estimate of the characteristics of the population

Variable types: categoric, discrete and continuous

Relative scale: choosing sensible quantities to give accurate data

Range and interval: choosing sensible values to identify, unambiguously, the pattern in a relationship

Choice of instrument: to give the necessary sensitivity, accuracy and repeatability

Repeatability: repeating measurements (sampling the behaviour of variables) to get an estimate of the associated errors

Accuracy: how it links to ideas of repeatability, choice of instrument

Tables: their use as organisers

Graph types: their link to the nature of the variables

Patterns: collecting sufficient information to portray the pattern in a relationship

Multivariate data: the effect of many independent variables and the ways of separating out those effects

Interpretation: of first- and second-hand data

Running throughout – RELIABILITY AND VALIDITY

Concepts associated with design

Factors that can change are called *variables* – for example, in looking at physical human characteristics, hair colour is a variable. It varies from one individual to another. Hand span is another variable. To describe the variable we use the term *value*. In the example of variable hair colour the values could be black, brown, blonde or red, while in the variable hand span we can measure it with a ruler and the value would be numeric. There is a difference in these two types of variable. A variable that has values which can be described by labels are called *categoric* variables, while the sort of variable that can have any numerical value is called a *continuous* variable. There is another type of variable called a *discrete* variable when the value can only be an integer multiple, for example, the number of offspring produced.

When conducting an experiment or investigation we are usually looking for a relationship (or the absence of a relationship) between two variables. For example, to answer the question, 'Does a red spot squash ball have more bounce than a blue spot squash ball?', we are looking at the relationship between the type of ball and the bounce height. The variable ball type (a categoric variable) is the one that we change and is called the *independent* variable. The bounce height is measured for each type of ball and is called the *dependent* variable (in this case it would be a continuous variable). In schools that use the Cognitive Acceleration in Science Education (CASE) project materials these variables may be referred to as the input and outcome variables which describe what they do (Adey *et al.*, 1995). In carrying out the investigation there will be other variables to consider too, which may or may not influence the results. In the above investigation the surface of the floor could be important, as could the temperature of the balls. These variables will need to be held constant or kept the same, and are called the *control* variables (or fixed variable).

To be certain that the results of an investigation are really down to the effect of changing the independent variable on the dependent variable, all the other relevant variables must be held constant, with only the independent being allowed to change. This is called the *fair test*. It is also important to recognise that there will be variables that will not impact on the outcome of an investigation and need not be controlled. Many chemistry and physics-based investigations are easily manipulated to identify the independent/dependent/control variables and a fair test carried out; however, biology experiments are sometimes different. Field study data or long running studies can be described as a fair test if the conditions change for all elements.

Task 3.2

In an investigation to find out if brown sugar dissolves more quickly than white – what is the independent variable, the dependent variable and how would you make it a fair test?

A *sample* is one or more measurements taken from all of the possible measurements that could be made, for example, measuring the height of a cress seedling in a tray of cress. The *size* of the sample could be important in considering how true the result is –

the greater the number of readings taken, the more likely they are to be representative of the population, so the more cress seedlings measured the more closely we get to the height of the population. Obtaining a *representative sample* is important too – an appropriate sampling strategy must be used (random/stratified/systematic).

Concepts associated with measurement

Relative scale refers to the decision relating to the values chosen for the independent and control variables; for example, it would not make sense to try to dissolve huge amounts of solute in a small amount of solvent in an investigation about dissolving. Nor would it be sensible to have a very narrow mass range (e.g. 0.1 g, 0.11 g), since the *range* of the values for the independent variable has to be wide enough to detect any pattern in the dependent variable with the *interval* between values small enough so the detail of the pattern may be seen, with a sufficient *number* of intervals to make out this pattern.

Task 3.3

If you were to extend the investigation in Task 3.2 to see if the temperature of the water mattered – what would the *range* of water temperature be, and what size *interval* would you have?

In many schools the choice of instrument is governed by what is available but it is important to consider which instrument is most appropriate. For example, in measuring 15 ml water it would be better to use a 25-ml measuring cylinder than the 100-ml one! It is one of nature's facts that repeated readings of the same quantity with the same instrument will never give exactly the same answer (*repeatability*). The more repeat readings you do the closer the average will get to the 'true' value. The *precision* of the measuring instrument is the degree to which you can read the instrument; for example, a digital stop-watch will give you a reading accurate to one-hundredth of a second. However, unless it has been calibrated this reading may not be accurate. *Accuracy* is a measure of how true the value is.

Concepts associated with data handling

By convention we record results in tables, but these can have more uses than just 'somewhere to write the results'. Tables present information about the experiment design. The first column of the table is the independent variable with the column headed with the name and units (if appropriate), and the values of this variable in the cells in that column. Depending upon the nature of these values we can determine if this is a categoric, a discrete or a continuous variable. The number of values chosen reflects the range and interval. The second column is the dependent variable with a similar description. However, it does not give any indication of the control variables or measurement techniques.

Independent variable (unit)	Dependent variable (unit)
Value	Value
Value	Value

Graphs are used to display the data recorded in the table, with the independent variable on the x axis and the dependent on the y. When the independent variable is categoric and the dependent continuous a *bar chart* is drawn; for example, if the time taken for different types of sugar to dissolve had been recorded. If both variables are continuous then a line graph is drawn to allow for interpolation and extrapolation; for example, if the time taken for a quantity of sugar to dissolve in water of different temperatures had been recorded. Using a graph enables you to see if you have collected enough data to see the *pattern* clearly.

Task 3.4

What sort of graph would you draw for the data collected in Task 3.2? Task 3.3? Why are they different? Why is the second graph type more useful?

Overarching concepts

To be satisfied that the outcome of an investigation is 'true', all aspects of the investigation have to be evaluated in terms of reliability and validity. In addressing the two questions *Are the data reliable?* and *Are the data valid?* ideas associated with making each measurement should be considered. The evaluation should also include a consideration of the design of the investigation, the ideas associated with the measurements, the presentation of the data and the interpretation of patterns and relationships.

SUGGESTIONS FOR FURTHER READING

If you would like to explore further some of the issues touched upon in this chapter, the following should be of interest to you.

Gott, R. and Duggan, S. (1995) *Investigative Work in the Science Curriculum*, Oxford: Oxford University Press
This book provides an excellent overview of the research into the teaching of investigative skills and the explanation of 'concepts of evidence'. Further details may be found on Gott, R., Duggan, S. and Roberts, R., http://www.dur.ac.uk/richard.gott/Evidence/cofev.htm.

Gott, R. and Duggan, S. (1998) 'Understanding scientific evidence – why it matters and how it can be taught', in M. Ratcliffe, *ASE Guide to Secondary Science Education*, Glasgow: Stanley Thornes
This chapter is a useful summary of the 'understanding of evidence' and the rationale for teaching it explicitly in order to produce an 'informed citizen'.

Roberts, R. and Gott, R. (2002) 'Collecting and using evidence', in D. Sand and V. Wood-Robinson (eds), *Teaching Secondary Scientific Enquiry*, London: ASE/John Murray
This chapter illustrates how some of the ideas of evidence may be applied in secondary school science.

4 The Living World

ROS ROBERTS

INTRODUCTION

Biology is an active enquiring science. Working biologists, whether in academic or research institutions, working in hospitals or out doing fieldwork, draw on both substantive and procedural ideas while doing their work. The procedural ideas needed for biology are considered in Chapter 3.

Some of the major substantive ideas that are necessary to be able to understand the detail of *Life Processes and Living Things* (Sc2 of the current National Curriculum for Science) are going to be considered here. These form a *conceptual framework* for an understanding of biology. They underpin the thinking of biologists but are not always made explicit in texts or in school. The framework may be used to make sense of the diversity of biology and the myriad detail that is specific to Sc2. These notes, therefore, are about the framework in which the detail of Sc2 may be understood. There are many texts (such as Roberts (1991) or Jones and Jones (1997)) that could be used as a source of detailed information about the content of Sc2 if you feel you wish to explore these ideas further.

LINKS WITH THE IDEAS OF CHEMISTRY AND PHYSICS

At their most basic level, biological systems are composed of substances that interact. The interaction of the substances in biological systems may be explained by the substantive ideas used in chemistry and physics. The living world may be described at this level and, indeed, to be able to understand biological systems, an understanding of chemistry and physics *is* necessary. There are, however, biological phenomena that are a consequence of the way biological systems work. Some of the ideas that may be used to explain these phenomena are considered here. They form the framework on which the detail may be built.

A SYSTEMS APPROACH: MAINTENANCE AND CHANGE

Biology is a diverse science. Genetics, evolution, animal behaviour, plant physiology and microbiology are just some of the areas studied by biologists. How can we make sense of this diversity? One approach is to consider phenomena that affect all biological systems, regardless of their level of complexity; two phenomena will be considered here: the ideas of maintenance and change.

Biological systems

Different levels of organisational complexity are studied in biology, and this is reflected in the National Curriculum. The systems we need to consider are, with increasing levels of complexity:

- chromosomes and their genes
- cells
- whole organisms
- populations and communities
- ecosystems

Although we consider all these to be *biological* systems, only cells and organisms are *living* systems. A living system is a homeostatic, self-regulating system whose function is to maintain itself, the system. (We shall consider *how* this takes place later.) It is the active maintenance of its integrity that makes a living system different from other systems. By 'integrity' we mean that the entity is in an organised state whereby it can carry out the processes it needs to (from the idea of integrity meaning 'wholeness' or 'oneness'). It is important to understand a living system as an entity, a self-maintaining unit. All living systems are discrete entities that have boundaries which delimit them from the external environment. The size of an organism as an entity differs, from the single cell of a bacterium to the huge structures of a whale or an oak tree, but all are *discrete* entities.

Other biological systems differ from these living systems in that they are not *actively self-maintaining*, nor are they discrete entities with boundaries (although Lovelock's 'Gaia hypothesis' (1979) considers the Earth to be a living system). The distinction between living systems and other biological systems is important when we consider maintenance and change in systems.

Task 4.1

- Look up the definitions of all the systems mentioned above. What are their main components?
- Which of these systems is most emphasised in the National Curriculum?

In biology, in each of these systems, we study two things: how conditions are maintained and disruptive change is prevented, and the causes and consequences of change in the system.

An understanding of these two phenomena, which affect all biological systems, provides a robust conceptual framework to which the details of each system may be added. It enables us to 'see the wood from the trees'. In the following account, we will try to develop a basic understanding of these phenomena and consider how they may be applied to the different biological systems. A point worth noting is that since each of the systems listed is intricately associated with the other systems, what happens in one system will affect other systems. Thus what happens in the genes of an organism can eventually affect the whole Earth as an ecosystem and, in turn, factors in the ecosystem can affect the genes of individual organisms. This is discussed further at the end of this chapter, but it should be borne in mind as you read this next section.

How conditions are maintained and disruptive change is prevented

All biological systems have processes acting to maintain the system, correcting any disruptive changes that might occur. The following are examples of this in each of the biological systems.

- At the level of *chromosomes*, there are processes that act to correct most of the damage which may occur in the molecular structure of the DNA. A change to the sub-units of the DNA, caused by radiation or reaction with certain substances, may be corrected by processes initiated by the chromosome. DNA is a self-repairing molecule.
- *Cells* are able to maintain themselves. The concentration of substances inside all living organisms' cells is different from that outside. Substances need to be taken into the cell in the right quantity to maintain this difference and cells have to be able to get rid of substances that would upset the composition of the cell. All living cells are able to maintain a difference between their internal and external composition. This self-maintenance involves the cell in chemical changes. For instance, some substances (such as hormones or ions such as Na+) are moved into and out of the cells by a series of chemical changes involving proteins in the membranes around the cells. Cells are membrane-bound systems. They also contain membranes inside them which act to compartmentalise the cell contents and function as transport systems. The membranes are very fragile. They too need to be maintained. If damage to membranes cannot be repaired the cell will be unable to maintain itself. The synthesis of new substances and structures to maintain cells is vital for the cell.
- Living *organisms* carry out various chemical changes that enable them to maintain themselves. They do things to keep themselves in a state that enables them to carry on maintaining themselves. Some organisms, for instance, are able to carry out their chemical changes only if their cells are maintained at a nearly constant

temperature. Birds and mammals are able to maintain the temperature of their bodies. They have ways to conserve heat energy and have mechanisms to lose heat if the internal temperature rises above the optimum. An inability to keep conditions around their cells at or near the optimum results in the cells, and consequently the organism, not working properly. All organisms need to take in substances that enable them to carry out the chemical changes necessary for self-maintenance. For instance, most animals take in oxygen and substances derived from their food. Plants take in substances for photosynthesis and use the products, along with minute traces of substances from the soil, to maintain themselves. Whatever the substance, it needs to arrive at the organism's cells in the quantities necessary for the cells to be able to maintain their conditions. All organisms have evolved structures and mechanisms to be able to maintain their supply of essential substances. For instance, plants require light energy to be able to raise the energy level of an electron in a chlorophyll molecule so that carbon dioxide can react chemically with water to make glucose and oxygen. They can move their leaves to optimise the amount of light falling on them and they grow towards the source of the light. Plants also control the balance between glucose production by photosynthesis and the use of glucose by the plant. Organisms that consume others also behave in such a way that they optimise their intake of the substances that they require. Many organisms act to control the conditions surrounding their cells by altering the composition of the fluid in contact with the cells.

- The size of many *populations* is often maintained at a fairly constant level over a period of time. The population size of many predators is controlled, at least in part, by the availability of food, and the size of the prey's population is determined by the rate of predation and the availability of its food source. The long-term consequences of this are populations that remain at fairly constant levels. Competition occurs for resources, and individuals able to compete best can self-maintain and survive.

- At the *ecosystem* level there is evidence that, during the Earth's history, levels of substances, such as carbon dioxide in the atmosphere, have fluctuated within certain limits. Interactions in the ecosystem occur, involving living organisms and their surroundings, that result in the maintenance of fairly constant conditions.

So, in all of these systems, we can identify a phenomenon that acts to prevent disruptive change in the system and results in maintenance of the system. The mechanism by which each of these forms of control acts is called negative feedback.

Task 4.2

Look at Sc2 in the National Curriculum document and map on to it each of the examples mentioned in the paragraphs above.

NEGATIVE FEEDBACK MECHANISMS

Active self-maintenance occurs in living systems, both at the level of the cell and the whole organism. This self-maintenance depends on detection–correction mechanisms which use negative feedback. These mechanisms detect any change from the optimum required conditions (known as the set point) and act to correct that change. In other biological systems, such as populations or ecosystems or even on the molecular scale, there is an analogous phenomenon; a dynamic equilibrium is established where systems react to counteract change. The ideas of negative feedback may be used to explain this; negative feedback acts to correct any change but, in contrast to living systems, the set point does not have a value that is 'optimum' for the system. Living systems have the capacity to use negative feedback to restore conditions to the optimum to enable the system to survive. In other biological systems negative feedback occurs, but there is no level that is optimum for the system.

The controversial Gaia hypothesis, put forward by James Lovelock, proposed that the Earth could be considered as a single, self-regulating, *living* system, in which both the biotic and abiotic components are shown to interact in such a way that they are able to maintain conditions as 'a fit place to live' (at least in the broadest sense, not necessarily the anthropocentric (people-centred) sense). As a living system, the Earth should be controlled by homoeostatic processes. Lovelock proposes that the fluctuations seen in the Earth (such as in atmospheric gases, surface temperature and the acidity and alkalinity of the oceans) provide evidence that supports such an hypothesis. In particular, Lovelock drew attention to the discovery that over many millions of years the heat output from the sun had increased to a level that should have made the Earth too hot for life. However, Lovelock suggests that as the earth heated up, plants evolved and spread over the Earth taking in carbon dioxide from the atmosphere, so cooling the Earth by allowing more outgoing radiation. Vegetation provided the necessary feedback to control the Earth's temperature (Job, 1999). There is some support from eminent scientists (such as Lynn Margulis) for this view, sometimes called 'Earth System Science'.

Negative feedback is the mechanism that acts to correct a change in the value of a variable in a system, whether that is the light intensity in the eye, the concentration of sodium ions in a cell or the number of rabbits in a population. In many biological systems negative feedback mechanisms are extremely complex. Many negative feedback mechanisms involve diverse components which, in the case of living systems, are controlled and integrated to bring about the self-maintenance. The interactions that result in long-term fluctuations in carbon dioxide levels in the atmosphere are still not understood. Feedback at the molecular level, for instance, in the control of the production of a digestive enzyme in bacteria, is comparatively quite simple. However, regardless of the detail, the maintenance of systems occurs through negative feedback.

The principle of negative feedback can be illustrated by the maintenance of the correct temperature in an oven. Suppose a thermostat is set to maintain an oven temperature of 200 degrees Celsius (200°C). If the temperature is below this value, a current is sent through the heating elements and heat energy is transferred, causing a rise in temperature. If the temperature rises above the set point, the current is switched off and the temperature drops. Thus the oven is maintained at or near the set point by a process of negative feedback (Figure 4.1).

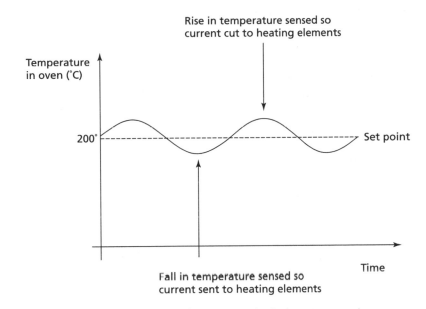

Rise in temperature sensed so
current cut to heating elements

Fall in temperature sensed so
current sent to heating elements

Figure 4.1 The results of negative feedback acting to maintain the temperature in an oven

To be able to maintain the value of any variable in a *living* system, some component of the system (at whatever level) has to be able to 'detect' or 'sense' the variable and bring about a response which changes the value of the variable to bring it back to the set point or optimum. In whole organisms we can often identify the components of the feedback mechanism: the sensor or receptor, the regulator or control centre, the effectors that bring about the response and often a means of communication between these components. Without any part of that mechanism functioning properly, the value of the variable would not be able to be controlled and change would occur. The consequences of this will be considered below.

Task 4.3

For this exercise you need to work with a friend. Each person in turn should do the following while the other should note his or her observations.

1 In a clear space, away from any obstacles, stand as still as you can on one leg with your arms out horizontally.
2 Stand like this for one minute.
3 Note any observations about movements made or sensations felt while doing this.
4 After a brief rest, repeat the exercise but this time with your eyes closed.
5 Discuss your observation with other members of the group.

You were told to stand still. This was the condition that you had to maintain. Draw a flow diagram of what took place when you did this with your eyes open.

The second exercise, with your eyes closed, may have given you some clue as to how you were able to maintain your balance. Discuss in your group how you were able to sense when you were not maintaining conditions (there may have been more than one sensor involved) and what you did to restore conditions.

Here are some specific examples of negative feedback in different systems.

● The single *cell* of an *amoeba* involuntarily takes in water by diffusion if it is put into fresh water. To prevent this intake from damaging the system, excess water is collected in membrane-bound 'bubbles' known as contractile vacuoles. These move to the surface of the cell and expel the water to the outside. The faster water enters, the greater the rate of formation of contractile vacuoles. Cells in multicellular organisms also use negative feedback mechanisms. They are able to maintain a concentration gradient of ions across the cell membrane, an active process that, in mammals at least, is estimated to use about half of the ATP (adenosine triphosphate, see p. 46) the organism produces from respiration. (The importance of respiration is considered later.)

Task 4.4

Draw and annotate the feedback loop for the amoeba.

During the time it takes for a contractile vacuole to form and ultimately empty, draw two sketch graphs showing:

● the amount of water in the cell;
● the size of the contractile vacuole.

● Whole *organisms* use negative feedback. Some of the 'activities' in this chapter are examples at this level and most textbooks describe human examples. However, *all* living organisms use negative feedback to prevent disruptive change occurring, not just mammals. Most plants have evolved so that their roots grow down in response to gravity. To be able to respond to gravity the plant must have some way of detecting the direction of the force. It is believed that large starch grains in the cells at the tip of the root change their position in response to gravity. If the root position is changed from vertical to horizontal, the plant responds to the change in direction by the upper side of the root growing more quickly than the lower surface. This unequal growth restores the direction of growth to the vertical. The exact mechanisms which initiate this growth response are not completely understood.

Task 4.5

The amount of light falling on the light-sensitive cells in the retina of a mammalian eye is controlled by negative feedback.

Identify the sensor, regulator, effectors and the means of communication used in the feedback loop that controls light intensity in the eye.

Draw three sketch graphs showing (1) the light intensity outside the eye; (2) the light intensity inside the eye; and (3) the size of the pupil while someone is in a room with normal lighting and then a brighter light is suddenly turned on.

● Negative feedback may be seen acting at the level of *populations*. The size of the population of cod in the North Sea is determined by variables that limit the size of the population; both density-independent factors such as the temperature of the water or levels of pollution, and density-dependent factors such as their food supply, infectious disease or predation and fishing. Fluctuations in the population around the 'carrying capacity' are determined by density-dependent factors. Since species interact with each other, whole *communities* are also affected by complex and changing interactions, but none the less often exhibit a high degree of stability as a result of negative feedback (Figure 4.2).

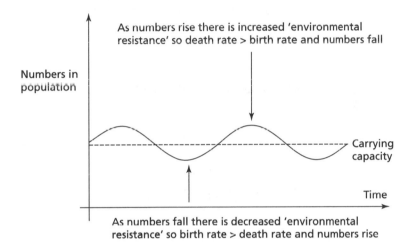

Figure 4.2 The results of negative feedback acting to maintain the size of a population

Since the ability of any living system to self-maintain is ultimately dependent on the 'programme' in its genes (since the genes code for the production of proteins that affect the functioning of the system), systems that survive must have the genes that 'programme' for successful self-maintenance. By the same argument, systems that fail are not as successful at self-maintenance, whether it is because they succumb to disease, cannot run fast enough or cannot compete as successfully for a resource. So what are the features of successful living systems?

Cells and organisms have negative feedback mechanisms that enable the system to respond to change and correct it. They also have structures that are produced by the system that help to prevent change affecting the system in the first place.

Let us consider the difference between *passive structures and active mechanisms* for self-maintenance, using the mammalian eye as an example. The mammalian eye is able to detect light. It must be maintained in optimum conditions for the light-sensitive cells to function at their best. Many factors could change the conditions in the eye. Over millions of years, organisms have evolved structures that reduce the effect of these changes. Bony eye sockets limit the damage to the eye from blows. Eyebrows help to maintain optimum conditions for sight by directing sweat away from the eye. The tough white sclera helps to maintain the shape of the eyeball. All of these are structures that are produced by the organism and help to maintain optimum conditions in the eye by protecting the eye from change, but the structures themselves do not respond directly to changes. Active mechanisms, on the other hand (such as blinking or changing the size of the pupil when the intensity of the light changes), are able to respond to a change and act to maintain the optimum conditions for the eye.

Task 4.6

In Sc2 there are several examples of structures found in living systems whose function is to help maintain the system. List the structures specified and, for each state, how it enables the system to prevent change from affecting it.

THE CAUSES AND CONSEQUENCES OF CHANGE IN THE SYSTEM

The discussion so far has considered how relatively stable conditions are *maintained* in systems by *correcting* or *preventing* change from affecting the system. However, biological systems are all subject to change, whether relatively short term or over the millennia. Again, it is worth distinguishing between living systems (cells and organisms) and other biological systems.

- In *cells* and whole *organisms* there are *three* distinctly different causes of change. First, there is the normal genetically 'programmed' change. For instance, growth and maturation are changes that occur in an organism. They occur in a controlled fashion with the integration and co-ordination of many processes. They are changes that maximise the chances of the individual being able to maintain itself and survive. Second, change in the system can be the result of a system being unable to correct the disruptive change, either because there is no mechanism functioning to restore conditions or because the conditions are outside the range that the usual negative feedback mechanisms can correct for. This will cause a change in the system. Third, an uncorrected change may occur in a gene on a chromosome, thus affecting the 'programming' of the cell, so that a novel protein may be made, which may or may not enhance the chances of the organism's survival.

- Biological systems such as *populations, communities and ecosystems* are also subject to change because of change to the individuals that make up the populations and communities. The creation of a lake by geological or human processes enables aquatic plants to colonise. As they take in substances from the water, affect the light penetration and accumulate dead material on the bottom, conditions change. This will affect the numbers and types of plants growing there. The presence of these populations and communities of organisms in an area will slowly alter the conditions there. This change to the environment, by the organisms living there, makes the conditions more suitable for other species. Competition results in the earlier populations being replaced by others. Thus communities change over long time-scales, a process known as succession.

From your own experience and from texts, list some examples of succession and explain how the organisms present at each stage cause the environment to change and become more suitable for other species.

Humans often deliberately disrupt succession in order to manage habitats for conservation. Look up some examples of this.

A genetic change in an individual can ultimately affect whole populations and communities. Any change to the individual will affect the way in which the individual functions. This in turn will affect its survival. If the genetically different individual has an advantage over others and this advantage can be passed on to its offspring, populations and whole communities may ultimately be affected by this genetic change.

So, biological systems do change. During a period of change, negative feedback mechanisms are not acting to correct any change (although in the case of living systems, 'programmed' change is under other forms of control, which we will not consider here).

EXAMPLES

In a **living system**, a change to the value of a variable in the system means that the system will not be operating under optimum conditions. If the value deviates too far from the optimum it may result in the breakdown of the system. This is what happens during illness and death. It can occur for different reasons.

In living systems (cells and whole organisms) which have evolved to self-maintain using negative feedback, their negative feedback mechanisms will only work successfully within a range of external conditions. There are limits to the value of an external variable that can be successfully corrected. If the value exceeds the level that negative feedback can correct for, there will be disruptive change.

Detection-correction mechanisms can only function within a *range of conditions*. For instance, body temperature in humans can be maintained at or around 37 degrees Celsius (37°C) so long as the external temperature is within certain limits. If the temperature outside the body is very high no amount of sweating or drinking can restore the internal temperature to 37°C and the body's temperature rises dangerously, perhaps even leading to death. Similarly, in extremely cold conditions the body may be unable to produce and conserve enough heat energy to be able to maintain the internal temperature at 37°C. This results in a change from the optimum and hypothermia sets in which, if uncorrected, leads to death. Deviation from the set point that is too extreme or lasts for too long can result in the disintegration of the system.

At the cell level, if a substance diffuses into a cell at a faster rate than the cell is able to expel it, conditions inside the cell will change. Thus for all the myriad variables that an organism can detect and correct, there are limits to the range of values for each variable that can be tolerated. If external conditions are outside the range that the detection–correction mechanisms can cope with, the internal conditions will change. If this change is to a variable which could damage the system, the inability to maintain the value of the variable at or near the optimum will result in the death of the system.

Task 4.8

Draw three sketch graphs showing (1) the light intensity outside the eye; (2) the light intensity inside the eye; and (3) the size of the pupil while someone is in a room with normal lighting and then very intense spotlights are shone in their eyes, then the light is returned to normal, after which the room is plunged into darkness.

All living systems are, by definition, able to self-maintain in the conditions under which they are naturally found. If they didn't, they'd be dead! Biology studies the success stories – organisms that are living are successful at maintaining themselves in the conditions under which they are normally found. We say they are adapted to a particular set of conditions. Since self-maintenance can only take place within a range of conditions over which the detection–correction mechanisms can function adequately, the distribution of organisms may be seen to be governed by the limits of the mechanisms for self-maintenance.

Task 4.9

In a freshwater stream, the types of organisms found upstream and immediately downstream from a sewage outfall are different. How is each type of organism adapted to the conditions in which it is found?

What would be the consequences of a clean-water organism being swept downstream to the polluted site? Try to explain your answer with reference to self-maintenance.

Factors outside the system can bring about a change. Infections in mammals caused by bacteria and viruses are usually controlled by a negative feedback mechanism involving the production of substances in the blood that restore the level of the pathogens to the set point. However, some diseases cannot be controlled in this way. Fatal diseases such as forms of, say, plague or meningitis are caused by organisms that the body is unable to control. Similarly, toxins could be considered to be any substance whose levels cannot be controlled by the system, either because the system has no mechanism to control them or because the levels are outside the range that the feedback mechanisms can cope with. The inability of many plants, for instance, to maintain their conditions in places such as spoil heaps, by getting rid of excess metal ions from their cells, will disrupt the functioning of the cells and may result in death. Bacteria can be killed by antibiotics. Plants can be killed by herbicides. These are substances that cause changes to the organisms that cannot be corrected.

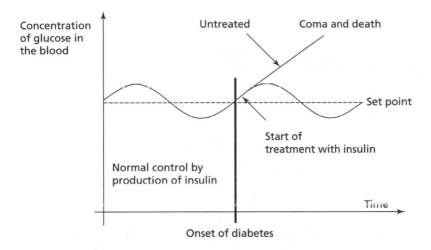

Figure 4.3 The control of blood glucose before and after the onset of diabetes mellitus

Sometimes disruptive change occurs when a component in a negative feedback mechanism fails to function. This is the case with diabetes mellitus. Insulin is normally produced by the body as part of the mechanism to control the level of glucose in the blood. If insulin production is disrupted the negative feedback will not work, causing a rise in blood sugar levels. Administration of insulin by injection is an intervention that aims to restore the component in the negative feedback mechanism. Untreated diabetes would result in death if the level of blood glucose accumulated to such an extent that the system was damaged (Figure 4.3).

Change in *population* size shows a similar pattern as a consequence of change to one of the factors that was limiting the population. A rise in a population will cease when some density-dependent factor is in short supply, or when there is a change in a density-independent variable. However, predicting when that will occur is very difficult. The exponential growth of the human population is an example. Similarly, a drop in the size of a population might lead eventually to loss of the species from a given area or even extinction. With complex and little-understood systems, predicting the consequences of change is very difficult. Witness the debate on global warming! (Figure 4.4).

Predicting the consequences of change is not just a problem for us when we consider large systems. It has particular relevance to living systems when we are trying to determine whether they are alive (Figure 4.5).

IS IT ALIVE? IS IT DEAD?

If you compare a fish swimming in a tank with one laid out on a fishmonger's slab, you can see that the living fish is doing things that the dead one isn't. If you observe a tree in winter you'd find it much harder to determine whether it was living or not. We often describe what living things do, for instance, moving, taking in substances and

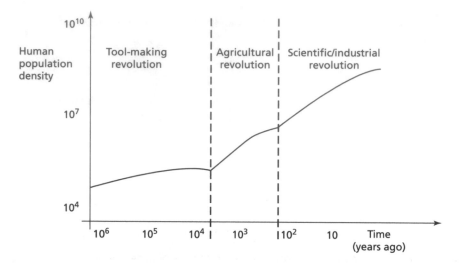

Figure 4.4 Log plot of three major phases in the growth of the human population

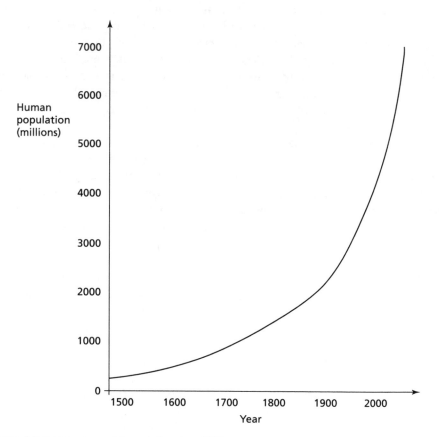

Figure 4.5 Increase in world population since 1500

so on, but all we end up with is a list of things living organisms can do without really understanding why these contribute to an understanding of what we mean by living.

To be able to answer the question 'Is it alive?' we must be able to understand that, to be living, an organism must be maintaining its conditions within certain limits. (If it is 'healthy' it is able to maintain optimum conditions. However, changes from the optimum can often still be tolerated; the system may not be healthy but it is still living.) Then, we need to determine whether the thing in question is *actually* maintaining itself at that time.

To see whether something is alive means that we have to consider time. Self-maintenance by negative feedback takes time. We have to see whether the system is correcting changes to variables so that it is maintaining itself. For many living systems with which we are familiar, we know, from past experience, when we can say conclusively that the system has permanently stopped maintaining itself. It is dead. However, when we consider some systems such as bacterial spores, dehydrated seeds or desiccated brine shrimp eggs, distinguishing between 'living' and 'dead' is not so straightforward.

How long it takes a living system to make the correction of the value of the variable depends on several factors. First, it depends on how quickly the value of the variable is changing. If living things have structures that act to reduce changes affecting the system, the change may be so slow that the time-scale needed to see if it is correcting that change can be very long. Dehydrated seeds or trees in winter are good examples. They have structures that reduce the effects of any change in the value of a variable on the system. Change occurs very slowly in these instances, and determining whether the system responds to the change and acts to correct it similarly takes a long time. Since some systems can tolerate a fairly wide range of values for a variable before initiating any correction mechanism, there can also be delays in determining whether the system *is* maintaining itself. Systems such as bacterial spores or brine shrimp eggs seem to stop all self-maintenance. However, they can 'revive' at a later date, often years, or even thousands of years, later. They seem to be in 'suspended animation'. How can you distinguish this from death? Can something that is in 'suspended animation' be considered to be either alive or dead? Answering the question 'Is it alive?' is not always easy. In some cases the answer may have to be 'Wait and see!'

Task 4.10   Many texts list the characteristics of living things. What do they claim they are? Do all living things show these characteristics? For instance, do all living things reproduce? Worker bees don't! How suitable are they, in your opinion, for developing an understanding of 'living'?

SELF-MAINTENANCE DEPENDS ON CHEMICAL CHANGES

Detection-correction mechanisms involve living systems doing things. They must be able to detect the value of each variable and be able to respond to it. Such responses in turn depend on chemical changes in the cells. Nearly all the chemical changes that occur in living cells only take place with the involvement of a substance called ATP (adenosine triphosphate). ATP has to be present for the chemical change to take place. During the reaction, ATP is chemically changed into a substance called ADP (adenosine diphosphate) and a phosphate ion. ATP concentrations are therefore depleted by the chemical changes involved in self-maintenance. Without ATP there can be no self-maintenance. Without self-maintenance there is no life. So, to be able to continue to self-maintain, an organism must be able to replenish its supplies of ATP. It does this in a series of chemical changes that are known as respiration. Respiration occurs in *all* living cells *all* the time and produces ATP essential for self-maintenance. ATP needs to be produced continuously. For instance, it is estimated that there is only 5 g of ATP in a human at any point in time but a person requires at least 40 kg of ATP in twenty-four hours; that requires a lot of respiration!

Since the production of ATP by respiration depends on a supply of substances (e.g. glucose and oxygen) to every living cell in their body, structures and mechanisms have evolved that result in organisms' cells having a good supply of these substances. The structures and mechanisms involved in the acquisition and distribution of these substances in an organism are studied in detail in Sc2. For instance, the structure and functioning of the lungs and digestive system in mammals are studied to show how substances are acquired by the animal. The blood and heart are studied for their importance in the transport of the substances to the cells, and the removal of substances that would be toxic if they were allowed to accumulate and changed the composition of the cells. Leaves are studied to exemplify the structures and mechanisms which plants use to acquire the substances they need for survival.

ATP may be used to determine whether an organism is carrying out chemical changes which bring about self-maintenance. Since ATP is not stored in living things it has to be continually produced by respiration. Often, one of the easiest ways to determine whether something is self-maintaining is to check whether it is carrying out respiration. The production and use of ATP is a good sign of chemical reactions occurring in an organism. Since self-maintenance involves chemical changes taking place, it is a good bet, but not a certainty, that production and use of ATP may be taken as a sign of self-maintenance.

Task 4.11

The above description of respiration does not use the term *energy* at all. Students are easily confused by this abstract idea which is often used in very unspecific ways in biology in particular. Look at biology texts and list all the different ways in which the term *energy* is used. Why might students get confused?

RELATING THE FRAMEWORK TO MORE FAMILIAR IDEAS IN BIOLOGY

This framework of maintenance and change in different systems may be used to understand many of the most important ideas in biology. The survival of an individual organism depends on its being able to maintain fairly constant internal conditions and responding to change. The distribution of individuals is governed by the range of conditions over which an individual can maintain itself. *Ecology*, the scientific study of organisms and their interactions with each other and with the environment, can be understood from a systems perspective. *Population dynamics* involve the ideas of maintenance and change; long-term changes to communities result in succession. *Evolution* of a species and of a whole ecosystem can be understood by considering the consequence of change, either to the genes of an individual or in the conditions surrounding the individual, resulting in the survival of organisms best able to maintain themselves in the conditions at the time. Over many generations organisms best able to maintain themselves will survive and pass on their successful genes to their offspring. An organism that is successful is said to be adapted. *Adaptation* is the end result of the successful production of proteins which are determined by an organism's genes. It is the consequence of the species' past history. Individual organisms cannot adapt.

Task 4.12	Draw a concept map of all the interactions that can happen which bring about change in a biological system.

Although the ability to produce new organisms by *reproduction* is not a property of all living organisms, the long-term changes that are the consequence of evolution depend on organisms reproducing. During reproduction new living systems are produced that contain genes from the parents. Organisms which are successful at self-maintenance in the given conditions tend to be the most reproductively successful, producing offspring with genes that enable self-maintenance.

LINKS TO SC2

The Programme of Study for Sc2 contains a lot of detail. The aim of this chapter has been to provide you with a framework of some biologically important concepts so that some of the detail may be understood.

Task 4.13	Map the ideas developed in this chapter on to KS3 and KS4 of Sc2.

The important ideas considered so far are that:

- biological systems have mechanisms to maintain the system;
- living systems are able to actively self-maintain;
- negative feedback acts to correct change;
- negative feedback in living systems will act only within a range of external conditions, and this limits the distribution of species;
- change is the result of negative feedback not functioning;
- organisms need ATP to carry out chemical changes necessary for self-maintenance;
- ATP is produced during respiration which requires a supply of substances;
- all an organism's activities are controlled, ultimately, by the production of proteins;
- protein production is determined by genes, sections of DNA;
- organisms that are successfully maintaining themselves must have genes which produce proteins that enable them to be successful;
- if the DNA in genes changes, different proteins will be produced;
- only proteins that allow self-maintenance will be present in reproductively successful organisms;
- over many generations organisms best able to maintain themselves will survive and pass on their successful genes;
- an organism that is successful is said to be adapted.

SUGGESTIONS FOR FURTHER READING

If you would like to explore further some of the issues touched upon in this chapter, the following books should be of interest to you.

Jones, M. and Jones, G. (1997) *Biology; Cambridge Coordinated Science*, Cambridge: Cambridge University Press

and

Roberts, M. (1991) *The Living World*, Walton-on-Thames: Nelson
These two books provide a thorough overview of the biology needed to teach Sc2 in schools.

Lovelock, J. (1979) *Gaia – A New Look at Life on Earth*, Oxford: Oxford University Press
For those interested in Lovelock's view of the Earth as a living system this is worth reading, especially the introductory chapters.

5 The Material World

FRANK SAMBELL

INTRODUCTION

The human race is adept at fashioning its immediate environment to meet its needs. This may be seen in the way the built environment matches the use of materials to their properties. The strength, under compression, of concrete and the tensile strength of steel are harnessed to make tall buildings stable. The resilience and non-slip nature of solidified creosote makes roads safer. The safe handling of electrical equipment often depends on the insulating properties of plastics, and the transfer of electrical energy is made possible by the electrical conductivity of metals, particularly copper and silver. However, these materials, which are so common now, have not always been available.

The Earth is a rock of mass six thousand million, million, million, million kilograms (6×10^{27} kg) partly covered by water, most of which contains dissolved substances, and surrounded by an atmosphere containing largely nitrogen and oxygen. Apart from the use of wood and stone in the construction of buildings, surprisingly few natural materials find applications in everyday life.

Elements (substances in which all the atoms have the same atomic number) may occur naturally. Examples are copper, silver, gold, carbon, nitrogen and oxygen, and simple mechanical techniques may be used to separate these elements from other materials. Copper, silver, gold and carbon have been known since ancient times but most other elements have been isolated in the past 250 years. Robert Boyle (1627–1691) gave a definition of an element as 'a primitive and simple or perfectly unmingled body'. John Dalton (1766–1844) showed brilliant insight in describing the structure of elements in terms of *atoms* but it was not until the early 1900s as a result of research by H.G.J. Moseley that it became possible to identify and characterise elements.

There are about 106 known elements. Of these, ninety-two occur in nature either combined with other elements forming *compounds* or they are uncombined. The other elements have been made by nuclear reactions. Dimitri Mendeleev (1834–1907) brought order into the known properties of the elements by devising the *Periodic Table of Elements*.

This has been described as one of the great intellectual advances in science. We will return to the Periodic Table later in this chapter.

For the most part, if a natural substance is to be made into something more useful then it must be available in substantial deposits called *ores*. For example, aluminium is always extracted from deposits of bauxite despite the fact that it is the third most abundant element on Earth, occurring in most surface rocks, but in too low a concentration for commercial exploitation. The discovery (presumably accidental) of the properties of iron transformed the durability of some artefacts. Almost anything made from wood could be made in iron. It could be beaten into sheets to make the hull of a ship or moulded to make the beams and pillars of a bridge.

Early scientists delighted in experimentation, in discovering the properties of natural materials and, more crucially, in making new materials from the substances around them. The essence of chemistry is its capacity to make new substances as well as making the many thousands of substances used every day. The discovery and isolation of new materials was empirical; there was no underlying theory of the behaviour of materials. The impressive success of chemical theory in predicting the existence, preparation and likely properties of materials is testimony to the painstaking observation, testing, recording and analysis of data by the founders of modern chemistry.

This chapter will focus on the key ideas and principles of chemistry appropriate to the study of materials and their properties at Key Stages 3 and 4. Some of the details stray beyond the National Curriculum for Science but have a place in developing a fuller understanding of certain key ideas. The importance of experimentation and evidence in science (Sc1 of the National Curriculum) must not be underestimated and is the focus of Chapter 3. The knowledge base identified in this chapter should be developed through methodical working and logical thinking. Materials and their properties is about making new substances and understanding why they behave in the way they do.

The sections of the chapter are listed below in Figure 5.1 under one of two headings: 'The behaviour of materials' and 'Principles'. It is hoped that this will allow you to develop knowledge and understanding side by side or to take each section as a stand-alone topic.

CHANGING MATERIALS

In all chemical changes new substances are made. The term 'new substance' refers to a new chemical entity, something different from the substances we started with. It does not necessarily mean new to the world of science. The term does not include a substance in a different physical state. Changing carbon into carbon dioxide involves a chemical change because carbon dioxide is a different chemical entity from carbon. Changing liquid water into steam is not a chemical change as no new substance is formed. Liquid water and steam contain the same chemical entities. When referring to chemical change we use the word *reactants* to mean the substances we start with and *products* for what is produced. Reactants together with products make a *system*. For reactants to become products we need the *correct substances* and the *correct conditions*. The correct conditions for a reaction include the amounts of reactants, the temperature of the system, the pressure in the system

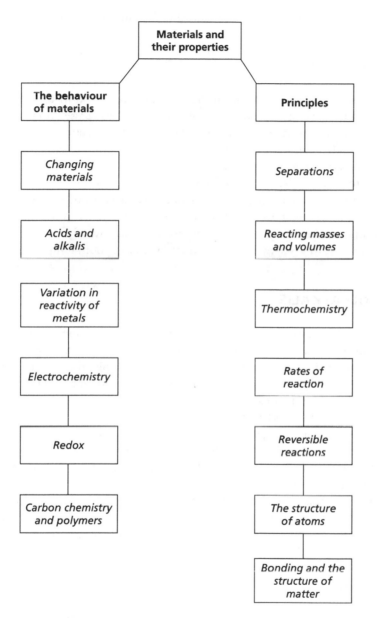

Figure 5.1 An organiser for the structure of the chapter

and the presence of a catalyst. Consider the chemical change for making ammonia from nitrogen and hydrogen. In equation form this may be written as:

$$N_{2(g)} + 3H_{2(g)} \rightarrow 2NH_{3(g)}$$

We can superimpose conditions in the following ways:

1   *amounts of reactants*: 1 volume of nitrogen: 3 volumes of hydrogen
2   *temperature of system*: 720 K
3   *pressure of system*: 250 atmospheres
4   *catalyst*: iron (Fe)

This tells us that when nitrogen and hydrogen gases are mixed in the ratio of 1:3 by volume, heated to 720 K at 250 times atmospheric pressure and passed over iron, ammonia gas is formed. What this does not tell us is how long the reaction will take, whether or not there are other conditions which could also produce ammonia and what proportion of the reactants are changed into products.

If there is to be an understanding of how and why chemical changes occur and how we might control these changes, we must explore what types of *particles* make up the reactants and products and how these particles are held together. It is worth remembering that the conditions necessary for substances to react vary widely, and the majority of reactions studied at Key Stages 3 and 4 occur at or near to room temperature.

ACIDS AND ALKALIS

Acids, such as hydrochloric acid, sulphuric acid and citric acid, change the colour of many vegetable and fruit juices. The juice from 'red' cabbage is magenta in colour. When an acid is added the colour changes to red. An alkali causes the colour to change to blue. Because these changes in colour are so marked, we can use red cabbage juice as an *indicator* to distinguish an acid from an alkali.

The three *acids* mentioned above are made by dissolving. In the case of hydrochloric acid, a gas is dissolved in water; in the case of sulphuric acid, a liquid is dissolved in water; and in the case of citric acid, a solid is dissolved in water. Without the water there are no acidic properties. An *alkali* is a solution of a base in water, and without water, alkaline properties are not evident.

The most common plant dye used as an indicator is *litmus*, extracted from a lichen. Litmus has a colour change similar to that of red cabbage juice: pale magenta in water, pink in acid solution and blue in an alkali. Because plant extracts vary in composition, mainly as a result of the different conditions in which the plants grow, their use as indicators is limited; they are not sufficiently reliable. Manufactured substances (such as Universal Indicator) are used more widely because their composition and purity can be controlled. To appreciate how best to use acids in making new substances we need to understand the cause of acidity (and alkalinity) in aqueous solutions. Hydrochloric acid is a solution in water of hydrogen chloride gas. The hydrogen chloride does not simply dissolve in the water; it reacts with it.

$$HCl_{(g)} + H_2O_{(l)} \rightarrow H_3O^+_{(aq)} + Cl^-_{(aq)}$$

The $H_3O^+_{(aq)}$ *ion* [the hydrated proton] is often abbreviated to $H^+_{(aq)}$ [the hydrogen ion].

This ion is the cause of acidity in all aqueous solutions. It is the reaction of this ion with pigments which results in the colour changes of indicators in acidic solutions.

In a similar way, a base such as ammonia (gas) reacts with water to produce OH(aq) ions [hydroxide ions]. These ions are the cause of alkalinity in aqueous solutions.

$$NH_{3(g)} + H_2O_{(l)} \rightleftharpoons NH^+_{4(aq)} + OH^-_{(aq)}$$

The arrows pointing in opposite directions indicate that the reaction is *reversible*. It can go from left to right or from right to left depending on the conditions. This is referred to in the section on reversible reactions below.

In all solutions in water both the $H_3O_{(aq)}$ ion and the $OH_{(aq)}$ ion are always present. If the concentrations of these two ions are equal the solution is *neutral*. An excess of $H_3O^+_{(aq)}$ over $OH^-_{(aq)}$ makes a solution acidic. What makes a solution alkaline?

- The greater the excess of $H_3O^+_{(aq)}$ $\rightarrow$ the stronger the acid.
- The greater the excess of $OH^-_{(aq)}$ $\rightarrow$ the stronger the alkali.

Task 5.1

From around your home, find some examples of strong and weak acids and alkalis that you could use to exemplify acids and alkalis in your teaching.

We represent this variation in strength of an acid or an alkali by using the pH scale. In most everyday uses the pH scale ranges from 0–14 (any value including non-integral). Values outside this range are possible but rare.

- A solution with a pH of 7 is *neutral*.
- For *acidic* solutions: $0 < pH < 7$
- For *alkaline* solutions: $7 < pH < 14$.

Remember that we can refer to acidic and alkaline solutions as *weak* or *strong* according to the pH. The terms *dilute* and *concentrated* do not have the same meaning. We can have a dilute solution of weak acid or a concentrated solution of a weak acid. The same applies to alkaline solutions.

Acids and bases (or alkalis) react together to make salts. In the example below, the salt formed is sodium chloride.

Sodium hydroxide + hydrochloric acid $\rightarrow$ sodium chloride + water

     alkali   *acid*   *salt*

If the amounts (in *moles*) of the acid and the alkali are equal, the pH of the sodium chloride solution is 7. It is a neutral solution. There are two points to consider when developing this basic idea.

1   Equal amounts of acid and alkali mean equal numbers of *moles* of hydrogen ions and of hydroxyl ions (see 'Reacting masses and volumes' below).

2   If either the acid or the alkali is weak then the final solution will not have a pH of 7. If the acid is weak the solution will have a pH greater than 7 and if the alkali is weak the pH will be less than 7.

Reactions between acids and alkalis involve the same fundamental process. This is the interaction of hydrogen ions and hydroxyl ions in solution.

$$H^+_{(aq)} + OH^-_{(aq)} \rightarrow H_2O_{(l)}$$

Because this involves attraction between oppositely charged ions the reaction is rapid and occurs at room temperature and pressure.

Reactions involving organic acids and organic bases are slow by comparison, often requiring a *catalyst*. With organic compounds bonds must be broken and new ones made. These processes need both time and energy. The most well-known organic bases are alcohols and they react with organic acids to form *esters*. An ester is the organic equivalent of a salt. Esters are important in perfumes and food flavourings because of their fragrances.

Acids, bases and salts are widely used and several occur naturally. Table 5.1 shows you some examples. You may wish to add to this list from your own reading.

Table 5.1 Occurrence of acids, bases and salts

Naturally occurring acids	Where found
• Hydrochloric acid	• Human stomach
• Ethanoic acid	• Vinegar
• Methanoic acid	• Red ant stings
• Citric acid	• Citrus fruits
• Tartaric acid	• Grapes
• Lactic acid	• Sour milk
Naturally occurring alkalis	**Where found**
• Ammonia	• Urine
• Various metal hydroxides	• In combination with other salts of the metal as minerals and ores
• Copper (11) hydroxide	• In malachite
• Magnesium hydroxide	• In dolomitic limestone
Naturally occurring salts	**Where found**
• Sodium chloride	• Underground deposits (e.g. Cheshire)
• Calcium carbonate	• Limestone (marble) deposits
• Barium sulphate	• Barytes deposits
Manufactured salts	**Use**
• Sodium carbonate	Reduces hardness in water (bath crystals)
• Sodium glutamate	• Flavour enhancer
• Sodium ethanolsalicylate	• Soluble aspirin

THE VARIATION IN REACTIVITY OF METALS

Substances, even those similar in type, vary in the ease with which they react. This variation in reactivity is particularly evident in metals because they are so widely used in everyday life. It is clear from observation that iron corrodes in air and gold does not. Iron is more reactive than gold. We can compare the reactivities of metals by observing how vigorously each one reacts with the same reactant. To illustrate this we can compare calcium with iron.

If we put a small piece of each metallic element separately in water, we will see that the metal calcium reacts vigorously with a lot of effervescence. Under identical conditions iron reacts slowly. Repeating this for all metals would give a comparative list (as follows), although differences in behaviour are sometimes slight.

Potassium
Calcium
Magnesium
Zinc
Iron
Lead   Reactivity with water decreasing
Hydrogen
Copper
Gold

This comparative behaviour has been recorded for all metals with a wide range of reagents. With few exceptions the order of reactivity is the same for all reagents. It is clear from the above list that zinc is more reactive than copper. If a piece of zinc is put into a solution of a copper salt, the zinc will go into solution and the copper will be displaced. The copper settles to the bottom of the vessel.

This list is a small part of the *reactivity series* of metals. It is qualitative and, as we will see in the section on *electrochemistry* (below), it can be written with a quantitative scale. This is helpful in describing how much more reactive one metal is than another. There is an important point to bear in mind when using the reactivity series. The metals near the top of the series are very reactive and will react with water. If one of these metals is added to an aqueous solution of another metal, there are two possible displacements: (1) displacing the metal which is in solution, and (2) displacing hydrogen from the water. The reactivity series of metals should therefore include hydrogen which although not strictly a metal has many properties in common with metals. On the short list above, hydrogen is placed between lead and copper. To illustrate the usefulness of this list consider what happens when zinc (a grey metal) is put into a solution of a copper salt (a blue solution). The zinc quickly becomes coated with a brown deposit and the blue solution becomes paler in colour.

$$\text{Copper (in solution)} + \text{zinc} \rightarrow \text{zinc (in solution)} + \text{copper}$$

The zinc is more reactive than the copper and so dissolves in preference to the copper. Looking at the reactivity list we could predict that magnesium will displace copper from a solution of a copper salt and also that copper will *not* react with a solution of a zinc salt. Remember where hydrogen has been placed in the reactivity series? Another prediction we could make is that both zinc and magnesium will displace hydrogen from solutions of acids and that copper will not react with acids. (Nitric acid is an exception to this generalisation. Copper reacts with nitric acid but does not produce hydrogen.)

So, what is produced when copper reacts with nitric acid and why does it behave in this way? The fact that metals differ in their reactivity is made use of in two ways of protecting iron from rusting. In one method the clean iron is coated with zinc. In moist air the zinc reacts and dissolves in preference to the iron; therefore as long as there is some zinc on the iron, the iron will not rust. This process is called *galvanising*. The principle is the same in protecting iron pipelines underground from corrosion. Blocks of magnesium are fastened at intervals along the pipeline. How does this protect the pipeline?

The *Periodic Table of Elements* is an excellent guide to trends in reactivity among the elements. The elements in group 1 (the *alkali metals*) and group 2 are predominantly metals. Their reactivity *increases* going down the group. The elements in groups 6 and 7 (the *halogens*) are predominantly non-metals. Their reactivity *decreases* going down the group. Moving from left to right across the periodic table there is a gradual change from metallic to non-metallic properties. Group 8 (sometimes called group 0) consists of the *noble gases*. These are much more stable than other elements in the periodic table.

Task 5.2	
	Looking at the Periodic Table, which is the most reactive metal and which is the most reactive non-metal?

ELECTROCHEMISTRY

In the section on reactivity of metals we came across the idea of displacement.

$$\text{Copper in solution} + \text{zinc} \rightarrow \text{zinc in solution} + \text{copper}$$

When we write *copper in solution* we mean copper ions [Cu^{2+}] in an aqueous solution. Thus this is written $Cu^{2+}(aq)$. The word *equation* may be written in symbols as:

$$Cu^{2+}_{(aq)} + Zn_{(s)} \rightarrow Zn^{2+}_{(aq)} + Cu_{(s)}$$

Copper ions are changed into copper atoms and zinc atoms are changed into zinc ions. For these changes to happen, the copper ions must gain 2 electrons and the zinc atoms must lose 2 electrons.

$$Cu^{2+}_{(aq)} + 2\ e^- \rightarrow Cu_{(s)}$$
$$Zn_{(s)} \leftarrow Zn^{2+}_{(aq)} + 2e^-$$

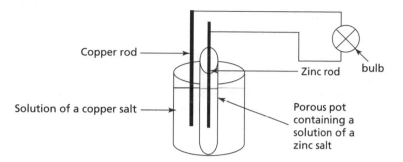

Figure 5.2 A simple chemical cell

Electrons are transferred from zinc atoms to copper ions. These transfers occur randomly in solution but we can make the transfer more controlled as in a simple cell. This is shown in Figure 5.2.

From the activity series of metals it may be seen that zinc is more reactive than copper. This is a natural tendency resulting from the internal structure of the atoms. If the zinc and the copper are attached (as shown in the diagram), electrons flow from the zinc to the copper through the connecting wire. Zinc dissolves and copper is deposited on to the copper plate. As the zinc dissolves, zinc ions go into solution and the electrons released build up on the zinc. Electrons are then available to flow to the copper and convert copper ions into copper. Thus electrons flow from zinc to copper through the connecting wire and an electric current is produced. The diagram represents a *simple cell*. When zinc reacts with copper ions in solution, heat is produced. When the reaction is carried out in a cell, the equivalent amount of electrical energy is released. The bigger the difference in reactivity between the metals, the bigger the voltage produced by the cell. Each metal contributes to this voltage and this contribution is the *electrode potential*. Knowing the values of electrode potentials allows the metals to be listed in precise order. This is the *electrochemical series*.

Electrode reaction	E^0/V	
K^+/K	−2.92	*Potassium is the most reactive metal*
Ca^{2+}/Ca	−2.87	
$Mg^{2+}//Mg$	−2.38	
Zn^{2+}/Zn	−0.76	
Fe^{2+}/Fe	−0.44	
Pb^{2+}/Pb	−0.13	
$H^+/\frac{1}{2}H_2$	0.00	
Cu^{2+}/Cu	+0.34	
$Au^{3+} Au$	+1.50	*Gold is the least reactive meal*

If a simple cell is made with a copper rod and a zinc rod in a conducting solution such as a salt dissolved in water, the copper will be the positive terminal of the cell and the zinc will be the negative terminal. The voltage of the cell will be the difference between +0.34 and −0.76 V; that is, 1.10 V.

Task 5.3

If a simple cell is made with a zinc rod and a lead rod, which of the metals will be the positive terminal and what will be the voltage of the cell?

We have seen that a chemical change can produce an electric current. An electric current can produce chemical change. This is *electrolysis* (Figure 5.3). For an electric current to bring about chemical change in a substance, the substance involved must conduct electricity. Therefore it must consist of ions which are free to move. For this to be possible the substance must be in one of three states:

1   ionic and in solution (e.g. sodium chloride dissolved in water);
2   ionic and molten (e.g. liquid sodium chloride);
3   covalent and producing ions in solution (e.g. hydrogen chloride dissolved in water).

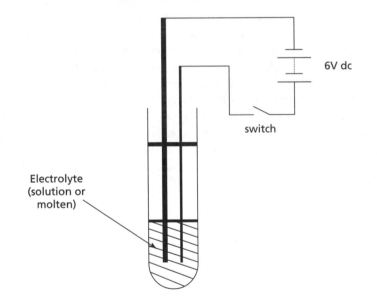

Figure 5.3 Electrolysis

More details on this are given in the section on 'bonding' below.

The general name for a substance which conducts electricity and is decomposed as a result is an *electrolyte*. The rods carrying the electric current into and out of the electrolyte are *electrodes*. The electrodes are electrically charged. The electrode carrying a positive charge is the *anode* (+) and the electrode carrying a negative charge is the *cathode* (−).

During electrolysis the positively charged ions travel towards the cathode. These ions are called *cations* (pronounced cat-i-ons). During electrolysis the negatively charged ions travel towards the anode. These ions are called anions (pronounced an-i-ons). It is these ions which carry the charge through the electrolyte during electrolysis.

To illustrate the main features of electrolysis, consider what happens during the electrolysis of molten sodium chloride. The electrolyte consists of sodium ions Na+ and chloride ions Cl^-. During electrolysis the cations (Na+) migrate to the cathode where they lose their charge (are discharged).

$$Na^+_{(l)} + e\text{-} \leftrightarrow Na_{(l)}$$

Sodium is produced by electron gain. Electron gain is *reduction*. The chloride ions migrate to the anode where they are discharged.

$$Cl^-_{(l)} \rightarrow Cl_{(l)} + e^-$$

Chlorine atoms are produced by electron loss. Electron loss is *oxidation*. These principles can be remembered with the acronym *OILRIG*:

O oxidation
I is
L loss (of electrons)
R reduction
I is
G gain (of electrons)

This is referred to again in the section on 'redox' below.

If the sodium chloride is dissolved in water the electrolysis follows a different path. The ions present in a solution of sodium chloride are:

$$Na^+_{(aq)} \text{ and } Cl^-_{(aq)} \text{ from the sodium chloride}$$

$$H^+_{(aq)} \text{ and } OH^-_{(aq)} \text{ from the water}$$

Whenever water is present there is the possibility that the ions from the water will be discharged in preference to the ions from the solute. The *ease of discharge* of the ions needs to be considered. In terms of energy it is easier to discharge $H^+_{(aq)}$ and $Cl^-_{(aq)}$ than it is to discharge $Na^+_{(aq)}$. Therefore at the cathode (–):

$$2H^+_{(aq)} + 2\ e^- \rightarrow H_2$$

Hydrogen atoms are produced first. Then pairs of atoms combine to form molecules. At the anode (+):

$$2Cl^- \rightarrow Cl_2 + 2e^-$$

Chlorine atoms are produced first. Then pairs of atoms combine to form molecules.

There are other possible reactions dependent on the concentration of the solution of sodium chloride. These equations are *ionic* equations. Because each represents half of the total reaction they are called *half equations*. The equation for the reaction at the cathode is often called the *reduction half equation*. The anode reaction is represented by the *oxidation half equation*.

Task 5.4

Explain why the words *reduction* and *oxidation* are used in these terms.

Now try to write the half equations for the reactions at the anode and cathode occurring during the electrolysis of a solution of copper (11) chloride.

REDOX

In the section on electrochemistry we noted two fundamental changes:

1   changing positively charged ions into neutral atoms or molecules
   (e.g. $Cu^{2+} + 2e^- \rightarrow Cu$)

2   changing negatively charged ions into neutral atoms or molecules
   (e.g. $2Cl^- \rightarrow Cl_2 + 2e^-$)

The process of electron gain is *reduction*. The process of electron loss is *oxidation*.

There are many examples of reduction and oxidation reactions. One well-known example of a reduction is the conversion of copper (11) oxide to copper by heating with carbon. The loss of oxygen is often the criterion for describing this as a reduction but the fundamental change is the conversion of copper (11) ions to copper atoms by gaining electrons.

When calcium is burned in oxygen, calcium oxide is formed. The calcium has gained oxygen so the reaction would be described as an oxidation. However, the fundamental change is the loss of electrons by the calcium.

$$Ca_{(g)} \rightarrow Ca^{2+}_{(g)} + 2e^-$$

The oxygen gains these electrons to form the oxide ion.

$$\frac{1}{2}O_{2(g)} + 2e^- \rightarrow O^{2-}_{(g)}$$

There are two reactions going on together. One is the oxidation of calcium. The oxygen is the *oxidising agent*. The other reaction is the reduction of oxygen. The calcium is the *reducing agent*. The oxidation and reduction reactions go on together and the overall reaction is a *redox* reaction.

The redox reactions discussed thus far have been ionic reactions. Some redox reactions do not involve ions as the substances are molecular (see the section on 'bonding' below). In the burning of hydrogen in oxygen, water is produced.

$$2H_{2(g)} + O_{2(g)} \underset{\leftarrow}{\rightarrow} 2H_2O_{(l)}$$

Clearly the hydrogen has gained oxygen and has been oxidised. The oxygen has gained hydrogen and has been reduced. This is a redox reaction with no ionic changes.

Some definitions of oxidation and reduction

Oxidation

Reduction

Gain of oxygen by an element
Loss of hydrogen from a compound
Loss of electron(s) by an atom or ion

Loss of oxygen from a compound
Gain of hydrogen by an element
Gain of electron(s) by an atom or ion

CARBON CHEMISTRY AND POLYMERS

Carbon Chemistry was previously known as Organic Chemistry because the substances known were derived from living organisms. Examples are sugars and oils from certain plants. During the sixteenth, seventeenth and eighteenth centuries an increasing number of organic substances were isolated, and analysis showed that they contained carbon and hydrogen. The nineteenth century saw a dramatic change with the preparation, by Wohler, of urea. This was the first deliberately synthesised organic substance and its preparation paved the way for the rapid growth of preparative organic chemistry.

Carbon has a special place in chemistry due to the remarkable ability of its atoms to bond to other atoms of carbon. This is an example of *catenation*. An atom of carbon can form four covalent bonds with other atoms. Consider a molecule of methane in which an atom of carbon is bonded to four atoms of hydrogen. In the section on 'Bonding' below, we will see that a covalent bond is represented by a single line:

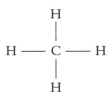

This molecule has four covalent bonds, each bond being two electrons shared between the carbon atom and a hydrogen atom. Because the covalent bonds carry the same type of charge (negative) there is repulsion between the bonds. This results in the molecule taking a three-dimensional structure (Figure 5.4). This shape is a regular tetrahedron.

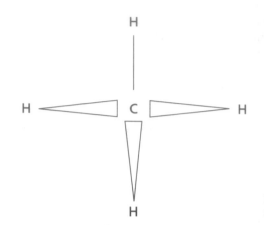

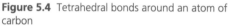

Figure 5.4 Tetrahedral bonds around an atom of carbon

This molecule, methane (CH_4), is the simplest *hydrocarbon*. Almost any number of carbon atoms can combine to form long chains, and the number of compounds of carbon and hydrogen only can be many millions. Other elements, replacing atoms of hydrogen in organic molecules, increase the number of possible organic compounds by many more millions. This sets carbon chemistry apart from the chemistry of other elements. There are far more compounds of carbon known than the total number of compounds of all other elements.

Methane is the first member of a series of hydrocarbons called *alkanes*. Other members are:

Ethane C_2H_6
Propane C_3H_8
Butane C_4H_{10}

The general formula for an alkane is C_nH_{2n+2} and n can have any whole number value. An alkane, for which n = 6, has the formula C_6H_{14}.

All the bonds in the alkanes are single covalent bonds (see 'bonding' below). Particularly important is the fact that the bonds between the carbon atoms are *single covalent bonds*. If the bonding between carbon atoms in a molecule consists of single bonds only, the molecule (and, by association, the compound) is said to be *saturated*. In writing a formula such as C_6H_{14} there is no indication of structure. The arrangement of atoms in a molecule can make a dramatic difference to the physical properties of the compound. With a molecule such as C_6H_{14} containing twenty atoms, there will be many different ways of arranging the atoms. These different structural forms with the same molecular formula are *isomers*.

Task 5.5

Find out what you can about isomers and sketch the several forms of C_6H_{14}.

Another important series of hydrocarbons is the *alkenes*. In these compounds, the bonding between the carbon atoms is a *double covalent bond*. Remember that a single covalent bond consists of two electrons. Therefore a double bond consists of four electrons. The simplest alkene is *ethene*, C_2H_4. The structure of ethene is:

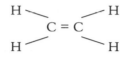

This is often written as: $CH_2 = CH_2$.

The presence of a double bond between the carbon atoms makes the molecule (and compound) *unsaturated*. The general formula for an alkene is C_nH_{2n}. The alkene next in the series after ethane is propene. The naming of alkenes follows the name of the corresponding alkane, replacing -ane with -ene.

Task 5.6	
	Name the alkenes with n = 3, 4, 5, and write the formula for each, making clear the position of the double bond.

As a guide we can do the first one together. To start with, let us write the structural formula for propene. Remember that the molecule will contain one double bond. Therefore write:

$$C = C$$

There is one more carbon atom so the skeleton structure is:

$$C = C - C$$

There are six hydrogen atoms to bond to the three carbon atoms and this gives:

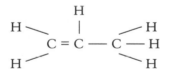

This would often be written as: $H_2C = CH.CH_3$. Other variations are: $CH_3.CH = CH_2$; $H_3C.CH = CH_2$. However you write the formula, make clear where the double bond is and remember that a dot in these formulae means a single bond.

The term *saturated* indicates that no more atoms can be accommodated in the molecule. Therefore for saturated molecules to react with other substances, atoms in the saturated molecules must be replaced by atoms from the attacking substance. We call this type of reaction *substitution*. To illustrate this, consider the reaction between methane and chlorine. All the bonds in the methane molecule are single bonds so any reaction must involve substitution.

$$CH_4 + Cl_2 \rightarrow CH_3Cl + HCl$$

One of the atoms of hydrogen has been replaced by an atom of chlorine producing chloromethane. There are still four atoms bonded to the atom of carbon.

Substitution is a dominant reaction in the chemistry of alkanes but the most well-known reaction of alkanes is *combustion* (oxidation by oxygen). The burning of alkanes in oxygen or air releases a lot of energy as heat and light and so alkanes are good fuels.

$$CH_4 + 2O_2 \rightarrow CO_2 + 2H_2O \qquad \text{energy released}$$

Maximum energy is released with complete combustion when the products are carbon dioxide and water. Incomplete combustion is less efficient and some carbon monoxide is produced.

Task 5.7

Try writing balanced chemical equations for the complete and incomplete combustion of propane, C_3H_8 and butane, C_4H_{10}.

The double bond in the molecule of an alkene makes alkenes very reactive. Since a single bond is more stable than a double bond, there is always a tendency for the double bond to be the focus of any reaction. Unsaturated molecules such as alkenes react by *addition* rather than by substitution. Let us compare the reaction of chlorine with an alkane and with an alkene.

As we saw in the above section, chlorine and methane react by substitution and the product is chloromethane. An atom of hydrogen has been replaced by an atom of chlorine. When ethene reacts with chlorine one of the bonds in the double bond breaks, leaving the two carbon atoms joined by a single bond and an atom of chlorine bonded to each of the two carbon atoms.

$$H_2C = CH_2 + Cl_2 \rightarrow H_2C.(Cl).CH_2Cl$$

Another way of showing the structure of this molecule is:

$$
\begin{array}{ccc}
 & & Cl \\
 & & | \\
H_2C & \!\!\!\!-\!\!\!\!- & CH_2 \\
| & & \\
Cl & &
\end{array}
$$

Another, and more important, reaction of ethene is *polymerisation*. In this reaction many thousands of molecules of ethene combine to form one large molecule called *polyethene*. As in the above reaction, the double bond in each molecule of ethene opens and the resulting *units* link together to form one long molecule. One way of representing this molecule is:

$$-----\left(\begin{array}{cc} \overset{\displaystyle H}{\underset{\displaystyle H}{|}} & \overset{\displaystyle H}{\underset{\displaystyle H}{|}} \\ --C & - & C-- \\ & & \end{array}\right)_n-- \quad \text{(n is the number of molecules (or units) joined together)}$$

This large molecule is an example of a *polymer* and the small molecule from which it is made is a *monomer*. In this example the monomer is ethene and the polymer is polyethene, or more commonly, polythene. This polymer is formed by the adding together of thousands of small molecules. There is no other product than the polymer. This type of polymer is an *addition polymer*. Addition polymers are typical of the polymerisation of alkenes. Each of the units is saturated, but what happens at the ends of the polymer?

Sometimes a hydrogen atom migrates from one end of the polymer to the other. This leaves a $H_2C=CH-$ group at one end and a H_3C- group at the other end. Another possibility is that some other molecule in the system reacts at the double bond (there are catalysts and promoters in the system). Whichever reaction occurs, any double bond in the polymer is of little consequence and the polymer is essentially saturated and has the properties of an alkane. Combustion apart, polymers of this type are chemically stable and of relatively low density.

Vinyl chloride is similar in structure to ethene. One of the hydrogen atoms in ethene has been replaced by an atom of chlorine. The formula is $H_2C = CHCl$.

Task 5.8	What would be the structure of the addition polymer made from vinyl chloride and what is its common name?

Polymerisation is a study in its own right and you may be interested in reading more about this important topic (see suggestions at the end of this chapter).

SEPARATIONS

Substances found in nature are rarely pure. Sometimes the impurity imparts aesthetic and monetary value, as in diamonds and other gems. In general there is a need to separate materials at some stage of processing to isolate a substance from its impurities. The importance of *purity* in substances used in food preparation and health care cannot be overemphasised. The tragedies associated with the drug thalidomide were, through later research, found to be the result of impurities in the drug. Table 5.2 gives a summary of the more common separation processes.

Techniques of separation are used to purify substances and, having separated the components, each can be identified. Hence these separation processes have been extended to be suitable for analysis in, for example, drug detection and the causes of atmospheric pollution.

Table 5.2 More common separation processes

Separation	Technique	Property used
Sea water and sand	Filtration	Different particle size. Holes in filter allow small molecules of water to go and retain the bigger sand particles
Ethanol and water	Fractional distillation	The liquids have different boiling temperatures
Dyes in ink or in food colouring	Chromatography	Components have different solubilities in a common solvent and are held to different degrees on common adsorbent
Salts (e.g. potassium chloride and potassium chlorate in water)	Fractional crystallisation	Salts have different solubilities in water. The less soluble will crystallise first

REACTING MASSES AND VOLUMES

The actual masses of atoms are very small and have little meaning for everyday use. It is of more value to use relative masses. The mass of one atom of carbon-12 is about twelve times the mass of one atom of the simplest form of hydrogen. Taking the mass of one atom of carbon-12 to be twelve atomic mass units (amu), the *relative atomic* mass of hydrogen is about 1 amu (actually 1.008). An alternative way of conveying this is to write Ar (C) = 12 where Ar represents relative atomic mass. For hydrogen, Ar (H) = 1. Similarly, for oxygen, we can write Ar (O) = 16. The symbols for atoms may be used in the representation of molecules. Carbon dioxide may be written as CO_2. Adding relative atomic masses gives a value for the *relative molecular mass* (Mr). The Mr value for carbon dioxide may be calculated as follows:

$$Mr = (1 \times 12) + (2 \times 16) = 12 + 32 = 44$$

Using the system above we can write Mr (CO_2) = 44.

Mr values may be calculated in a similar way for any compound. At the beginning of this section it was noted that one atom of carbon has a mass which is twelve times the mass of an atom of hydrogen. In other words, Ar (H) = 1 and Ar (C) = 12. If we put together a sufficient number of hydrogen atoms to make a mass of 1 g then the same number of atoms of carbon would have a total mass of 12 g.

The relative atomic mass in g or the relative molecular mass in g is called a *mole*. Thus one mole of hydrogen atoms has a mass of 1 g, 1 mole of carbon atoms has a mass of 12 g and 1 mole of carbon dioxide molecules has a mass of 44 g. Note how important it is to state the type of particle in the substance. For example, 1 mole of hydrogen *atoms* has a mass of 1 g but 1 mole of hydrogen *molecules* has a mass of 2 g. The mole is the unit of amount of substance, and the symbol or formula used to represent a substance indicates 1 mole of it.

The number of particles in 1 mole of any substance is the *Avagadro constant*. It has a value of 6.023×10^{23}. This is an important idea because it is the interaction between particles which leads to chemical change. Measuring the amounts of substances in moles ensures that we know the relative numbers of particles in the system. Consider the reaction between iron and sulphur, $Fe + S \rightarrow FeS$. This implies that 1 mole of iron reacts with 1 mole of sulphur to make 1 mole of iron (11) sulphide. If $Ar(Fe) = 56$ and $Ar(S) = 32$, then 56 g of iron react with 32 g of sulphur to make 88 g of iron (11) sulphide.

By putting together equal numbers of moles we have equal numbers of particles. Working on a smaller scale we could use 7 g of iron and 4 g of sulphur and still have equal numbers of moles ($\frac{1}{8}$ of a mole in each case). The mole is a convenient way of indicating a fixed number of particles. We could refer to:

- a mole of hydrogen atoms
- a mole of oxygen molecules
- a mole of sodium ions
- a mole of electrons

You may be able to think of other examples.

To recognise the usefulness of these ideas we can explore the quantitative aspects of a chemical change. Consider the breakdown of ammonium nitrate when it is heated.

$$\text{Ammonium nitrate} \rightarrow \text{dinitrogen monoxide} + \text{water vapour}$$

The balanced symbol equation would be:

$$NH_4NO_{3\,(s)} \rightarrow N_2O_{\,(g)} + 2H2O_{(g)}$$

For every mole of ammonium nitrate decomposed, 1 mole of dinitrogen monoxide and 2 moles of water vapour are produced.

Recalling Mr values and converting these into masses it may be seen that 80 g of ammonium nitrate will produce 44 g of dinitrogen monoxide and 36 g of water vapour. Therefore whatever mass of ammonium nitrate is decomposed, $\frac{44}{80}$ of that mass is the mass of dinitrogen monoxide produced and $\frac{36}{80}$ of that mass is the mass of water vapour produced. This process applies to any system so long as the ratios are derived from a *balanced* chemical equation. Look again at the above equation. You will see that the reactant is a solid and the products are gases. It is convenient to measure the *mass* of a solid and the *volume* of a gas.

1 mole of any gas has a volume of 24 litres (dm^3) at room temperature and pressure (r.t.p.). Volumes of gases are affected by changes in temperature and pressure, and it is convenient to quote the value under average conditions in this country.

Referring again to the above equation, we could write: 1 mole of ammonium nitrate produces 2 moles of dinitrogen monoxide, or 80 g of ammonium nitrate produces 24 litres of dinitrogen monoxide, measured at r.t.p.

Task 5.9

Calculate the volume of dinitrogen monoxide which would be produced by the decomposition of 1 g of ammonium nitrate.

What would be the volume of water vapour produced?

THERMOCHEMISTRY

This section is concerned with energy changes in chemical reactions. The reaction of hydrogen with chlorine to form hydrogen chloride may be represented by the equation:

$$H_{2(g)} + Cl_{2(g)} \rightarrow 2HCl_{(g)}$$

In each of the molecules of hydrogen, chlorine and hydrogen chloride the atoms are bonded covalently.

It is evident that for the reactants to become the products, the bonds between the atoms of hydrogen and between the atoms of chlorine must break, and new bonds must be formed between atoms of hydrogen and chlorine. Thus:

H---H and Cl----CL becomes H---Cl and Cl---H

Whatever the mechanism of the reaction the overall energy change depends solely on the initial and final states of the system (*Hess's Law*). To break the bonds in 1 mole of hydrogen molecules requires 436 kJ of energy. To break the bonds in 1 mole of chlorine molecules requires 242 kJ of energy. Each of these values is known as a *bond energy*. This makes a total of 678 kJ of energy taken in by the system. Making the bonds in 2 moles of hydrogen chloride molecules releases 862 kJ of energy. Therefore there is a release overall of 184 kJ of energy. This reaction is *exothermic*. There are reactions in which energy is absorbed. Such changes are *endothermic*. Try to find examples of endothermic changes.

In chemical systems, energy is referred to as *enthalpy* (symbol H). Changes in enthalpy have the symbol ΔH (pronounced delta aitch). The reaction referred to above could be represented by the equations:

$$H_{2(g)} + Cl_{2(g)} \longrightarrow 2HCl_{(g)} \Delta H = -184 \text{ kJ}$$

$$\tfrac{1}{2} H_{2(g)} + \tfrac{1}{2} Cl_{2(g)} \longrightarrow HCl_{(g)} \Delta H = -92 \text{ kJmol}^{-1}$$

The sign indicates loss of enthalpy (an exothermic change). A positive value for ΔH indicates an endothermic change.

RATES OF REACTION

In the section on thermochemistry above, we saw that a chemical change involves the breaking and making of chemical bonds. These processes are never instantaneous; they take time. The time taken to change reactants into products varies considerably from one reaction to another. For example, the rusting of iron is a relatively slow process, taking several days for any noticeable change to occur. By contrast, the explosion of gunpowder when ignited is very fast reaction. A study of the rate at which reactants are changed into products can often help in deducing how the reaction occurs. Standard GCSE texts will describe how the rate of reaction can be measured for each of two well-known reactions, namely:

1. the decomposition of hydrogen peroxide solution;
2. the reaction between sodium thiosulphate and dilute hydrochloric acid.

The data from these studies will show the following important features of rate of reaction:

(a) The higher the concentration of a reactant, the faster the reaction.
(b) The rate of reaction increases as the temperature of the system increases.
(c) the smaller the size of the particles in a reactant, the faster the reaction.
(d) Some substances can increase the rate of a reaction without undergoing any permanent change. Such substances are known as *catalysts*.

These summaries help to explain some well-known features of reactions. For example:

*   The reaction between dilute hydrochloric acid and calcium is vigorous. With concentrated hydrochloric acid the reaction is violent.
*   The reaction between zinc and dilute sulphuric acid is slow at room temperature. When the mixture is heated to 50°C–60°C, the reaction is brisk.
*   A sugar lump will not ignite when heated with a lighted wooden spill. If the sugar is first sprinkled with a trace of cigarette ash it burns vigorously.
*   The reaction between dilute hydrochloric acid and a piece of marble (calcium carbonate) is very slow. Crushing the marble into a fine powder makes the reaction vigorous.

Task 5.10

Try to explain each of these changes in terms of the factors which affect the rate of reaction and in terms of particle theory.

How is the breakdown of starch in our bodies speeded up?

Try to find examples of other changes, in the natural world or in a laboratory, which are examples of the effect on rate of: concentration change; temperature change; catalysts; and particle size.

REVERSIBLE REACTIONS

The burning of natural gas (methane) is a one-way process.

$$CH_{4(g)} + 2O_{2(g)} \rightarrow CO_{2(g)} + 2H_2O_{(g)}$$

When methane reacts with oxygen it is completely converted into carbon dioxide and water vapour. These products cannot be changed back into methane and oxygen. This change is *irreversible*. The situation is very different when we consider the effect of heat on ammonium chloride.

$$NH_4Cl_{(s)} \rightleftarrows NH_{3(g)} + HCl_{(g)}$$

Initially the ammonium chloride breaks down, producing ammonia and hydrogen chloride. However, these two gases can react to form ammonium chloride. The overall effect is that both reactions occur together. The reaction can go from left to right or from right to left as indicated by the two arrows. Usually, two half-arrows are used like this instead of full arrows.

The two gases may be detected using moist litmus paper. What would you expect to see? This reaction is *reversible*. If the gases can escape into the atmosphere then all the ammonium chloride will be changed into ammonia and hydrogen chloride. If the vessel containing the ammonium chloride is sealed then only some of the ammonium chloride will decompose. Ammonia and hydrogen chloride will combine to form ammonium chloride and the two reactions (forward and backward) will eventually occur at the same rate. The amounts of ammonium chloride, ammonia and hydrogen chloride in the vessel will remain unchanged although the forward and backward reactions are still taking place. The reaction is said to be at *equilibrium*. As reactions are still going on this is a *dynamic equilibrium*. The equation is best written as:

$$NH_4Cl_{(g)} \rightleftharpoons NH_{3(g)} + HCl_{(g)}$$

The chemical industry makes huge quantities of ammonia which is a precursor for making nitric acid and fertilisers. The manufacture of ammonia makes use of the reaction between nitrogen gas and hydrogen gas

$$N_{2(g)} + 3H_{2(g)} \rightleftharpoons 2NH_{3(g)}$$

Note that the reaction is reversible. In industry the nitrogen and hydrogen gases are heated, compressed and passed over a catalyst. About 8 per cent of the reacting gases are converted into ammonia. The ammonia is removed and the unchanged nitrogen and hydrogen are recycled. Instead of a one-stage process to make the ammonia the reactants are recycled many times. This is an important process and you may find it helpful to read more widely about it.

THE STRUCTURE OF ATOMS

Atoms display a wide range of properties. Our understanding of how this happens stems from our knowledge of the internal structure of atoms. All atoms are built from three types of particle:

1   The *proton* which carries a single positive charge and has a mass approximately the same as that of a hydrogen atom. Protons are found in the nucleus of an atom.
2   The *electron* which carries a single negative charge and has a mass approximately 1/2000 of the mass of a proton. Electrons are found in energy levels surrounding the nucleus of an atom.
3   The *neutron* which has no charge and a mass almost the same as that of a proton. Neutrons are found in the nucleus of an atom.

The number of protons in an atom is the *atomic number* (Z). The number of protons plus the number of neutrons is equal to the *mass number* (A). These numbers are often written alongside the symbol for an atom in the periodic table, e.g.:

$$^{1}\text{H (mass number) and } _{1}\text{H (atomic number) } = \, _{1}^{1}\text{H}$$

Because A and Z represent numbers of particles they have integral values. The atomic number determines the atom and hence the element. An atom with an atomic number of 1 is hydrogen. An atom with an atomic number of 6 is carbon. An atom with an atomic number of 12 is magnesium. The simplest atom is that of hydrogen. It has 1 proton in the nucleus of the atom and 1 electron in an energy level relatively distant from the nucleus. Adding more protons to the nucleus produces an atom of a different element:

H atom (1 proton in nucleus) + 1 proton $\rightarrow$ He atom (2 protons in nucleus)

Changing the number of neutrons in the nucleus does not change the identity of the atom. Only the mass of the atom changes. For example, starting with H atom (1 proton in the nucleus), adding 1 neutron produces a different form of hydrogen (1 proton + 1 neutron in the nucleus). This is deuterium, sometimes called 'heavy hydrogen' because the mass of an atom of deuterium is about twice the mass of the simplest atom of hydrogen. An atom with 1 proton + 2 neutrons in the nucleus is also a form of hydrogen. This is tritium. These three forms of hydrogen are *isotopes*.

Isotopes are forms of an element in which the atoms have the same atomic number but different mass numbers. Separate atoms with the same atomic number but different mass numbers are *nuclides*. All elements have isotopic forms. The existence of isotopes accounts for the non–integral value of the *relative atomic mass* of an element. Elements are isolated from naturally occurring materials and are a mixture of isotopes. Some atoms in the element have one mass, some atoms have a different mass but all have the same atomic number.

In everyday use we must work with this mixture of isotopes and instead of identifying the masses of individual atoms we use the average mass of the atoms in the mixture. This is the relative atomic mass. If masses are to be compared, there needs to be a standard of mass. In work with atoms the standard of mass is the *atomic mass unit (amu)*. This is equal to one-twelfth of the mass of a C–12 atom. Remember this is the nuclide of carbon with mass number 12. In general, values of relative atomic mass are given to the nearest integer. For example, chlorine has two common isotopic forms, one of mass number 35 and the other of mass number 37. In natural chlorine the ratio of atoms of mass 35 to those of mass 37 is 3:1. The relative atomic mass is the *average mass per atom* in a natural mixture of isotopes. For chlorine this will be:

$$\frac{(3 \times 35) + (1 \times 37)}{4} = \frac{142}{4} = 35.5$$

This is usually quoted as 35.5 but there is a developing tendency to use 35 as this is the more abundant isotope.

BONDING AND THE STRUCTURE OF MATTER

To our eyes the paper on which these words are printed seems to be a continuous sheet. Mirrors seem to have a smooth, continuous surface. Our skin covers our body with what seems to be a continuous protective layer. A piece of copper, beaten into a thin sheet, appears continuous too. There are powerful microscopes that allow us to see the detail in these materials. For example when we look very closely at a thin sheet of copper, we see that it is not continuous at all but consists of small, spherical particles arranged in a regular array (pattern). The packing of these spheres leads to much of the sheet of copper being empty space. The particles in copper are atoms of copper. Atoms are the smallest particles in *elements*. Each element has its own specific atom.

Atoms can combine with other atoms (the same or different) to form *molecules*. These are the smallest particles in *compounds* and in some elements (such as hydrogen, H_2). Some molecules, such as water, are relatively small (three atoms combined). Others, such as carbohydrates, are *polymers* and have many thousands of atoms joined together. Because molecules consist of many atoms combined together, they are rarely spherical. Many large molecules are long threads. This means that the arrangement of particles we see in copper is not seen in carbohydrate polymers. Copper consists of spherical atoms packed together. This sheet of paper consists of woven threads of cellulose polymers.

All materials consist of molecules, large or small. The terms are relative. Even the largest of molecules is small by everyday standards. For example, the diameter of a hydrogen atom is about 10^{-13} cm. It would take 10 million, million hydrogen atoms touching in a line to make 1 cm. Now imagine 1 g of cane sugar. This mass of sugar contains almost two hundred thousand million, million, million molecules of sugar.

If the particles in a material are relatively far apart so that the forces of attraction between them are small and the particles are in rapid and random motion, the material is a *gas*. If the particles are closer together so that the forces of attraction are much stronger than in a gas, the material is a *liquid*. If the particles are very close together the forces of attraction are so strong that the particles are held in a rigid array as a *solid*. Solids, liquids and gases are the *three states of matter*. Which state a particular substance takes depends on its temperature and pressure. A change of state occurs at a *melting* temperature or at a *boiling* temperature. Changes of state are reversible:

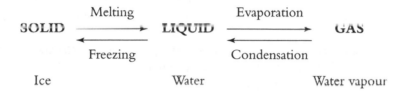

The change from solid to gas without passing through the liquid state is known as *sublimation*.

In the section on the structure of atoms, we saw that atoms are spherical in shape with a central nucleus which is surrounded by an electron field (electron cloud). When atoms join together to make molecules, only the electron fields are involved. The nuclei are deep within the atoms and take no part in chemical reactions. Why should atoms join together? The answer lies in stability with the product(s) being more stable than the reactant(s). Consider two atoms of hydrogen colliding. If conditions are appropriate the atoms will combine to form a molecule which is a more stable structure than the separate atoms. An atom of hydrogen has one electron in its electron field. This electron moves in a region of space called an orbital. When two hydrogen atoms join together the two electrons involved in the bonding share the combined orbital. This greater freedom of movement results in a lower energy state. In this type of bonding the two electrons involved are shared between the two atoms. Remember, a shared pair of electrons is a covalent bond. This can be expressed in a slightly different way.

It has been known for a long time that the noble gases are among the most stable of elements. Furthermore, it has been recognised that the reactivity of atoms is linked to the arrangement of electrons around the nucleus. Electrons are found in *energy levels* (electron shells or electron sub-shells) around the nucleus. The shell nearest to the nucleus can accommodate a maximum of two electrons. Other shells or sub-shells can accommodate a maximum of eight electrons. We can now view bonding between atoms as the result of the rearrangements of electrons so that all the atoms involved end up with a filled shell or sub-shell.

One way of achieving this is by *electron sharing* as indicated above. Another is by *electron transfer*. The following will illustrate the two types of bonding between atoms. An atom of hydrogen may be represented as shown in Figure 5.5. This gives the symbol and the number of electrons in each energy level. Remember that atoms are spherical particles and these energy levels are spherical too. A more stable arrangement would have two

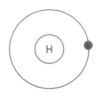

Figure 5.5 Representation of an atom of hydrogen

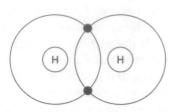

Figure 5.6 Representation of two atoms of hydrogen joined together

electrons in the outer energy level (i.e. completely filled). Two atoms of hydrogen join by sharing the two electrons (Figure 5.6). The shared electron pair is a covalent bond. In diagrams, a covalent bond is represented by a line. Thus H---H indicates a covalent bond between the two atoms of hydrogen. The two atoms of hydrogen are identical. Therefore, the negative charge in the covalent bond is shared equally between the two atoms.

An atom of chlorine may be represented as shown in Figure 5.7. In this example, three energy levels are being used. There are two electrons in the first level, eight in the next level and seven in the outer level. This totals seventeen, equal to the *atomic number*.

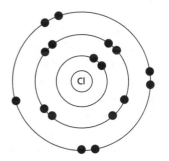

Figure 5.7 Representation of an atom of chlorine

Both the atom of hydrogen and the atom of chlorine have one *unpaired* electron. In the molecule of hydrogen chloride the two unpaired electrons are shared by both atoms to make a more stable electron arrangement than in the separate atoms. The atom of hydrogen will have access to two electrons in its outer energy level and the atom of chlorine will have access to eight electrons in its outer level (Figures 5.8). Therefore there is a covalent bond between the atom of hydrogen and the atom of chlorine. This would be written as: H---Cl.

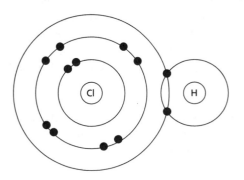

Figure 5.8 Representation of a molecule of hydrogen chloride

Because the two atoms are different, the negative charge in the bond is not shared equally between the two atoms. This separation of charge makes this bond a *polar* bond. We say that the bond has a *dipole*. Physical properties such as melting temperature, boiling temperature and solubility are determined by the existence of the dipole. The atoms of sodium and chlorine may be represented as shown in Figure 5.9.

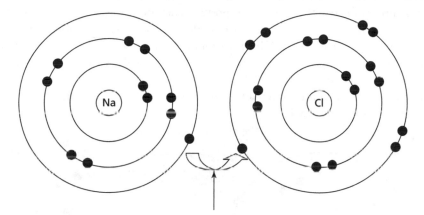

Electron transferred from atom of sodium to atom of chlorine

Figure 5.9 Representation of electron transfer between an atom of sodium and an atom of chlorine

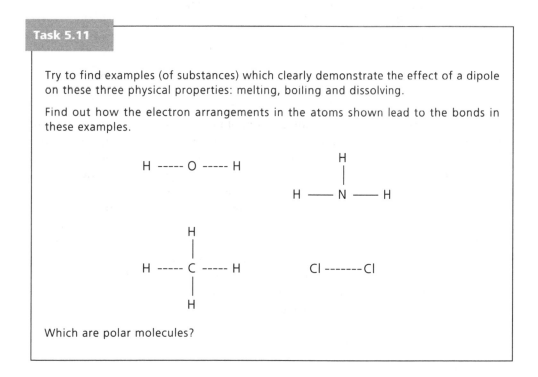

Task 5.11

Try to find examples (of substances) which clearly demonstrate the effect of a dipole on these three physical properties: melting, boiling and dissolving.

Find out how the electron arrangements in the atoms shown lead to the bonds in these examples.

H ----- O ----- H

H — N — H (with H above N)

H ----- C ----- H (with H above and H below C)

Cl ------- Cl

Which are polar molecules?

A more stable arrangement may be achieved by the transfer of one electron from the atom of sodium to the atom of chlorine. This gives both atoms completely filled outer energy levels. The chlorine atom has *gained* one electron, adding to the seven already in that energy level. By *losing* one electron, the sodium atom now has eight electrons in its outer level, previously its penultimate level.

This transfer affects only the arrangement of electrons in the atoms. The nuclei of the atoms remain unaffected, the number of positive charges in the atom does not change. Therefore the sodium atom, having lost one electron (negatively charged), becomes a particle with one positive charge. This is a sodium *ion*, represented as Na^+. On the other hand, the chlorine atom gains one electron, becoming a particle with one negative charge. This is a chlorine *ion* represented as Cl^-.

The transfer of electrons between an atom of magnesium and an atom of oxygen may be represented as in Figure 5.10.

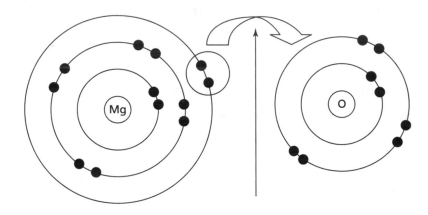

Figure 5.10 Representation of electron transfer between an atom of magnesium and an atom of oxygen

By the transfer of two electrons from the atom of magnesium to the atom of oxygen, both atoms will acquire eight electrons in the outer energy level. The magnesium atom becomes a positively charged magnesium ion Mg^{2+}. The oxygen atom becomes a negatively charged oxygen ion O^{2-}. Try to work out the rearrangement of electrons which occurs when two atoms of potassium react with one atom of oxygen.

The transfer of electrons from one atom to another results in the formation of charged particles called *ions*. In a compound the ions are of opposite charge (one negative and one positive) and are held together by an electrostatic force of attraction called an *ionic bond*.

Remember that a *covalent bond* is a pair of electrons shared between two atoms. An *ionic bond* is an electrostatic force of attraction holding ions together. Because a covalent bond consists of electrons positioned between two nuclei, a covalent bond has *direction* which leads to covalent substances having *shape*. For example:

1   *For the molecule of hydrogen, H_2*
     H——H   The shape of the molecule is linear.

2   *For the molecule of water, H_2O*

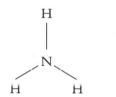

The shape of the molecule is bent.
The three atoms are in the same plane.

3   *For the molecule of ammonia, NH_3*

The shape of the molecule is pyramidal.
One N—H bond is in the plane of the paper.
Two N—H bonds lie in front of the plane of
    paper.

4   *For the molecule of methane, CH_4*

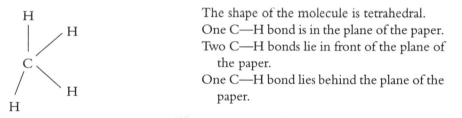

The shape of the molecule is tetrahedral.
One C—H bond is in the plane of the paper.
Two C—H bonds lie in front of the plane of
    the paper.
One C—H bond lies behind the plane of the
    paper.

Compounds of carbon are covalent and so have shape. As carbon compounds are the basis of living organisms shape plays an important part in biochemical systems. For example, molecules of a particular shape fitting into receptors allows the body to recognise substances by taste.

In substances with ionic bonding the charge on the ions is spread uniformly over the spherical surface of the ions. Therefore the attraction between ions (ionic bond) can be in all directions in 3-D. A positively charged ion is surrounded by negatively charged ions and each negatively charged ion is surrounded by positively charged ions. This gives a 3-D structure called an *ionic* lattice. Consider sodium chloride as a typical ionic compound. Even a small amount of sodium chloride contains many millions of ions of sodium and an equal number of ions of chlorine. These ions are spherical, and in solid sodium chloride they pack together to take up the least volume possible. This is close packing of spheres.

There are several different types of structure possible depending on two things: the relative sizes of the ions and the magnitude of the charges on the ions (Figure 5.11). In an ionic lattice, since the ions are packed closely together the forces of attraction are very strong. What properties do you think this gives the ionic structure?

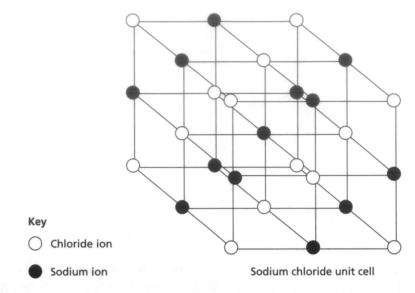

Key

○ Chloride ion

● Sodium ion   Sodium chloride unit cell

Figure 5.11 Representation of the structure of the ionic lattice of sodium chloride. This structure is repeated in three dimensions throughout the sample of sodium chloride. Such a repeating structure is a *unit cell*

SUGGESTIONS FOR FURTHER READING

If you would like to explore further some of the issues touched upon in this chapter, the following books should be of interest to you.

Porter, A., Wood, M. and Wood, T. (1994) *Science Companion – Essential Science for Key Stage 3*, Glasgow: Stanley Thornes
This is a useful basis for secondary science teaching. It shows how Materials and their Properties fits with other aspects of science.

ASE (n.d.) *Teaching Secondary Chemistry*, Hatfield: Association for Science Education
This is a readable textbook for GCSE chemistry and one of a set of three science texts.

Baggley, S., Cammis, C., Gow, J. and Noone, P. (1998) *Understanding and Applying Science 4*, London: John Murray
This text sets Materials in the context of wider science and includes some useful practical work as extension exercises.

NOTE

Science has many synonyms for the word *material*. The choice of word depends on the context. Those mentioned in this chapter are *chemical, material, matter, product, reactant, reagent* and *substance*. Each has the following meaning:

- *Chemical*: Abbreviation for chemical compound. A substance composed of two or more elements in definite proportions by weight.
- *Material*: A substance of which a thing is made.
- *Matter*: The substance of which the physical universe is composed. Matter is characterised by gravitational properties and by its indestructability under normal conditions.
- *Product*: A substance formed in a chemical reaction.
- *Reactant*: A substance taking part in a chemical reaction. A reactant is written on the left-hand side of the equation which represents the reaction.
- *Reagent*: A substance used to produce a characteristic reaction in chemical analysis.
- *Substance*: A type of matter with characteristic properties and, generally, a definite composition.

6 The Physical World

DOUGLAS NEWTON AND FRANK SAMBELL

INTRODUCTION

A rocket stands on the launching pad, its engines ignite, and the rocket lifts, accelerates, leaves the Earth's atmosphere and takes its satellite into orbit. Why did the rocket need engines? Why don't things just drift effortlessly into space? Why did the rocket burn up in the atmosphere when it fell back to Earth? Why did the satellite circle the Earth repeatedly, even though it had no engines? When the astronauts looked back at the Earth, they could see a large, tight swirl of cloud. Under the storm, high waves make small ships bob up and down, and lightning flashes from cloud to cloud and cloud to masthead. Why don't ocean waves sweep ships along with them and throw them on to some beach hundreds of miles away? Why are there lightning flashes? Why did lightning strike the masthead and not the deck? While this is happening, less dramatic events occur in every home. Someone switches on a lamp in the kitchen. It flashes then goes out. She feels in the drawer for a torch and goes to the fuse-box. Having replaced the fuse, she tries the switch again and the lamp works. She makes some sandwiches and begins to wrap them. The plastic stretches but not enough, so she puts the sandwiches in to a bag and holds the pack together with an elastic band. Why did the lamp go out? Why does a torch give off light? Why was the light confined to a beam? Why did the plastic film and the elastic band behave differently? All these events, spectacular and otherwise, involve physical processes. Why events like these happen as they do – or happen at all – is what this aspect of science is about.

Ideas about *forces*, *motion*, *energy* and *waves* help explain and understand such events. These powerful ideas have a wide range of application and help bring together various kinds of physical processes into a coherent whole. The physical processes studied in the secondary school are drawn from, for instance, *electricity*, *light*, *sound*, *properties of materials and objects*, and *radioactivity*. Such a list is never exhaustive but is a sample of what is felt to be important at a given time. As time passes, developments in science and what is relevant to people's needs change and the science programme is adjusted to reflect that.

The scientists who work in the fields described in this chapter tend to be described as physicists although, in practice, some would be more specific. Society and the opportunities people have were different in the past. In Western societies, women generally avoided learning and working in science. Unwarranted beliefs about what is an appropriate interest or career for a girl are still evident. Attitudes develop early in children and shape their motivation and decisions. They can impede learning and deny choices, particularly in this aspect of science. You should avoid adding to the problem. Much of what you teach stems from the work of physicists from earlier centuries – almost exclusively men. If ignored, the subliminal message this can convey is obvious. You should work towards removing self-imposed barriers and limits on your students' interests and achievements, whatever they are.

The aim of this chapter is to describe important aspects of what you must teach in Physical Processes (Figure 6.1). The order of the topics tends to reflect popular ordering in recent years but this does not mean that you must teach the topics in this order. Nor is it necessary to teach a topic in its entirety in one year. In fact, it is likely to be more productive if topics are revisited to revise, add and refine ideas. Remember that the National Curriculum allows students to take a reduced amount of science as a single subject, or a larger amount of science as a double subject at Key Stage 4 and in the GCSE. What follows reflects the minimum requirements of the National Curriculum for Physical Processes. Particular schemes of work and examination syllabuses take this core and add to it. A list of reading is provided at the end of the chapter so that you can develop and extend your teaching skills further.

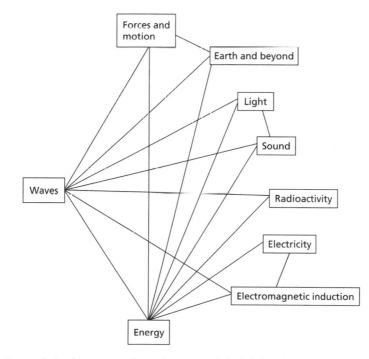

Figure 6.1 Some relationships among the topics commonly included in Physical Processes

ENERGY

At Key Stage 2, children may have used the word *energy* in connection with motion, electricity, light and sound, but they are likely to use the word loosely. In Design and Technology, the children will probably have made buggies propelled by elastic bands and, in some cases, by springs and electrical motors. This may provide you with a concrete starting point to explore the meaning of the concept of energy and energy transfer.

Teaching about energy

Energy is an abstract concept that can be meaningless to younger students. How to make it meaningful while doing justice to the science can be a contentious matter. Some take the view that it is entirely beyond young students' abilities while others see it as so central to our lives that we cannot deny it a place in elementary science. The latter view prevails and so the debate is largely one of what to teach and how to teach it. Traditionally, the favoured approach has been to describe *forms of energy*, how they 'flow' from place to place, and how they are *transformed* from one form to another. For instance, chemical energy in a battery can be transformed into electrical energy, and then into light and heat energy in a torch bulb. Some argue that labelling these so-called intermediate forms of energy (e.g. electrical energy) can obscure the process of energy transfer. Accordingly, another approach concerns itself less with labels for forms of energy and simply describes the transfer of energy from one place to another. Thus an electrical current *transfers* energy from the battery to the torch bulb. In this approach, forms of energy (e.g. chemical) may be treated as *energy stores*. Although we suggest that you talk of energy in terms of energy transfer and energy sources, do bear in mind that this may foster a belief in energy as an invisible substance. This can be countered if you give students a rudimentary grasp of the concept of energy, albeit limited to certain concrete and mechanical instances. At times, you will still have to talk of certain forms of energy (e.g. kinetic and potential energy).

The concept of energy

There is something unsatisfying about teaching when you do not help students build a mental picture of ideas. To argue that the idea is mathematical or abstract is not to say that we should not try to make it meaningful. Energy is a state or condition with the potential for change. When the state or condition does change, we may try to use that change to do something for us. You will recognise in that change a formal definition of energy as the capacity to do work. The problem is that this is often quite meaningless to pupils. What do we mean by 'capacity' and 'work'? Consider a stretched elastic band. It can return to its original size. When it does so, we can get it to propel a buggy. In other words, being stretched gives the elastic band the capacity to do work. This capacity comes from the state or condition that will change if we let it. The more the band is stretched, the more it might do. We tend to say that the more it is stretched, the more energy there is stored or available. If the band is used like a catapult, when it is released it can exert a force on a buggy that makes it move. In the same way, a coiled or compressed spring is an energy store and may also be used to make a buggy move. Even a book poised on the edge of a table is an energy store. When it falls, its height above the floor changes and, if it was attached to a buggy via a string, it could make the buggy move. When lying on the table top, we often say that the book has *potential energy* (literally, the potential to make energy available). Just before it hits the floor, it is moving fairly fast. You might use the book in this way to break open a nut. In other words, there is the capacity to do work in the state of moving – something that is often referred to as *kinetic energy*. This is used to advantage when wind turns a generator to produce electricity.

The conservation of energy

The amount of energy in an isolated system is constant. In other words, when energy is transferred from one place to another, the amount lost by the source is the same as that gained by the various recipients, in total. A helpful analogy is to say it is like having exactly £20. You give (transfer) £10 to Ben, £8 to Nadia, and £2 to John. When you add up what you transferred, it amounts to £20, so the books balance. If they could only receive money from you, their total could not be £21 or £19. If they, in turn, transferred it to others in the class, it might be spread around a bit more, but the total would still be £20. In the same way, energy might be transferred from a battery to a lamp at the rate of 100 joules per second. The lamp may transfer 40 joules per second of light energy and 60 joules per second of thermal energy. First, the books balance ($100 = 40 + 60$). Second, since it is light we want, a lot of energy is 'wasted' as heat. In effect, the lamp is only 40 per cent efficient. You will also find that Sankey diagrams are recommended to summarise and display such an account of energy flow. For this example, see Figure 6.2.

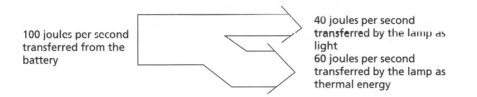

Figure 6.2 Sankey diagram to represent energy flow

The swing of a pendulum is often cited as an instance of the Conservation of Energy. When the pendulum is held to one side it is, potentially, a source of energy (potential energy). Suppose this amount is ½ joule. When released, the pendulum swings down and, at its lowest point, is moving fairly quickly. It still has ½ joule of energy but now it is kinetic. The pendulum, of course, continues and is carried up until its potential energy is ½ joule, again. (Note that talking of *transferring* energy in the pendulum does not seem right: the pendulum would be transferring energy from itself to itself. This is a case where *transforming* energy from potential to kinetic can make more sense.) In reality, as the pendulum swings, some energy is continually transferred to the air and string through friction so there is less available in each successive swing to maintain motion, and eventually the pendulum comes to rest.

The Conservation of Energy is sometimes confused with the conservation of energy (no capitals). The conservation of energy refers to the need to use energy sources (e.g. coal, gas, oil, nuclear fission) sparingly, since they are limited in quantity. This entails ensuring that we get the most out of such sources by making, for instance, car engines efficient and reducing heat loss from houses. In the latter case, energy transfer is reduced by, for instance, lining lofts with a poor conductor of heat and installing double glazing. The problem, of course, is that these need energy for manufacturing and fitting, and the real saving is what is left after these factors are taken into account. The equation is further complicated by environmental effects that arise by burning some fuels. For instance, sulphur emissions (often as sulphurous acid) can produce acid rain that can severely damage plant life many miles away. It also seems likely that carbon dioxide emissions are changing the composition of the atmosphere so that more heat is retained near and on the Earth's surface. This could have serious implications for climate. Some sources of energy are renewable. Trees, for instance, can be planted, cropped and replaced. The advantage is that although they produce carbon dioxide when burned, this is taken up again when new trees grow. Energy extracted from the wind and from water (rivers, tides and waves) is also usually called renewable. These renewable sources are maintained by the Sun's energy, a source that will last for millions of years.

Work, power and energy

The unit of energy is the joule, abbreviated to J (after James Joule, the Victorian scientist who laid much of the foundation for the study of energy). Roughly speaking, 1 J is the amount of energy which has to be transferred to lift a cup of tea from a table to the mouth. Work done is energy transferred to achieve some end, so it is also measured in joules. If the task is to move a large crate across a room, the greater the force needed, the greater the energy that has to be transferred. Similarly, the greater the distance the crate has to be pushed, the greater the energy that has to be transferred. This force–distance effect is captured in the formula:

$$\text{Work done (J)} = \text{Force (N)} \times \text{Distance (m)}$$

For a book at a certain distance above the floor (height, h), gravity pulls down on it with a force mg (mass × acceleration, mass in kg and acceleration in ms^{-2}). Thus, the potential energy of the book relative to the floor is mgh joules (force × distance). Kinetic energy turns out to be $\frac{1}{2}mv^2$ (v is the velocity in ms^{-1}). This means that when the book hits the floor, its potential energy has become kinetic energy and $mgh = \frac{1}{2}mv^2$. This type of calculation is required in problems to do with the pendulum.

Power is the rate of doing work; that is, the number of joules transferred per second. Power is measured in watts (W). Thus a 60 W light bulb transfers 60 Js^{-1} into light (and heat). Before the last century, horses did a lot of the tasks that are now done by machines. A good horse, working hard and at a steady rate, has a power of about 750 W. This was referred to as a horsepower (1 HP) and it enabled people to compare the power of horses with that of the new machines being developed.

Some misconceptions or alternative frameworks relating to energy

Pupils' concepts of energy may be influenced by expressions such as 'full of energy', and pictures that appear to show that certain foodstuffs make you glow with energy. Similarly, news items about the energy industry can lead to various confusions between sources of energy and energy itself, and between force, energy and power. In other words, pupils may use these terms interchangeably. Make an effort to use such terms carefully yourself and take time to reinforce their meaning. Energy transfer may also be dealt with by your colleagues who teach design and technology. Consult them to find out which approach they use – it will not support understanding if teaching is radically different in science and D&T.

Energy at Key Stage 3

At Key Stage 3, pupils can be taught about important energy sources and their origins, the distinction between renewable and non-renewable resources and how electricity is generated by using these resources. They can learn about energy and its transfer (conduction, convection, radiation and evaporation) and the Conservation of Energy. Keep the explanations concrete.

1 What do we mean by *energy*?

Find out what pupils' concepts of energy are by asking questions and discussing responses with the pupils. Begin the process of establishing a scientific concept of energy in a concrete way using, for example, a stretched elastic band, a compressed spring and a bent stick. Ask the pupils to identify what changes when you release each item, and to suggest how the change might be made to do something more or less useful. Use this to arrive at a meaningful, simple definition of energy.

2 Gravity and energy

Extend the account to objects held above floor level. Introduce the terms *potential energy* and *kinetic energy*. Apply them to falling objects, to a toy car running to and fro on a concave surface and to a pendulum.

Example of an investigation: Why does the toy car eventually stop? Ask the pupils to hypothesise about the cause, design an investigation to test their hypothesis, predict outcomes and carry out the test. Afterwards, discuss what happens to the energy 'lost' due to friction.

---

3 Chemicals and energy

Compare a dead and decayed battery with a new battery to make the point that the substances inside batteries change. (For safe and easy handling, keep the decayed battery in a transparent bag. Do not let the pupils handle it.) Extend the account of energy to include this kind of change. Explain that food and fuels are sources of energy in a similar way. Show that a peanut can be a source of energy by inserting a pin into the nut, holding the pin with tongs and setting the peanut alight.

> *Example of an investigation*: Which peanut has more energy available, one straight from the shell or a roasted peanut? Ask the pupils to consider what the effect of roasting might be and predict which peanut will have more energy available. They should design an experiment to test their prediction (e.g. burning peanuts under matching boiling tubes of water).

4 Heat and energy

The above activity has introduced heat, so this is a convenient point to pursue it further. Describe thermal energy in terms of molecular motion. Heat different materials for the same length of time (for example, use a Bunsen burner to heat a kilogram of water and a kilogram of iron), hence demonstrating that the same amount of thermal energy produces different temperatures. Ask the pupils to explain the difference between the water and the iron in terms of molecular motion. Describe evaporation in terms of molecular motion.

> *Example of an investigation*: The aim is to store the sun's heat during the day so it can be transferred into the house at night. Which material would be the best to use: water, soil, brick? Ask the pupils to devise an investigation to find the best material to use. Will a drop of water that is spread out evaporate more quickly than one which is not spread out? Ask the pupils to predict which will evaporate more quickly and to justify their predictions. Ask them to investigate the effect of surface area on evaporation to test their ideas.

5 Conduction, convection, radiation

Demonstrate conduction, convection and radiation. (There are fairly standard pieces of equipment for doing this in the classroom.) Describe these as processes of energy transfer. Relate the effects to everyday applications.

> *Example of an investigation*: Which materials are good conductors of heat? Ask the pupils to test a range of materials in rod form, perhaps using heat-sensitive paper as the temperature sensor.

6 Renewable and non-renewable sources of energy

Ask the pupils what life would be like when there are no more fossil fuels. Talk about how electricity is generated using a variety of sources of energy, including wind and moving water. Ask them to supplement this evidence by using books, wall charts, CD and website sources of information.

7 Transferring energy and the Conservation of Energy

Ask the pupils to draw diagrams to represent energy transfer events. Convert them to simple Sankey diagrams. Distinguish between the Conservation of Energy and the conservation of energy.

Review the pupils' grasp of the concept of energy and compare it with the one they had to begin with. Point out the change to the children to let them see that they are learning and making progress in science.

Energy at Key Stage 4

At this stage, there is a greater emphasis on quantifying energy.

1 How much energy?

Review the work at Key Stage 3 on energy. Introduce the joule as a unit of energy and give it meaning by exemplifying the energy needed to do some everyday tasks, such as lifting a cup of tea from a table to your mouth (roughly 1 J). Ask the pupils about the energy involved in lifting such a cup vertically over twice the distance, and taking it upstairs through a vertical height of 4 m. Similarly, ask what the effect would be if it was a mug of tea with twice the mass of the cup of tea. Hence arrive at: Work done (J) = Force (N) × Distance (m) and ask the pupils to practise its use in a variety of contexts.

2 Power

Explain the scientific meaning of power. Ask the pupils to weigh themselves, then to time themselves climbing a set of stairs and hence calculate their own power.

> *Example of an investigation*: Show the pupils a small, low-voltage, electric motor. Ask how they might calculate its power. Ask them to design a practical arrangement and try it out.

3 Potential and kinetic energy

Ask the pupils to recall the meaning of potential and kinetic energy, and show them how to calculate these for some everyday phenomena (e.g. a 100 g cup of tea on a table

70 cm above the floor, a 70 kg person walking at 4 kmh^{-1}). Explore instances of the conversion of potential energy into kinetic and vice versa.

Example of an investigation: How much energy is 'lost' each time a ball bounces? Illustrate that the height of rebound of a ball diminishes each time it bounces. Discuss what is meant by 'lost' in this instance. Why? What happens to the energy? Ask the pupils to investigate how much energy is lost in successive bounces of a ball.

4 Transfer of thermal energy

Revisit conduction, convection and radiation. Talk about the need to be economical with sources of energy and how this is achieved in the home. Extend this to the need for an economical use of energy resources in general and some environmental implications of energy generation. Show that the problem is not a simple one.

Example of an investigation: Which material is best at keeping heat in? Discuss what this means scientifically. Ask the pupils to examine, hypothesise and predict about a range of materials, then test them; for example, beakers of equally hot water may be lagged with different materials and the temperature of each taken regularly.

5   Generating electricity

This aspect of energy may be taught as an extension to work on electricity (see below) or as a unit attached to Energy. You should include:

- the motor effect and the electric motor (see also the investigation of the power of an electrical motor, above),
- electromagnetic induction and the ac generator,
- transformer action,
- the generation and transfer of energy from the power-station to the home.

Various kits are available for hands-on experience of motor and dynamo action. The supply of electricity from the power-station to the home is often modelled on a small scale using safe voltages.

ELECTRICITY AND MAGNETISM

The students will have had some hands-on experience of simple electric circuits, particularly at Key Stage 2. Generally, they should be able to set up a circuit to make a light bulb or buzzer work and to draw a simple circuit diagram. These circuits will usually have included on-off switches. Many students will have tested various materials for conductivity and will know that a complete circuit is needed for a circuit to function.

Not all students will understand why a complete circuit is necessary. They will have been made aware of the dangers of mains electricity and this should be reinforced. Up to the end of Key Stage 4 all practical work with electricity uses low-voltage direct current. Low voltage is normally up to 12 volts and is recommended for safety reasons. The use of direct current is a matter of convenience, since most low-voltage supplies are cells or batteries. Most students will also have handled magnets and tested various materials with a magnet. They are likely to know that a magnet has poles and that a compass is a magnet that responds to the Earth's magnetic field.

Circuits

A *complete circuit* is one where the electricity can flow from one terminal of the battery, around the circuit and to the other terminal. Current flowing through a circuit will tend to take the path of least resistance. A *short circuit* is a complete circuit that bypasses components because an easier route is available. Usually this occurs when a circuit has not been constructed properly. For instance, if a wire bypasses a bulb most of the current will tend to go through the wire so the bulb will not glow. Sometimes, the current in a low-resistance short circuit can be strong enough to cause heating and start a fire.

A *series circuit* is one in which the components are all connected in a single loop. The current flows from one terminal through each component in turn to the other terminal (Figure 6.3). A *parallel circuit* is one in which there is more than one loop powered by the same source. In effect, the loops share the same power supply (Figure 6.4). Components commonly used in circuits at this level include:

- batteries (e.g. multiples of 1.5V and low-voltage bench supply);
- switches of various kinds (e.g. on-off, off-on (*not* gate));
- filament bulbs (and their semi-conductor equivalent, the light-emitting diodes);
- buzzers (low-voltage sound producers);
- resistors (including light-dependent resistors which change resistance according to the amount of light which falls on them and thermistors which change resistance according to the temperature);
- semi-conductor diodes (devices which allow current to flow in one direction only).

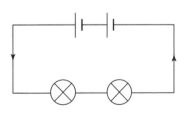

Figure 6.3 A series circuit – two batteries in series and two filament lamps (bulbs) in series

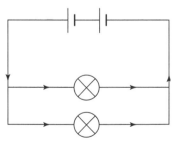

Figure 6.4 A parallel circuit – two batteries in series but two lamps in parallel

The *current* is the rate of flow of electrical charge. Electrical charge is measured in *coulombs*. The rate of flow is therefore the number of coulombs per second that passes a point in a circuit. Coulombs per second are normally called amperes, usually abbreviated to *amps* (A). Batteries are rated by their *voltage* (V). This is an indication of the energy per unit of current they can deliver to a circuit (joules per coulomb). In practice, batteries themselves tend to resist the flow of electricity, and some of the energy is lost as heat in the battery, overcoming this resistance. In the same way, the current transfers energy to each component in the circuit. A voltmeter connected across a bulb may, for instance, read 1V, indicating that 1 joule per coulomb is being transferred to the bulb. This voltage of 1V across the bulb is known as the *potential difference* between the terminals of the bulb.

Ohm's Law

For many components, the current (in amps) through them increases as the potential difference (in volts) across them increases. For some components, when the conditions are right, the current is directly proportional to this potential difference. In other words, when the potential difference is doubled, the current doubles. A material or component that behaves like this is said to obey *Ohm's Law*. For example, a resistor made from carbon obeys Ohm's Law fairly well provided that the current does not heat the resistor. This means that a graph of current against voltage will be a straight line passing through the origin. A filament bulb, on the other hand, does not obey Ohm's Law because the filament's resistance changes as it is heated. In this instance, the current–voltage graph will be a curve that passes through the origin. For a material or component that obeys Ohm's Law, where the current is proportional to the voltage, this is expressed as $V = RI$ (where V is the potential difference in volts, I is the current in amps and R, the constant of proportionality, is the resistance of the component in ohms, Ω). *Resistance* is a measure of the ability of a component or material to oppose the current.

Electrical power

Electrical power describes the rate of energy transfer in a circuit or in the components of a circuit. So, for instance, a current might transfer 3 joules per second (usually called watts, W), to the filament of a bulb, a process we would notice because of the light and heat it emits. The rate of energy transfer depends directly upon the potential difference (voltage) across the bulb and the current through it. That is, $P = IV$, where P is the power (in watts), I is the current (in amps) and V is the potential difference (in volts). In this case, if the current was 2A then $3 = 2 \times V$. So the potential difference across the bulb must be 1.5V. The above formula has other forms: $P = I^2R$ and $P = V^2/R$. (You can prove this for yourself by substituting $V = RI$ into $P = IV$.)

Magnetic fields and electromagnets

A magnet is an object that attracts certain materials, the most obvious being ferrous-based (iron and steel). (A magnet may attract articles made from 'tin'. In reality, 'tin' is actually sheet steel with a thin coating of tin to prevent rusting.) The zone of influence around a magnet is called its *magnetic field*. Traditionally, these are revealed with iron filings (with safety considerations) or plotting compasses.

A wire with a current flowing through it has a magnetic field around it. When the wire is wound into a cylindrical coil, the magnetic field around the coil is similar to that around a bar magnet. However, an important difference is that the field disappears when the current is switched off. This makes it possible to have *electromagnets* which can be switched on and off as in scrap-yard cranes. These devices are also used in electrical bells, buzzers and relays.

Mains electricity

Mains electricity commonly refers to the electrical power supply in homes. In the UK, this supply is 240V alternating current (ac). This means that the current is flowing to and fro (at 50 cycles per second in the UK). Because the supply is alternating, the voltage actually varies throughout the cycle and reaches a peak of above 300V. The 240V is a kind of average. The danger associated with mains electricity largely arises from the combination of a high voltage and its alternating nature which can interrupt the heart's rhythm. The transmission of mains electricity to a home (via pylons, for instance) is often at a much higher voltage, making pylons dangerous places to play.

The dangers of the mains supply make it necessary for electrical plugs to have an earth connection. In the event of certain faults in a circuit, this connects the body of the appliance directly to the ground. The fuse is likewise a safety device which breaks the circuit if the current becomes excessively large.

Household appliances generally need more power than the components of classroom circuits. For instance, a heater might be rated at 2 kW (2000 W). Since P = IV, 2000 = I × 240. This makes I about 4 A. The fuse in the plug would have to be greater than 4 A if it was not to melt and break the circuit on normal running. A 5-A fuse would be too close to 4-A fuse and might melt in normal use. Typically, a 13-A fuse would be used.

We have to pay for the power transferred to our electrical appliances through the mains services. Calculations based on watts and seconds of use give large numbers, so generally kilowatts (kW) and hours of use are used. For example, the 2-kW heater on for three hours would 'consume' 2 × 3 = 6 kW-hr of energy. If the tariff was 10p per kW-hr, this would cost 60p.

Some misconceptions or alternative frameworks relating to electricity and magnetism

The best-known misconception concerning electrical circuits is that only one wire from a battery to a component is needed. This is associated with a consumption view of electricity – current flows from the battery to the component and is consumed there. This is a particularly difficult conception to modify, even when students accept the need for a complete circuit. They may, for instance, be surprised to find the same current on either side of a filament bulb in a series circuit. Of lesser consequence can be a belief that electricity will flow from a socket on a wall if the switch is left on and there is no plug in place.

Some practicalities to do with managing activities about electricity

Working with circuits will involve large quantities of components which may not be reliable. Check everything beforehand, and be highly organised about how you manage, distribute and collect the components. Have available a simple test meter for you to check bulbs, batteries and wires in use. Be prepared for a large number of requests for help with faulty circuits. As soon as is reasonable show the students how to test components themselves.

Electricity and magnetism at Key Stage 3

At Key Stage 3 students are taught to make series and parallel circuits, and to measure current and voltage in them. A concerted attempt is made to change misconceptions about current flow. The elements of magnetism and magnetic fields are explored and related to subsequent work on electromagnets.

1 Exploring circuits and measuring current

Explore the students' ideas about electricity, electrical circuits and current flow. Ask them to construct various series and parallel circuits. Introduce the ammeter and ask them to try it in a simple series circuit.

> *Example of an investigation*: Ask the students to find the current in one arm of a series circuit and then to predict what it will be in the return arm. Get them to test their predictions and to explain what they find. Repeat this with the loops of a parallel circuit where the loops are identical (e.g. one bulb in each) and different (e.g. one bulb in one loop and two in the other).

2 Measuring voltage

Prepare a collection of various low-voltage batteries for the students to examine. Ask them to identify the voltage of each and suggest what that tells us about the batteries. Show them how to measure the voltage using a voltmeter.

Example of an investigation: Ask the students how they can use the batteries they have to make a larger voltage. Let them try out their ideas and test them with the voltmeter. Get them to predict the effect of connecting two matching batteries so that they oppose one another and test their prediction and explain what they find. Ask them to explore the effect of connecting identical batteries in parallel. They will find that this arrangement does not increase the voltage but is like having a larger battery that will last twice as long.

3 Measuring the voltage across circuit components (potential difference)

Example of an investigation: Ask how a battery's voltage might be shared out among the components of a series circuit (e.g. one containing three identical filament bulbs). Get the students to test their ideas and to explain what they find. Ask them to short-circuit one bulb, observe what happens and predict what will have happened to the voltages across each bulb. Let them test their ideas and explain findings.

4 Electrical language

The meaning of words in electricity is important for understanding. Explain the origins of words such as electricity and electron (tell the story of Electra, the Greek goddess), charge (originally meaning filling something with electricity, e.g. charging a glass with wine), volt (after Volta), amp (after Ampére) and galvanism (after Galvani who made frogs' legs twitch when he connected dissimilar metals).

5 Strength of magnets

Example of an investigation: Ask the students to think of ways they can measure the strength of a magnet. Give them bar magnets of different strengths and ask them to investigate the problem and find out which is the strongest.

Example of an investigation: Ask if a magnet's influence can pass through paper. How does the thickness of the paper affect the strength of the influence? Get them to investigate their ideas.

6 Electromagnets

Ask the students to investigate the magnetism around current-carrying wires with a plotting compass. Ask them to suggest how they can make the effect stronger (e.g. by bending the wire into other shapes). Get them to test their ideas. Conclude with exploration of a solenoid.

Electricity and magnetism at Key Stage 4

At Key Stage 4 students will learn about resistance, its effect on a current in circuits, and the relationship between resistance, voltage and current. They will also learn about mains electricity and electrical power.

1 Resistance

Ask the students to construct a series circuit containing a filament bulb and ammeter. Then get them to add a resistor (e.g. a 5-ohm carbon radio resistor) in series with the bulb, and note and explain its effect. Introduce the terms *resistor* and *resistance* and the ohm (Ω) as the unit of resistance. Show the students how to use a multimeter to measure resistance.

Example of an investigation: Ask the students to predict the effect of connecting resistors in series and in parallel, and to test their predictions with a multimeter. They should then include the combinations in the series circuit and explain why the effects are what they expect.

Example of an investigation: Issue light-dependent resistors as an unknown device. Ask the students to find out what they do and to incorporate one into their series circuit to demonstrate its effect.

---

2 Testing various components

With the series circuit (above) set up with the ammeter and resistor, include a voltmeter in parallel with the resistor. Ask the students to record the current and voltage. The next step is to increase the voltage by including another battery in series with the first. Current and voltage are again recorded. Ask the students to predict what the current and voltage would be if a third battery was added. If possible, let them test their response.

Example of an investigation: In the above circuit, the voltage across the resistor should double if the current doubles (provided that the resistor remains cool). This is an example of a component that obeys Ohm's Law. The relationship is best seen in a graph of current against voltage, when a straight line through the origin is obtained. The question is: Which other components obey Ohm's Law? Let the students investigate filament bulbs, diodes and light-dependent resistors to find out.

Example of an investigation: The resistance of a thermistor changes as the temperature changes. Ask the students for possible applications of a thermistor and have them investigate its properties.

3 Power and household appliances

Prepare a display of various household appliances that have their power requirements marked on them. Show these to the students and discuss their meaning. Ask the students to rank the appliances according to how much it would cost to run each one and try to calculate costs from genuine tariffs (e.g. as on electricity bills).

Example of an investigation: Demonstrate energy transfer to water using a low-voltage laboratory immersion heater. Include an ammeter and voltmeter in the circuit so that the students can calculate the power input. Ask them to record the time and the increase in temperature so that the output may be measured. How do the two compare? Ask the students to explain the results.

4 Electrical plugs

Dismantle an electrical plug and explain the components. Issue lengths of three-core cable, plugs and appropriate screwdrivers. Get the students to wire them. Ask them to calculate the current drawn from the mains by an appliance in (3) above and they should then select an appropriate fuse from the range you make available and fit it to the plug.

FORCES AND MOTION

A concrete concept of a force will have been introduced in Key Stages 1 and 2. Children will know a force as a push or a pull, and that forces cause various kinds of motion. They are likely to name particular forces such as a magnetic force, friction and the force of gravity. The children should have been introduced to the newton as a unit of force and used newton meters to measure forces in simple contexts such as measuring the friction between a shoe and various surfaces. They are likely to have measured forces and their effects on items such as elastic bands and plastic bags. The difference between mass and weight may have been explained but the children's understanding of it may, as yet, be incomplete.

The notion of a force

Forces are what we call the influences that make objects move, change their motion or alter their shape. The parts of your body are held in place by forces: you get the world around you to do what you want using forces; you are held in place on the surface of the Earth by the Earth's gravitational force; the Earth is held on orbit by the pull of the Sun; and the Sun responds to the gravitational forces of the contents of the galaxy. In short, life, the universe and everything in it are influenced by an uncountable number of forces, large and small, all the time. These influences are often named according to their source so that there are friction, elastic, gravitational, magnetic and electrostatic forces, and surface tension. Forces have size or *magnitude*. The magnitude of a force is measured in newtons (N) and it takes about 3 to 5 N to raise a jar of jam steadily upwards from a table. Note that the direction (upwards) is also mentioned, because forces also have *direction*. Having both size and direction makes a force a *vector* in constrast to energy, which has only size (e.g. 10 J) and so is a scalar.

The effect of balanced, unbalanced and resultant forces

Suppose we wish to make a block of wood move across the surface of a table: we need to apply a force to the block of wood.

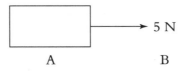

A   B

To move the block from A to B requires a force in the direction shown by the arrow.

If more than one force acts on the same block, we need to know the *resultant force* before we can say what happens to the block. If the forces are as in the diagram below, they are unbalanced, and the overall force is one of 3 N to the right and the block will move to the right.

If, however, the forces are equal and opposite, as in the diagram opposite, the resultant force is zero and there is no movement (although the block may stretch, depending on its material).

This is not the whole story, however. In this case, the block stays still because it was stationary to start with. Had the object been moving steadily, adding balanced forces to it would make no difference: it would continue to move at that steady speed. It would take an unbalanced force to make a difference. For example, for a rocket to leave the Earth, a force must act on the rocket. This force comes from the engine on the rocket. Once the rocket is well away from the Earth, the engine may be switched off. The rocket will continue at the speed it reached until some other force acts on it. If a change in direction is needed, an unbalanced force is needed, so the motor (or a small steering engine) is switched on for a time to provide the force.

Forces and acceleration

Unbalanced forces cause things to accelerate. Suppose a force of 10 N makes the block accelerate at the rate of 2 m/s^2. A force of 20 N will make the block accelerate at the rate of 4 m/s^2. The ratio of force to acceleration is constant: $10/2 = 5$; $20/4 = 5$. This constant is the *mass* of the block, 5 kg. This is expressed as:

$$\text{force/acceleration} = \text{mass}$$

or

$$\text{force} = \text{mass} \times \text{acceleration}$$

where the force is in N, the mass is in kg and the acceleration in m/s^2. The formula shows that the same unbalanced force will be something of small mass increase in speed at a greater rate than something of large mass which, of course, matches experience. Note that the same argument (and formula) applies to decelerating objects.

Rotation and turning

Forces can also make things turn about a pivot or fulcrum. The steering wheel of a car, for instance, is turned by an upward push on one side and a downward pull on the other. A pair of forces like this is known as a *couple*. Forces used in this way are common: taps, doorknobs, fitting a nut to a bolt, spinning a ball, are all examples. When fitting a nut to a bolt, the size of the turning effect is important. If excessive, it can make the bolt shear off. If insufficient, the nut may come loose. The turning effect, *moment* or *torque*, is calculated by multiplying the size of the force by the distance to the pivot. In the case of a spanner that is 20 cm long, pulled by a force of 100 N, the moment is 100 N $\times$ 0.2 m or 20 Nm. Torque wrenches are used to measure the size of the turning effect needed to fit a nut.

Another device which uses the turning effect is the crowbar. In essence, this is a lever with the pivot close to the object being extracted, rather like a screwdriver being used to prise open a tin of paint. In the laboratory, lever action is usually investigated using a wooden ruler on an edge that serves as the fulcrum. This tends to disconnect turning effect from the real world and can lack interest unless you make an attempt to reconnect it. When levers are balanced on a fulcrum, the sum of the turning effects on one side matches the sum of those on the other. This is known as the *Principle of Moments*.

The force of gravity

Everything on the Earth presses down on its surface. An adult male with a mass of 70 kg presses down with a force of 70 kilograms force (kgf). This is what we commonly call his weight, and some bathroom scales are calibrated in kgf. The cause of weight is the gravitational pull of the Earth, a pull that acts vertically downwards towards the centre of the Earth. If the man was free to fall, he would fall at the rate of 9.8 m/s^2, the acceleration due to gravity. To see what 70 kgf is in newtons, use:

$$\text{force} = \text{mass} \times \text{acceleration}$$

where 70 kgf = 70 kg $\times$ 9.8 m/s^2 about 700 N. On the Moon, the force of gravity is only one-sixth of what it is on the Earth (because the Moon has a much smaller mass than the Earth). The man would still have a mass of 70 kg on the Moon but he would press down (weigh) only 700/6 N, that is, about 117 N. To find his acceleration on the Moon if he was to fall, use force = mass $\times$ acceleration again: 117 = 70 $\times$ acceleration; that is, the acceleration is about 1.7 m/s^2, one-sixth of what it would be on the Earth, as you would expect. All objects would fall at this rate on the Moon, regardless of their mass. For instance, if the mass was 35 kg, the press would be 58.5N, and the acceleration would be 1.7 m/s^2 again. On the Earth, everything would fall at 9.8 m/s^2, regardless of their mass, if it was not for the friction of the air. Air resistance is what makes a feather fall more slowly than an apple. On the Moon, where there is no air, a feather and an apple released together both fall at the same rate and reach the ground together.

Friction

Friction is the force that opposes motion when something moves through a gas, a liquid, or over a solid or liquid surface. Air resistance is an example of a frictional force, and the friction between the soles of our shoes and the pavement enables us to walk forward. Some of the energy of motion is transferred to the materials and we sense it as heat. A bicycle or car tyre feels warm after prolonged use, but more spectacular is the heat generated by a spacecraft on re-entry to the atmosphere.

Another important effect of the force of friction is that all vehicles have a top speed, even though the engine (or cyclist) continues to try to push. The force which moves the car comes from the engine. This force is limited by the design of the engine. As the car picks up speed, the frictional force, predominantly from air flowing over the car, increases. The greater the forward speed, the greater the frictional force. Eventually the frictional force will be the same as the force from the engine and there will be no resultant force acting on the car. Without a resultant force there can be no acceleration, and the car will continue at a constant (maximum) speed. A similar situation arises when an object falls vertically through the air. Initially the object accelerates towards the Earth, the accelerating force being its own weight. As it picks up speed, the frictional force from the air increases. Eventually this upward force matches the weight of the object. The forces on the object are now balanced and there is no accelerating force. The object will now continue to fall towards the Earth at a constant speed called its *terminal velocity*. You may like to consider why someone in free fall and curled up will have a higher terminal velocity than someone who spreads out their arms and legs.

Pressure

Pressure is the force per unit area. For instance, a box with sides 2 m long standing on a flat surface, would be resting on a side of area 4 m^2. If the box contained waste cardboard it might weigh about 250 kgf, that is, about 2500 N. The force on each square metre of ground would be:

$$2500 / 4 = 625 \text{ N/m}^2.$$

In other words, the pressure on the ground would be 625 N/m^2. If this cube rested on your foot, the area would be much smaller, say, 0.02 m^2. The pressure you would experience would be 2500/0.02 = 125 000 N/m^2, probably quite painful. A drawing-pin is relatively easy to push into a pin board because the small area of the point results in a large pressure. A sharp knife cuts for the same reason.

Some misconceptions or alternative frameworks relating to forces

Many students will think that because an object is stationary, there are no forces acting upon it. In reality, of course, the forces are balanced. Similarly, students often think that an object moving at a steady speed must have a continually active force to keep it in motion. Of course this applies only to objects subject to friction. In rotation, students may think that the force acts in the direction of motion, rather than towards the centre of the circle. They may also think that a falling object (e.g. a satellite) is weightless. The terms *force*, *energy* and *power* may also be used as though they are all the same.

Forces at Key Stage 3

1 Forces

Elicit the students' ideas about the nature of a force. Remind them of the newton as a unit of force. Get them to feel forces of different sizes and estimate forces, testing their estimates with a force meter. Introduce and illustrate the direction of a force as an essential element of it.

> *Example of an investigation*: Ask the students to compare how various materials respond to an extension force. Provide the materials in similar form (e.g. lengths of cotton, linen, wool, plastic, 'rubber' thread). Discuss the nature of the response and introduce Hooke's Law as a special case when doubling the force doubles the extension. Hooke was particularly interested in the way bows responded to an extension force. Ask how knowing how materials stretch and compress would be of interest to us. Introduce springs and ask the students to test them.

2   Friction

Elicit students' ideas about friction. Ask if it is useful or a nuisance. Illustrate instances of each. Ask them to provide others. Talk of ways of reducing friction and increasing friction.

> *Example of an investigation*: Provide a variety of surfaces and a block of wood. Ask the students to investigate how the surface, area of contact and mass of the block affect the friction between the block and the surface.

> *Example of an investigation*: Ask the students to determine the best shape for an object if it is to fall as slowly as possible in water. Modelling clay and a tall tube full of water will probably be needed.

3   Turning effects

Ask the students to think of examples of forces which make objects turn. Ask what makes the turning effect greater. (It may help to get them to think of a steering wheel. The bigger the turning force and the larger the wheel, the greater the effect.) Show them how to calculate the size of a turning effect. If possible, illustrate it with a torque wrench.

> *Example of an investigation*: Give the students strips of wood (as a lever), fulcrums, a mass to attach to the end of the strip of wood and a force meter. Ask the students to place the lever on the fulcrum and find how the minimum force needed to lift the mass depends on the position of the fulcrum. From their data, ask them to find the relationship between force and distance on each side of the lever. (You will need to tell them what the weight of the mass is in newtons if the force meter is calibrated in newtons.) According to progress, you can develop this by adding a second mass to the lever at a different place to the first.

4 Pressure

Demonstrate that the same force on different areas has a different effect (e.g. stand on one upright kitchen tube and you will crush it; stand on a dozen held together by an elastic band, and they will take your weight. Explain that spreading a force over a bigger area dilutes its effect. Talk about the converse in connection with pin-points and knife edges. Ask the students to compare the effect of standing a brick on the head of a nail with the point on a block of wood, then reversing the nail so that the head is on the block of wood. Show and practise pressure calculations.

Forces at Key Stage 4

1 Speed and velocity

Discuss what is meant by speed and show the students how it is measured with the equipment you have. Show a distance–time graph and draw attention to the way that speed is indicated by the slope. Ask the students to collect data on an object moving at a steady speed, use it to construct a graph and determine the object's speed. Distinguish between speed (a scalar) and velocity (a vector).

2 Acceleration

Discuss what is meant by acceleration. Ask the students to invent data for a distance–time graph of a car, accelerating from rest. Discuss how the speed at different times might be obtained from such a graph. Remind the students that gravity makes falling objects accelerate but show that things falls too quickly for them to gather data for such a graph easily. Demonstrate that a slope, in effect, 'dilutes' gravity so that objects running down it accelerate more slowly and, if the slope is long, it gives them time to collect data. Ask the students to collect distance and time data for an object rolling down a long, shallow slope (e.g. a length of gutter), plot a graph, find velocities at two points and hence calculate the acceleration. (This is closely related to one of Galileo's demonstrations of the acceleration due to gravity.) Introduce velocity–time graphs and show that the slope indicates the acceleration. You should be explicit about the nature of deceleration and how it appears on distance–time and velocity–time graphs.

3 Newton's Laws of Motion

Give time to each Law so that the students develop an understanding of it (inertia, force and acceleration, action and reaction) – they are not as self-evident as they may seem to you. For instance, with the first, demonstrate instances of inertia (e.g. by covering a glass with a sheet of paper, placing a coin on the paper, then quickly pulling out the paper so that the coin falls into the glass. Ask the students to reflect on the inertia of a swing and the effort needed to deflect it or bring it to rest.)

Example of an investigation: For the Second Law, ask the students to investigate the effect of force and mass on acceleration. One way is to use a pulley with unequal masses of modelling clay suspended on either side. The force can be varied by moving clay from one side to the other, keeping the total mass in motion constant. The mass can be varied by adding clay to both sides but keeping the difference between the sides the same so that the force is constant. The students may think of other ways of addressing the problem.

For the Third Law, again show some examples and ask the students to think of others. For example, with two students on desk chairs with wheels, you can show that when one pushes the other, they both move apart. Furthermore, if the one being pushed has the greater mass, she or he will not respond as vigorously as the pusher.

4 Falling objects and terminal velocity

Example of an investigation: Ask the students to investigate the best shape for a parachute, square, circular, triangular, with and without a central hole. (This is more difficult for younger students than it seems, since the areas of the parachutes need to be the same.) Use this as an opportunity to talk about terminal velocity and ask the students to measure the speed of a falling feather to show it has reached its terminal velocity.

LIGHT

This is a topic that will have received some attention at Key Stages 1 and 2. In particular, students will probably have been taught about sources and reflectors of light and simple shadow effects. Students will know that some surfaces will reflect light better than others and some are more easily seen in a dim light. They may have done some work on colours and colour mixing, although the latter may have been in connection with mixing pigments in art. It is likely that attempts will have been made to dispel the idea that we see by the emission of light from the eyes and that light-coloured objects and mirrors emit light. These are not easy misconceptions to address and many students may use the right words but, underneath, hold on to earlier beliefs. At Key Stage 3 and with sound, this topic helps to underpin work on light and sound waves at Key Stage 4.

Rectilinear propagation

Light travels in straight lines. Just think of the books that use the above title. We must ask how meaningful those words are to Key Stage 3 students and use terms that mean something to them. That light travels in straight lines makes shadows sharp on a sunny day. It also explains how the Moon can block out the Sun's light during a total eclipse. To do otherwise, sunlight would have to curve around the Moon so that it could reach us on the Earth where the shadow would have been.

Reflected light

We see the world by the light that is produced by and reflected from objects. Rough objects tend to scatter light. Smooth objects, such as mirrors, tend to reflect light in a uniform way. White light comprises all the colours of the rainbow but certain objects reflect some of those colours more than others. For instance, a blouse that appears red in white light does so because it reflects more of the red light than the other colours. A white blouse tends to reflect all the white light falling on it. A black blouse absorbs all the light that falls on it so none is reflected. If you placed the red blouse in blue light, it would appear black because blue light contains no red light to reflect. This is why cars look so different in the yellow glow of some street lights. A blue car, for instance, is likely to appear black.

Refraction

As light enters an optically denser medium, it slows down. If it enters at an oblique angle, it slews towards the normal and moves on in a new direction. The more it is slowed down, the more it slews towards the normal. The refractive index, n, of a medium is an indication of its effect on light rays. Taking a vacuum as the baseline, its refractive index is 1.00. Travelling from a vacuum into crown glass, the refractive index is 1.52, into water it is 1.33 and into diamond it is 2.42. This means that diamond has more effect than glass which has more effect than water.

Some colours are refracted more than others. When light is sent through a triangular glass prism, blue and green light are affected more than orange and red light. The effect is to spread white light out into its constituent colours in the order red, orange, yellow, green, blue, indigo, violet. (The refractive indices listed above are for yellow light.)

Some misconceptions or alternative frameworks relating to light

Expect some students to behave as though they believe that we see by the emission of light from the eyes. At the same time, take care that they are not simply describing the direction of a gaze – some students may indicate this on their diagrams with arrows that we may mistake for the convention for drawing light rays. Similarly, students may 'accept' that light travels in straight lines, except when making it bend around obstacles conveniently explains things. A refracted ray striking a surface may also be represented as a curve because of the way we say light may 'bend' when it enters another material. Students often have difficulty ascribing the colour of a surface to the part of the spectrum it reflects, a difficulty that is compounded when filters are introduced. This may be due to a belief that colour is an inherent property of a surface, even in the dark, rather than an effect of the light. Such a belief probably stems from the overwhelming experience we have of a world that we view in white light.

Light at Key Stage 3

1 Light travels in straight lines

It is not difficult to convince students that light travels in straight lines. They see the edges of light beams in a mist and they have seen laser light effects. The problem is to convince them that it explains everyday effects, such as the way light gets behind furniture in a room. You need to combine straight line motion with reflection from walls, ceiling and furniture for this exercise; otherwise students are inclined to draw curved rays to fill in the gaps. Similarly, the fuzzy shadows we observe in a room need to be explained in the context of the effect of broad or multiple light sources. It may help to use a hand-operated water spray and produce a water shadow on a board. Two sprays (as with two lamps) can produce two, overlapping shadows and the sharp edges begin to be lost. At this point, repeat this with two small torches.

2 Reflecting surfaces

Example of an investigation: Issue cards of different colours including rough, smooth and polished white paper. Ask the students to investigate which reflects most light. They should aim to put the items in order from best to worst reflector. There are at least two messages in this task. First, some cards reflect more light than others. Second, a close examination should show that white card reflects white light, yellow card reflects yellow light, and so on.

Example of an investigation: Now add a mirror to the collection. Ask where they would expect it to be in the sequence and request reasons for their predictions. After trying it out, ask the students to explore the reflections of rays from the mirror and to explain why the angle of incidence is equal to the angle of reflection. This is easier to grasp if you get the students to use ray boxes rather than pins.

Example of an investigation: Issue a piece of transparent, coloured plastic sheet to use as a filter to each group. Let the students view the coloured squares through the filter. Ask them to attempt to explain what they see and construct a test of their explanation. You will need filters of other colours for the students to carry out their tests.

3 Refraction

You can demonstrate mechanical refraction using a pair of wheels on an axle and a tray which has a layer of sand in one half. Roll the wheels at an angle towards the sand. The wheel which enters the sand first will be slowed down. The other wheel will continue at a faster speed and make the axle change direction, in effect, refracting towards the normal (Figure 6.5). If you can establish this with the students, they can use it as an analogy to predict refraction effects with light rays. (Although useful, this analogy has its limits. For example, X-rays travel slightly faster in glass than in air.)

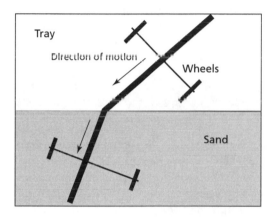

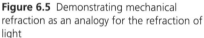

Figure 6.5 Demonstrating mechanical refraction as an analogy for the refraction of light

---

Example of an investigation: Ask: Which material 'bends' light the most: cooking oil, water, plastic or glass? Ask the students to investigate. It may be useful to have to hand the glass and plastic in the form of parallel-sided blocks and transparent, rectangular receptacles for the water and oil. Afterwards, introduce the concept of refractive indices and give them these for the materials tested so that the students can relate them to their results.

---

4 The spectrum

Display and discuss a spectrum in terms of the way some colours are refracted more than others. When a ray of white light passes through a prism it is refracted twice and the colours are spread out or *dispersed*. Demonstrate that recombining the colours gives white light (if the recombination was perfect).

Example of an investigation: Ask the students to predict and explain the colours they would obtain by mixing light of different colours. Ask them to test their predictions by colour mixing using coloured filters on light boxes.

SOUND

The pupils should have covered some aspects of sound at Key Stage 2. For example, by working with stringed instruments, they should know that sound is produced by vibrations although these may be too fast or too small to see. They should know how to make sounds louder by making the size of the vibration bigger (e.g. hitting a drum harder or pulling a string further out before releasing it). They should know that sound can travel through various materials and that we hear things when sound spreads out through the air and reaches our ears. How the ear works in simple terms may also have been covered. They may also be aware that an echo is a reflected sound. Some early misconceptions, such as the belief that words somehow travel invisibly from someone's mouth through the air to the ear, should have been dispelled or considerably weakened. At Key Stage 3 and with light, this topic helps to underpin work on light and sound waves at Key Stage 3.

The nature of sound

Sound is the result of vibration in a solid, liquid or a gas. A metal ruler, projecting over a table edge and held firmly in place, will vibrate when the free end is pressed. In the process, it repeatedly compresses and 'stretches' the air so that compressions (areas of higher pressure than normal) and rarefactions (areas of lower pressure than normal) spread out in the air from the ruler. These pressure waves (see section on 'Waves' below) are detected by our ears and interpreted as sound. Noise is sound that is unpleasant or annoying, so what constitutes noise is a subjective matter. Sound must have a medium to pass through. It cannot pass through a vacuum; hence rockets in space must be silent, unlike the way they are commonly depicted in science fiction films. Sound will reflect off surfaces and produce echoes.

The speed of sound

Sound travels at about 330 ms^{-1} in air at 0°C. Compared with the speed of light, 300,000,000 ms^{-1}, this is a snail's pace and it explains why we see the flash of lightning before we hear the thunder. The distance of the flash can be calculated by timing the interval between it and the beginning of the thunder (approximately 1 km for each second). Note, however, that a flash of lightning can take place at various heights as well as at different horizontal distances. The protracted roll of thunder is due to the length of the flash and echoes. Sound generally travels faster in liquids than in air and faster in solids than in liquids.

Loudness

If the ruler's vibrations are larger (i.e. they have a larger amplitude), the pressure waves are more intense. This is interpreted by the ear as a loud sound. Loudness as gauged by the ear is commonly measured in decibels (dB). Sound of more than 100 dB can damage hearing. The phon is another unit of loudness.

Pitch and ultrasound

If the ruler vibrates at a higher rate (by shortening the length over the edge of the table), the pressure waves in the air have a correspondingly higher frequency. The ear interprets this higher frequency as a higher pitched sound. Conversely, lower vibration rates produce lower pitched sounds. The frequency of a sound is measured in hertz (Hz), the number of complete waves that pass a point in one second. 256 Hz is Middle C on the piano; 512 Hz is Top C. Sound pulses in water will bounce off solid objects. Sonar takes advantage of this, and is used to detect shoals of fish, boats and the depth of water under a ship. Knowing the speed of sound in water and how long it takes for an echo to return, the distance to the fish, boat or sea bed can be calculated. In practice, this is done automatically. Many bats emit high-pitched sounds and use the echoes to gauge the location of obstacles and prey. The human ear can detect sounds between about 20 Hz and 20,000 Hz. The range of hearing tends to narrow as age increases. Sound with frequencies above the range of hearing is called ultrasound. Bone, soft tissue and fluids reflect ultrasound to different degrees; thus ultrasound is used to scan babies in the womb.

Quality of sound (timbre)

The same note on different musical instruments tends to sound different. This is because most musical instruments do not produce a note of only one frequency. In addition to the main note, they produce various overtones, notes that are related to the main note (e.g. twice and three times the frequency). These overtones are fainter than the main note and depend on the instrument, but affect the sound it produces.

Reverberation

In large halls, sound may bounce off walls and mix with the sound of the speaker's next words so that it becomes difficult to understand what is said. This reverberation of sound can be a nuisance in theatres and music-halls, so soft fabrics are used to reduce echoes.

Some misconceptions or alternative frameworks relating to sound

Sound is an invisible phenomenon that gives room for the imagination to work on and produce idiosyncratic understandings of its nature. Students do not generally see themselves as sitting in a sea of air that is alive with pulses and waves.

Sound at Key Stage 3

1 Vibrations

You should remind pupils of the work at Key Stage 2 and build on it. In particular, review the work on sound as the result of vibration, perhaps demonstrating this in different ways (e.g. by dipping a vibrating tuning fork in water). Make sure that they understand the nature of compressions and rarefactions. Introduce the hertz as the number of vibrations per second (frequency), and relate particular rates of vibration to some everyday sounds and their pitches.

Example of an investigation: Is the pitch of a sound related to the size of the object that makes it? Provide a range of items in different sizes (e.g. plant pots, wind chimes, xylophone bars, rulers). Ask the pupils to predict which will give high and low notes, justify their responses with reasons, then test their ideas.

2 Measuring loudness

Introduce the term *amplitude*, and relate it to loudness of a sound. You may have a decibel meter that can be used to measure the loudness of certain sounds, such as background traffic noise. Talk about reverberation, its effects and how it is reduced (see also investigation, below).

Example of an investigation: Ask the pupils to examine a wad of cotton wool, a newspaper, and corrugated parcel paper. Ask them to predict which they think would be the best for absorbing sound in a room. Press them to give reasons for their predictions. Get them to test their predictions using a small electrical buzzer suspended in a closed beaker as the source of sound. The pieces of material should be large enough to wrap around the beaker. A decibel meter will make the measurement of the volume of sound less subjective.

3 Sound travelling

Demonstrate in whatever way is possible in your laboratory, and with the appropriate safety precautions, that sound cannot travel through a vacuum. Talk about sound travelling through solids (e.g. railway lines), liquids (e.g. by ringing a bell under water) and gases (e.g. the high-pitched sound of a diver's voice in a helium-rich environment).

4 Travel and speed

Talk about seeing the smoke from a starting pistol before the sound is heard. Ask the pupils why they think this happens. Extend this idea to the delay between thunder and lightning. Together, measure the speed of sound. If there is enough distance outside, this is best done directly by starting a watch when a pupil some way off clashes two metal dustbin lids together, then stopping when the sound arrives. Repeating the measurement in the opposite direction allows an average to be obtained that compensates to some extent for the effect of winds. Often, you will not be able to position the pupil with the dustbin lids far enough away to make timing easy or reliable. In this instance, position the pupil as far as possible from a large wall, and time how long it takes for the sound to reach the wall and return as an echo. This generally works well but, of course, it introduces the complication of two-way travel. Contrast the speed of sound with the speed of light and work out a rule of thumb for calculating the distance of a lightning flash. Contrast the speed of sound in air, in water and in a solid material, such as wood.

Sound at Key Stage 4

At this stage, the wave properties of sound should receive particular attention.

1 The slinky spring as a wave analogy

A long, slinky spring provides a useful analogy to help pupils picture what is going on when sound travels through air. Stretch the spring along a smooth table with the far end held in place by a student. Transmit a pulse down the spring and draw attention to the longitudinal nature of the vibration that produced it. Transmit a strong pulse down the spring so that it reflects from the other end. Relate that to sound echoes. Transmit a string of pulses that are relatively far apart. Relate that to a low-frequency sound. Similarly, produce the parallel of a high-frequency sound. Conclude by making a pulse travel from both ends so that they pass through one another. Relate that to the way sounds can pass through one another without changing them.

2 Ultrasound

Discuss the nature and uses of ultrasound. Relate it to echolocation by bats.

3 Waves

Draw parallels between sound waves and light waves (e.g. echoes/reflections). Contrast the two (e.g. speed of transmission, sound needs a medium, longitudinal/transverse vibration).

WAVES

This topic tends to be introduced formally at Key Stage 4. Students will have had little formal experience of this topic at Key Stages 1 and 2, although they will understand the idea of waves in water and ripples in a pond. At Key Stage 3, they will have learned some of the properties of sound and light, but discussion of their wave properties is likely to have been limited except, perhaps, in the case of sound. The students will, however, have their everyday experience of water waves to draw on in your teaching and to use as an analogy in connection with sound and light. This section should be related to those on sound and light.

Characteristics of waves

Waves transfer energy from one place to another. In open water, as a wave passes by, a floating log simply bobs up and down. It does not move forward with the wave. Waves do not transport material. (Near the shore, waves tend to tumble forward, due to the drag on the sea bed in shallow water. This produces breakers and throws debris on to the beach, and is not the unimpeded behaviour of a wave.) Such waves move from one place to another and are referred to as *travelling* or *progressive* waves. The number of complete waves passing a point in a second is known as the frequency (formerly and meaningfully measured in cycles per second, now measured in hertz (Hz)). The distance between adjacent matching parts of a wave (like the tops of two adjacent waves) is the wavelength. The height of a wave above what it would be if the water was calm is the *amplitude*.

Observing water waves from above, you would see them approach a cliff and be *reflected*. Similarly, as they run into shallow water on a beach, they *refract* and change direction. As straight waves approach the narrow entrance of a marina, they pass through, but, in the process, the wavefront *diffracts* and spreads into the 'shadow' behind the marina walls. These are properties we look for if we wanted evidence of the presence of waves. For instance, we know that sound and light reflect off surfaces because there are echoes and the glare of the sun from a window. We know that they refract because sound curves up on a sunny day when the air is warm near the ground and we can focus the sun's light with a magnifying glass. We know that sound diffracts because we can hear what someone says about us, even though they are around a corner. Similarly, if light is shone through a very narrow slit, it spreads out like water waves entering the marina. This is powerful evidence that sound and light are waves. However, they turn out to be different kinds of waves. Waves in water are *transverse*; that is, they oscillate at right-angles to the direction of motion. Light waves are like this. Sound waves, on the other hand, are *longitudinal* waves; that is, they oscillate in the direction of motion.

The speed of waves

You can see that water waves often travel relatively slowly, perhaps at only a metre per second. Sound waves travel at about $330 \, \text{ms}^{-1}$ and light waves at $300\,000\,000 \, \text{ms}^{-1}$. Given the wavelength, λ, and the frequency, n, of a wave, the speed is

$$c \, (\text{ms}^{-1}) = n \, (\text{Hz}) \, \lambda \, (\text{m})$$

because if n waves pass a point in one second and each is of length λ, then a stretch of waves equal to n λ passes the point in one second.

Sound and light travel at different speeds in different media but, while sound travels faster in water and glass, light travels more slowly. The refractive index of a material is the ratio of the speed of light in a vacuum to the speed in the material. In glass, the index is about 1.5, so light travels about 1.5 times faster in air than in glass.

The spectrum

Picture yourself at the piano. If you were to play all the notes at once, the piano would produce a noise that would be a mix of all the frequencies of sound that the piano can produce. On the other hand, you could play each note in turn, beginning at the left and ending at the right. Spreading out the notes like this reveals the *spectrum* of frequencies that made up the noise. It is the same with light from the Sun. White light is the equivalent of the piano's mixed-note noise. Refraction through a prism reveals all the frequencies that made up the white light. The piano's notes, however, increase in steps. The Sun's 'notes' are continuous so that the frequencies run smoothly through the 'scale'.

The different colours of the visible spectrum (what we tend to think of as the rainbow) correspond to different wavelengths, and therefore different frequencies. The spectrum or 'scale' of white light consists of the colours (with their approximate wavelengths) listed in Table 6.1. In reality, this is only a small part of the full spectrum, most of which we cannot see. It begins with high-frequency gamma rays and low-frequency radio waves. This full spectrum is known as the *electromagnetic spectrum* (because the waves have electric and magnetic components), and is summarised in Table 6.2 (1 nm = 10^{-9} m).

Table 6.1 The different colours of the visible spectrum with their approximate wavelengths

Red	0.7×10^{-6} m
Orange	
Yellow	
Green	0.6×10^{-6} m
Blue	
Indigo	
Violet	0.4×10^{-4} m

Table 6.2 The full electromagnetic spectrum, most of which we cannot see (1 nm = 10^{-9} m)

Highest frequency ↑	Gamma rays (shortest wavelength)	less than 0.01 nm
	X-rays	0.001–10 nm
	Ultraviolet rays	400–200 nm
	Visible light	780–380 nm
	Infra-red rays	800 nm–1mm
	Microwaves	0.3–30 cm
Lowest frequency ↓	Radio waves (longest wavelength)	beyond 30 cm

Different wavelengths are reflected, absorbed or transmitted differently by different substances and different types of surface. This results in all types of electromagnetic radiation being used in everyday life. For example, uses of electromagnetic radiation include:

- communication systems (radar);
- radiant heaters, such as fires and cookers (infra-red);
- remote controls (infra-red);
- sunbeds (ultraviolet);
- security coding (ultraviolet);
- medical investigation (X-rays and other radioactive wavelengths);
- sterilising surgical instruments (gamma rays).

Seismic waves and tectonic plates

The Earth's lithosphere is broken into several large pieces called tectonic plates that move very slowly as a result of convection currents within the Earth's mantle. As these plates move, they can produce earthquakes. Much of our knowledge of the structure of the Earth has come from the study of shock waves from earthquakes. Earthquakes produce surface waves that can cause damage. They also produce two types of waves that can travel through the Earth:

1   p waves, which travel faster, are longitudinal and travel through liquids as well as solids;
2   slower travelling s waves, which are transverse and travel only through solids.

Abrupt changes in rock density make these waves refract, like light passing obliquely into a block of glass. Examination of the patterns of refraction allows seismologists to deduce the depth and nature of layers within the Earth.

Some misconceptions or alternative frameworks relating to waves

Students tend to believe that waves move materials from one place to another based on their experience of water waves. It is important to be clear that we are using water waves to give us a picture of the properties of waves and look for those properties in sound and light.

Waves at Key Stage 4

1 Water wave properties

Discuss water waves and describe features such as wavelength, frequency and speed. Point out that waves do not transport materials, and explain that the effect of the drag of the sea bed in shallow water makes us think differently. Demonstrate waves in a ripple tank and ask the students to calculate the speed of the wave. Observe the reflection, refraction and diffraction of wave pulses in the ripple tank.

2 Two kinds of waves

Use a slinky spring to demonstrate transverse waves like those in the ripple tank. Demonstrate a progressive wave and the reflection of a pulse. Point out the transverse nature of the action needed to produce such a wave. Now demonstrate a longitudinal wave as a series of compressions and rarefactions travelling along the spring. Again, show that a longitudinal pulse is reflected. Point out the longitudinal action needed to produce such a wave. Demonstrate that waves can pass through one another without change.

Example of an investigation: Ask: Do longitudinal waves travel through a spring at the same speed as transverse waves? Get the students to investigate. Ask them for other questions they might explore in a similar way. Later, you might relate this activity to p and s seismic waves.

3 Light and sound waves

Collect, through discussion, evidence that light and sound are examples of wave motion. Demonstrate the less obvious properties. (The students should be able to connect sound waves and longitudinal motion. To connect light and transverse motion, it might help to talk about polarised sunglasses and how crossed polaroids will block the light because it is a transverse wave.)

4 The spectrum of sound and the spectrum of light

Use an electronic keyboard to demonstrate 'white' noise and the notes that make it. Now show white light and pass it through a prism to produce a spectrum. Draw parallels between the sound spectrum and the light spectrum. For clear results, this needs to be carried out in subdued lighting with a fairly intense beam of light. Slowly adjust the orientation of the prism to produce a sharp spectrum. Students can look for other examples of refraction of white light (e.g. when bright light passes through a glass tank or aquarium or through a clear plastic ruler). Do not forget to make it clear that the light spectrum is continuous whereas the keyboard noise was made up of discontinuous frequencies of sound.

5 The electromagnetic spectrum

Explain that the visible spectrum is just that: what we see. Add in the rest and discuss the applications of the parts of the spectrum. Relate effects to reflection (as when ghost images appear on a TV picture), and refraction and diffraction (as with radio waves) and penetrating power (as when X-rays are used in hospitals).

6 Seismic waves

Ask the students to research the cause of earthquakes and begin with what they find to explore the properties of seismic waves and what they can tell us about the interior of the Earth.

RADIOACTIVITY

This topic does not tend to be addressed until Key Stage 4. Any prior knowledge has often been acquired informally, perhaps through reading and the media. It tends to be associated with certain dangerous materials used by the power and weapons industries. The terms *radioactivity*, *radiation* and *radioactive substances* are often used imprecisely in everyday language in expressions such as 'They had to wash the radioactivity off their protective suits'.

The nature of radioactivity

The nuclei of atoms contain protons and neutrons. The protons carry a positive charge and repel one another, but nuclear forces generally overcome that repulsion and bind the particles together. In large nuclei, such as that of uranium and radium, the repulsion can be so great that pieces are ejected, a process known as decay. Nuclei which decay spontaneously are said to be radioactive. Radioactivity, then, is a property of some nuclei. A piece that is commonly ejected consists of two protons and two neutrons. This is, in effect, a helium nucleus, usually described as an alpha (α) particle. Much of the energy that bound this particle to the nucleus is released as electromagnetic radiation, typically as gamma (γ) rays. Some relatively small nuclei, such as potassium, can also be unstable and there are other ways that nuclei can break down. One of these is when a neutron decays into a proton by emitting an electron, usually referred to as a beta (β) particle. α and β particles and γ rays emitted by nuclei are examples of radiation produced by a radioactive nucleus.

Radioactivity in nature

Fast-moving particles from space bombard the Earth continually. These so-called cosmic rays collide with gases in the atmosphere and produce showers of particles that can be detected by a Geiger counter. Natural radioactive substances in the Earth itself, such as uranium, add to the background radiation. Artificially produced radioactive materials (e.g. from medical uses, power and weapons industries) account for about 13 per cent of the background count. Some natural background radiation is present at all times, and it can be partly responsible for a low mutation rate that enables evolution.

Characteristics of α and β particles and γ rays

α-particles are positively charged, relatively heavy particles and tend to be emitted at relatively low speeds. The are brought to rest by less that 20 cm of air at normal pressure or by a sheet or two of paper. β-particles are fast-moving, negatively charged electrons. They are generally stopped by about 1 m of air and can often penetrate thin aluminium sheets. Thin sheets of more dense metals (e.g. copper) bring them to rest. γ rays are electromagnetic waves that are more energetic that X-rays. They have great penetrating power, and thick sheets of lead and concrete are used to absorb them.

α and β particles knock electrons from the outer shells of gas and vapour atoms and hence leave trails of ions in the air. If γ rays do interact with gas atoms, electrons may be emitted. These then behave like β particles and produce trails of ions. However, in the case of γ rays, this is not a strong effect. The Geiger counter, electroscope and cloud chamber respond to the presence of ions and so indicate readily the presence of α and β particles. The Geiger counter can be made to amplify and detect the slight ionisation produced by γ rays and so can detect the presence of γ rays.

Half-life

Half-life, often shortened to $T_{1/2}$, is the time it takes for one half of the radioactive atoms in a pure sample of a radioactive element to decay. Carbon-14 is a radioactive form of the normal carbon-12. Beginning with 1 g of carbon-14 now, there will be ½ g left after 5,700 years and ¼ g left after 11,400 years, and so on. Half-lives have a wide range (e.g. that of radium-221 is only 30 seconds while that of uranium-238 is 4,500 million years).

Harmful and beneficial effects of radiation and some uses of radioactive sources

Radiation can kill living cells, so radioactive materials have to be handled with due regard for safety. Radiation affects, for instance, the layer of living skin cells that lies under the surface layer, the bone marrow where many blood cells are produced and the hair follicles. This means that radiation can produce skin sores that will not heal, anaemia, baldness and even death. Pierre Curie was in the habit of carrying a piece of radium in his waistcoat pocket. His perpetual tiredness and skin sores near the pocket may have been partly due to that habit. Similar to excesses of ultraviolet light, radiation can also disrupt genes and cause cancerous growths.

Paradoxically, well-directed doses of radiation may also be used to kill cancerous cells. The effect of radiation on cells may also be put to use in sterilising hospital instruments and food. Food sterilised in this way will keep for longer. Just as X-rays are used in hospitals to reveal the internal bones of the body, the more penetrating γ rays are used in industry to check for faults inside metal components. Smoke detectors contain a weak source of α particles. These ionise the air and the ions are detected with the help of an electronic circuit. Smoke in the air affects the ionisation and the change is detected by the circuit, triggering an alarm.

The extent to which a radioactive substance has decayed may be used to gauge the age of an object. The best known method is radiocarbon dating. Cosmic rays that collide with nitrogen-14 (the normal nitrogen found in air) tend to change it to radioactive carbon-14. Plants and animals take in this carbon-14 along with normal carbon-12 from the air and from food, respectively. Carbon-14 decays at a known rate (half-life 5,700 years). By measuring how much has decayed in, say, a piece of charcoal, the age of the charcoal can be calculated, indicating the date at which the tree stopped growing. Some rocks may be dated in a similar way. In this case, the radioactive substance is uranium-234 with a half-life of 4,500 million years.

Nuclear fission is the splitting of a nucleus into fragments. When uranium-235 is struck by a neutron it becomes highly unstable and fragments, usually into two pieces, emitting more neutrons and releasing energy. This energy is used to generate steam which turns turbines. These turn dynamos that generate electricity. In practice, the rate of fission has to be controlled using rods that absorb neutrons, and moderators that reduce the energy of the neutrons. Thermal energy is transferred from the radioactive core to water to produce steam using a coolant, such as a gas or liquid metal. Nuclear reactors do not produce carbon dioxide as do coal-burning power-stations and so do not add to global warming. They do, however, produce radioactive wastes that can have a long half-life and are difficult to dispose of.

Radioactivity at Key Stage 4

1 Nature of radioactivity

One way to begin is by getting students to talk about what they know (or think they know) about the topic. To start things off, you could ask them to list three things they know about radioactivity. This process informs you of prior knowledge and of misconceptions you will have to address. Many will know that a Geiger counter detects radiation (although they may know little of the nature of that radiation). You follow this exploratory activity by showing a Geiger counter and taking a background count. The existence of a background count often surprises Key Stage 4 students. You could talk about the various contributors to the background count and show that shielding the Geiger counter with different materials reduces it to different degrees.

2 Existence of radiation

Demonstrate the existence of radiation with a cloud chamber. This makes visible that which is normally invisible, but you must make it clear that the students cannot see the particles, only the trails they make. Explain that these particles are coming from unstable elements. Be explicit in what you mean by 'unstable element'.

3 Modelling decay

Model the way unstable elements break down using a large number of dice made by sawing cubes from a length of wood of a square cross-section). We could say that dice which come up with a five have decayed. We do not know which of the dice will 'decay' but we do know that there is a one-in-six chance of each one decaying on each throw. For example, out of 100 dice on the first throw, 17 might come up with a five, leaving 83. On the second throw of the 83, 12 might come up with a five, leaving 71. Proceeding in this way allows the students to draw a graph of the number of dice remaining (analogous to the number of atoms) versus throw number (analogous to the time). This leads into the concept of half-life and to the use of half-life in radiocarbon dating and the dating of rocks.

> *Investigation of the effect of changing the probability of decay*: This is an activity the pupils can do if you have enough sets of dice. To increase the probability of 'decay', given six-sided dice, they count two numbers as indicating decay (e.g. a 5 and a 4). Alternatively, the pupils can use coin-like discs with the faces numbered 1 and 2. Here, the probability of a 1 coming up is one half. This means that the disks 'decay' more quickly than the dice, so the 'half-life' of discs is shorter.

4 Different kinds of radiation

Demonstrate that radioactive materials can emit different kinds of radiation – α and β particles and γ rays – and distinguish between them. Relate the properties to harmful and beneficial effects and uses of radioactive materials. *Activity*: You may have access to software that models the action of a nuclear reactor and allows pupils to control it.

THE EARTH AND BEYOND

In earlier Key Stages, children are generally taught that the Sun, Earth and Moon are spherical bodies, that the Earth revolves around the Sun in a year and rotates on its axis in a day, and that the Moon revolves around the Earth in approximately 28 days. They are aware that shadows cast by the Sun change in position as the Sun appears to move across the sky and will often have used shadow sticks to mark out the times of day. Day and night will have been related to the Earth's rotation on its axis. The children are also likely to know something of the internal structure of the Earth, volcanoes, mountain formation and the properties of certain rocks and soils.

The solar system

The Earth rotates on its axis once every 24 hours. Just as houses can appear to move past a bus window, the Sun looks as though it is moving across the sky when actually we are moving under the Sun. At night, the stars seem to move across the sky, circling a point near the pole-star. The Moon does not follow the movement of the stars because it is revolving around us at the same time. The Earth's axis of rotation is tilted with respect to its orbit. This makes the Sun appear higher in the sky in summer than in winter. When it is higher in the sky, its light and heat are spread over a smaller area so the season is hotter.

We do not usually see the stars during the day due to the brightness of the sunlight. Air tends to scatter the red part of sunlight so that the light which reaches us is predominantly from the blue end of the spectrum, hence the blue colour of the sky. The way air scatters red light is often seen at sunrise and sunset.

The universe behaves as though it began as a small, intensely hot and dense speck that expanded rapidly in what has become known as 'The Big Bang'. As it expanded, it cooled. This allowed gases to form into clouds and then stars to develop as gravity acted on the materials in the clouds. These clusters of stars tend to be held together by gravity and to form galaxies. The Milky Way is just such a galaxy and our Sun is one star in it. These galaxies continue to move apart as the universe expands.

Many stars have been around long enough for us to have some idea of their lives. They begin life as balls of hydrogen gas. As gravity compacts the gas, the point is reached where nuclear reactions begin. The hydrogen is converted into helium, emitting large amounts of energy in the process. Our Sun's energy comes from this source and the energy makes life on Earth possible. (It is wrong to describe this as 'burning', since it is not like the chemical reaction of burning.) Eventually, the Sun's hydrogen will be exhausted. By then, the Sun will be a giant red star. The final stage is when this red giant collapses to become a white dwarf or else explodes in a massive supernova.

Orbits

The Earth revolves around the Sun due to the gravitational attraction between the two. This may seem odd to students: in their experience gravity normally pulls things to the ground, so why is the Earth not pulled to the surface of the Sun? Imagine a ball on a string. If you simply hold the string taut and release the ball, the ball does fall. But if you start by setting the ball going at right angles to the string, you can use your pull on the string to start the ball going in a circle. It is as though there is an invisible string between the Earth and the Sun. The Earth is already moving forward at a tangent to its orbit. At the same time, the Sun is tugging on the invisible string and the result is an almost circular orbit. A similar explanation can help explain the orbit of satellites. If you throw a stone onto the Earth, it moves away from you and, at the same time, curves to the ground. If you were able to throw it towards the horizon, it would curve to the ground out of sight over the horizon. An even harder throw would send the stone far over the horizon, falling all the time but, because the Earth is a sphere, never actually hitting the ground. In other words, it would be in orbit.

Sources of light and reflectors of light

The Sun is a star with a surface temperature of about 6000 C. Among other things, it emits light. We see the other stars at night because they emit light, too. This makes them sources of light. The Moon, however, only reflects light. We see it because it reflects sunlight. This is why we see the crescent that faces the Sun. A faint light can sometimes be seen in the shadow side of the Moon because the Earth also reflects the Sun's light and this can illuminate the Moon, although only dimly.

Satellites

The Moon is a natural satellite of the Earth. Other planets have natural satellites, often several. Artificial satellites are used to survey the Earth, to act as relays for communication signals, to monitor the weather, and as bases for 'gravity-free' experiments. Strictly speaking, they are not gravity-free since they are still subject to the Earth's and the Sun's gravity. However, as they are falling all the time (see above), anything in them is falling at the same rate and so floats around the interior of the satellite.

Some misconceptions or alternative frameworks relating to the Earth and beyond

Students often believe that astronauts float around when in orbit because they are beyond the reach of gravity. They also think of the Sun as burning its fuel of hydrogen. While most will see the Sun as a source of light, some also see the Moon as a source rather than as a reflector. This tends to be because they are thinking of its effect (it illuminates the Earth at night) rather than its cause (it is not self-generated light).

The Earth and beyond at Key Stage 3

While many students will be able to give you the correct response that the Earth is 'round' and that people do not fall off it due to gravity, they may still feel that those on the 'underside' should sense they are 'upside down' in some way. Similarly, they may know that satellites are in orbit without understanding why orbits exist. Some may still believe that objects, such as fluorescent paper, metal foil and mirrors, should shine in the dark. That the Moon merely reflects light could be hard for them to accept.

1 The Earth and its motion

Tell the students that you believe the Earth is flat and get them to convince you that you are wrong. Display some pictures showing the Earth seen from space. Explore the students' ideas about why people standing on the other side of the world feel just the same as we do. Use a globe and torch to remind them of the cause of day and night, and ask them to explain why the Poles have six months of daylight and six months of darkness. Similarly, use the globe to explain the seasons.

> *Example of an investigation*: Why is it cold in winter? Ask the students to express their reasons and devise a simple way of testing their ideas. For example, on a sunny day, they could present a piece of card at different angles to the Sun's rays for the same length of time and measure the temperature of the back of the card.

2 The solar system

Ask the students to tell you about the solar system. Ask why everything does not fall into the Sun. Use a ball on a string as an analogy for the pull-and-go action of the planets to explain their motion. Use the words *revolve* and *rotate*. Videotapes and software may help here. Talk about some of the things that artificial satellites can do and ask the students to research the topic to find out about their uses.

3 Sources and reflectors of light

Remind the students of reflectors and sources of light. Ask them to classify some everyday instances. Ask them about the Sun and the stars: sources or reflectors? Ask why we often see only a crescent of the Moon. Explain this as being due to the Moon being a reflector of light, and extend it to the planets.

The Earth and beyond at Key Stage 4

The concepts and explanations developed at KS3 are extended at KS4.

1 The solar system

Ask the students to review their knowledge of the solar system. Ask them about asteroids, comets and meteors and distinguish between them. Help students build a coherent mental picture of the solar system.

2 Stars

Ask the students if the Sun ever changes. You might, for instance, talk of sunspots. Point out that the Sun (a star) will change with time. What will happen to it? Talk about the formation and evolution of stars. Describe some evidence of the existence of planets beyond our solar system, such as the oscillation of stars as invisible large planets move around them.

3 Galaxies

Show the students some pictures of galaxies, including the spiral galaxy of the Milky Way (our own galaxy), if possible. Ask why stars tend to hang together, bringing into the discussion gravitation and galactic rotation. Emphasise the role of gravity by discussing the nature and properties of black holes.

4 The Universe

Describe the Universe in terms of gases, galaxies, electromagnetic energy and space. Point to indications that the Universe was once much smaller than it is now and describe expansion from a so-called 'Big Bang'. Is there life elsewhere? Ask the students about characteristics of life and what a life detector might do. How else might we know if intelligent life is out there? How would intelligent life know if we existed?

Task 6.1

1   Plan a practical investigation for students in Key Stage 3 relating to the Earth and beyond.
2   Construct a practical investigation for students in Key Stage 4 relating to some aspect of light or sound. What investigative skills/processes would be practised by this investigation (see also the National Curriculum for Science, Key Stage 4)?
3   How will you explain the concept of gravity to a student who asks you, *I know we've done all this work on forces, but what is gravity really?*

SUGGESTIONS FOR FURTHER READING

If you would like to explore further some of the issues touched upon in this chapter, the following should be of interest to you.

Miller, R. (2003) 'Teaching about energy', in *Strengthening Teaching and Learning of Energy in Key Stage 3 Science: Additional Support Pack* (pp. 101–19), London: DfES/QCA.
    This chapter in particular provides a very useful account of teaching about energy.

You should also consult issues of the *School Science Review* for teaching ideas.

7 Pupils' Learning in Science

LYNN D. NEWTON

INTRODUCTION

In order to explore ideas about teaching, we need first to think about what we know about learning. How do our students learn science? There are a number of major theories of how learning takes place generally and, of relevance here, how we *think* students learn science. Table 7.1 provides an overview of two key perspectives, and the main theories and concepts underpinning them.

If you look at the table, you will see that there is a progression in the control over the learning opportunities, from a learner-centred constructivist approach in the cognitive perspective, to a teacher-centred behaviourist approach. There is not space in this chapter to explore these theories in full, nor would it be appropriate – any text on the psychology of education could provide this information (see e.g. Borich and Tombari, 1997). However, the two perspectives will be discussed in this chapter in the context of science education.

For any teacher, his or her main role with any group of students is likely to be to provide guidance and support in the process of learning. To be a successful teacher it is important that you understand what we currently know about how your students learn so that you can employ appropriate teaching strategies in your science classrooms. The basic principles underpinning progress in learning are the same for any area of experience. However, what works for you in your lessons will depend upon a variety of factors, from student characteristics (such as age or ability) to time of week (first thing Tuesday morning versus last thing on a Friday), from content (ionic bonding versus sexual reproduction) to examination pressures (Year 7 internal tests to Year 11 GCSE Double Award examinations). As a teacher of secondary science, you will need to match the learning experiences you offer to your students' needs, abilities and interests, all within the framework of the National Curriculum Order for Science for Key Stages 3 and 4. The importance of such a match was emphasised in the Non-Statutory Guidance offered by the National Curriculum Council in 1989.

Table 7.1 Perspectives in education (adapted from http://www.nyucolp.org/explore)

PERSPECTIVES	CONCEPTS	THEORIST	THEORY
BEHAVIOURIST	◆ Reinforcement ◆ Stimulus/response	● Pavlov ● Skinner ● Thorndike ● Watson	■ Classical conditioning ■ Operant conditioning ■ Connectionism ■ Behaviourism
COGNITIVIST	◆ Automaticity ◆ Directed instruction ◆ Chunking	● Bloom ● Bruner ● Gagne ● Guilford ● Sternberg	■ Taxonomy of educational objectives ■ Discovery learning ■ Types of learning; learning hierarchies ■ Structure of the intellect; intelligence ■ Triarchic theory of intelligence
COGNITIVIST – Constructivist Approach	◆ Learning transfer ◆ Metacognition ◆ Problem-solving ◆ Schema development ◆ Computer-supported learning ◆ Collaborative learning ◆ Environmental enrichment ◆ Interaction ◆ Learner-centred instruction ◆ Scaffolding	● Dewey ● Piaget ● Ausubel ● Bransford ● Brown ● Gardner ● Lave ● Sticht ● Vygotsky	■ Theory of cognitive development ■ Advance organisers; meaningful learning ■ Anchored instruction ■ Cognitive apprenticeship ■ Multiple intelligences ■ Situated learning ■ Functional context ■ ZPD (zone of proximal development)

> Providing appropriate learning experiences . . . requires careful planning and sensitive teaching by teachers with a broad understanding of science and the ability to match the work to their pupils' capabilities. Activities must challenge all pupils and, at the same time, provide them all with success at some meaningful level.
>
> (NCC, 1989, p. A9)

This suggests a three-sided partnership:

1   *the science content*: the National Curriculum and its place in the broader curriculum framework;
2   *you as the teacher*: the quality of your planning, organisation and choice of methods, approaches and strategies;
3   *the students as learners*: their personal characteristics and what they bring to the learning situation.

Each of these elements might be expected to contribute to progress in students' learning.

LEARNING IN SCIENCE

We can say our students have learned something if they *know* something they did not know before, they *can do* something they could not do before or they *understand* something they did not understand before. However, not a lot is known about how students learn in the sense of what actually goes on in their heads when they achieve real understanding. There is a need to identify more explicitly how learning takes place and to recognise how teachers may support the process. Think about the different ways your students may be involved in the learning process.

1   *Passive involvement.* Your students can learn a lot from listening to others – their peers, you as their teacher or other adults. This is sometimes described as a didactic approach and involves passive receptivity on the part of the listener. The emphasis is on the learning and recall of factual knowledge, such as the rules, laws and generalisations that make up science as a body of knowledge (e.g. $V=RI$) but ignores the vital element of understanding (*Why does the brightness of the bulb alter if we alter the resistance?*). Factual recall of information is important and has a place in teaching and learning – it can be an important element in the construction of understanding. However, by itself, factual knowledge that is learned by rote may be a necessary but insufficient condition in the process of learning with understanding. The learning must be meaningful, and connect with the knowledge and understanding already owned by the learner.
2   *Active involvement.* This is fundamental to science, with the emphasis switching to direct experience. The learner interacts directly with artefacts and events, and is seen as actively constructing his or her understanding through this interaction. The teacher's role becomes one of providing or encouraging activities

to stimulate such interaction in a secure learning environment (e.g. electric circuit components (batteries, lamps, lamp holders and wires) for students to explore changing the resistance (wires of different materials) and observing and explaining the effects).

3   *Interactive involvement.* Both passive and active involvement incorporate aspects of language, but the third consideration for learning has language and interaction with significant others as its focus. Under the psychological umbrella of constructivism (the view that meaning and understanding are constructed) it gives priority to discussion and exploration of ideas by debate or argument as a major vehicle of learning and in which learning is negotiated between the participants of the process. In this mode, the influence of others on the construction of knowledge and understanding is acknowledged.

These kinds of involvement correspond roughly to the perspectives and approaches identified in Table 7.1. Each of these will be considered briefly below.

A BEHAVIOURIST PERSPECTIVE

From a behaviourist perspective, studies focus on observable outcome performance and how to set up learning environments to encourage the production of the desired outcomes. Behaviourism tends to be used synonymously with the term *conditioning*. In *classical conditioning*, through training the learner learns to respond to stimuli other than those originally used to call for a response (e.g. Pavlov's dogs salivating at the sound of a bell rather than when hungry or when smelling food). In education, the parallel would be learning multiplication tables, names of objects, foreign words, historical dates, mathematical and chemical symbols and so on. This is sometimes called *stimulus learning*. In another type of conditioning, *operant conditioning*, the learner, in making his or her response, provides the means by which the solution is achieved or the problem solved. The learning is a slightly more active process and, after the necessary earlier acquisition of the relevant vocabulary, terminology and other information (by stimulus learning), the learner must use the information in some way (Skinner's rats in their mazes). This is sometimes called *instrumental learning*. By reinforcement, usually in the form of some kind of reward, both kinds of learning can be fused. Such learning can lead to *automaticity*, where a procedure has been learned so thoroughly that it can be carried out quickly with minimal effort or thought.

The term *learning*, in everyday use, tends to be associated with one particular, restricted type of learning that reflects this behavioural perspective – rote learning of information by heart so as to be able to regurgitate it as needed. This, in turn, is often associated with repetitive activity, with little or no associated understanding. In science, the rules, laws and theories underpinning science as a body of knowledge have often been learned in this way. Generations of students have probably learned chunks of science off by heart, reproduced them on cue in the examination room, and then promptly forgotten them. Dates in history, rules of algebra in mathematics, sections of Shakespearian plays in English, we can all probably remember learning in this way. What about Ohm's Law in physics or

Boyle's Law in chemistry? Clearly very little in-depth understanding may have been achieved. Why is there a proportional relationship between current, voltage and resistance? What is the explanation underpinning the relationship between pressure and volume?

The behaviourist perspective is useful to you as a teacher, but it is inadequate for explaining the totality of school learning. While the learning of basic academic skills and factual information can serve a useful purpose in further learning, it is only part of the picture. Intervening between a stimulus and a response is the black box – the learner's total mental structure, a consequence of personal experience, previous teaching, attitudes and beliefs and a capacity to interact with and control the learning situation. Secondary science education has been criticised in the past for focusing on the learning of large amounts of factual information at the expense of developing a deeper understanding and an ability to use that knowledge and understanding in new contexts to solve problems. This development of the learner in the broader sense leads to questions about cognitive development and how to support this process.

COGNITIVISM AND SCIENCE EDUCATION

The second perspective shifts the focus to looking at learning in terms of what is happening in the human brain. Cognitive approaches emphasise good thinking or good information processing and the cognitive processes underlying them:

> earlier cognitive models of instruction . . . incorporate notions of discovery learning . . . and meaningful verbal learning . . . the most recent models [are] based on social learning theory . . . and social constructivist notions.
> (Borich and Tombari, 1997, p. 137)

Teaching based on cognitive theories recognises the growth in the quality of intellectual activity and capitalises on this by organising the learning activities to anticipate the next stage in development and support the progression in learning that is possible. Once begun, the motivation depends more on standards of intellectual achievement generated by the learner him- or herself than on external reinforcement. A spiral curriculum, in which areas of experiences are revisited, building on what has gone before takes place, fits with this perspective. Progression through the National Curriculum Key Stages, as described in the spiral strands of the programmes of study, also fits this view.

Piaget and a cognitive development model

Cognitive development theories are appropriate to the school situation in that they focus upon knowing and thinking. Piaget was probably the first cognitive psychologist to explain intellectual growth in terms of progression from perceiving and doing (through motor-perceptual activities in manipulative play and games) to symbolic representation and comprehensive understanding. His views have been very influential in education. Piaget identified four stages of cognitive development:

1   *The Sensori-motor stage* (birth to *c.* 2 years): characterised initially by reflex actions with a transition into more goal-directed activity; learning of object permanence and the beginnings of internal cognitive mediation by making use of imitation, memory and thought. (Mediation is thinking that uses symbols to represent objects or events.)

2   *The Pre-operational stage* (*c.* 2 years to *c.* 7 years): characterised by egocentrism and an increasing ability to mediate with the development of language and to think in symbolic form; dependence on immediate, first-hand experience; has difficulty seeing others' points of view.

3   *The concrete operational stage* (*c.* 7 years to *c.* 11 years): characterised by an understanding of the laws of conservation (length, mass and volume) and a readiness to engage in other mental operations using concrete stimuli; able to solve concrete, hands-on problems in a logical fashion.

4   *The formal operational stage* (*c.* 11 years to 15+ years): characterised by abstract thought, logical reasoning and other forms of higher-order conceptualisation; thinking becomes more scientific; develops a sense of social identity and concerns about social issues.

It is important with Piaget's stages to emphasise stage and not age. It is thought that all students progress through these stages in the order stated, but this may take longer for some than for others. At secondary school level, the focus is on the transition from concrete to formal operational thinking. In particular, there are three conceptual processes you need to be aware of when you plan for teaching that produces quality thinking and learning.

- *Assimilation*: expanding or enriching cognitive structures with new perceptions or information.
- *Accommodation*: adjusting or altering cognitive structures affected by new information.
- *Equilibrium*: restoring cognitive balance by altering cognitive structures to take into account new information; the result of accommodation.

Information-processing model

Learning is seen as taking place when the brain processes and makes sense of information received, and builds up mental structures (sometimes called models or maps) which become more and more sophisticated in the light of experience. This is very much an *information-processing model*, a model of learning that examines how we learn using the 'mind as a computer' analogy. With this model, cognitive theorists have assumed that cognitive or thought processes follow a fairly common sequence:

- arousal of intellectual interest;
- preliminary exploration of the problem;
- formulation of ideas;

- construction of explanations or hypotheses;
- selection of appropriate ideas;
- verification of their suitability.

This processing is, in fact, performed by the already existing cognitive structures, raising interesting questions about which comes first (a chicken-and-egg conundrum).

More recently, the *parallel distributed processing (PDP) model* suggests that learners may not always learn in this orderly sequence. Instead they draw upon sources of information simultaneously to construct meaning (Rumelhart, 1992).

Intelligence – one or more than one?

Bloom (1981) provides an interesting summary of the ideas about learning from a cognitive perspective and how they have changed over the last half century. The transition has been from a notion of a fixed and measurable ability called *intelligence* to a more optimistic view of the diverse and developing cognitive processing of learners and their learning potential.

The earlier cognitive psychologists viewed intelligence as a structure (hence the intelligence quotient, IQ tests and an IQ score), initially seen as a single general ability and later as a combination of many specific abilities such as verbal and spatial ability. This measure was used for selection to different schools and streaming within them. More recently there has developed a view of intelligence as a process. While intelligence may well have a structure, what is important is how we process information. Current psychologists seek to explain the cognitive processing underpinning intelligent behaviour.

According to Howard Gardner (1993), intelligence involves the ability to solve problems and construct solutions or products, be it in science or technology, art, music or language. He argues that we learn about intelligence by studying the cognitive processing used to solve problems. He suggests that there is not a single intelligence but an array of *multiple intelligences*. These different intelligences are summarised below.

- *Bodily kinaesthetic* → as in physical education and dance:
  Learners control their own body movements precisely and are often good with their hands, handling objects skilfully.
- *Interpersonal* → as in good team workers, group leaders and peer tutors:
  Learners have good social skills; they discern moods and emotions in others and respond appropriately.
- *Intrapersonal* → as in independence and responsibility for own learning:
  Learners have a detailed and accurate self-awareness; they are reflective and intuitive, and draw on self-knowledge to guide behaviour.
- *Linguistic* → as in languages and linguistics, including poetry and literature:
  Learners are sensitive to the sounds and rhythms of languages and the meanings of words; they are fluent readers and articulate speakers.
- *Logical-mathematical* → as in physical science and mathematics:
  Learners discern logical or numerical patterns and handle chains of reasoning; they

are good at problem solving and activities involving analysis of evidence and data; they can engage in speculative thinking, draw conclusions and make generalisations.

● *Musical* → as in music and composition:
Learners appreciate timbre, pitch and rhythm and musical expression; they produce their own musical expression.

● *Naturalistic* → as in natural science, environmental studies and outdoor pursuits:
Learners enjoy being out of doors; they care about the environment and have empathy with natural things.

● *Spatial* → as in art and design and geography:
Learners perceive the visual-spatial world accurately and manipulate their mental representations adeptly; they express their thoughts in visual form.

Sternberg (1989), while agreeing with Gardner about cognitive processing and problem solving, suggests that regardless of the problem, the learner uses a common set of cognitive processes to construct the solution. He identifies three components involved in *any* problem solving, representing information processes used to organise the information perceived through the senses. Sternberg calls this his *triarchic theory of intelligence*. The three components are:

1   *Metacomponents*: the executive skills involved in planning, monitoring and evaluating cognitive activity;
2   *Performance components*: the processes actually used to carry out tasks such as remembering, encoding or deductive reasoning;
3   *Knowledge-acquisition components*: the processes used to acquire new information such as comparing and recognising what is relevant and relating bits of information.

These different perspectives on intelligence as a process have implications for you as a teacher. From your point of view, successful learning is likely to take place in your science lessons when you recognise your students' strengths and learning preferences and build on their capacity to learn. Indeed, the Curriculum and Standards Pilot Guidance on *Teaching and Learning in Secondary Schools* (DfES, 2003, p. 2) states:

> The inclusion statement in the revised National Curriculum charges all teachers with the responsibility to remove barriers to learning. One significant potential barrier is the mismatch between students' preferred learning styles and learning opportunities.

The document provides a good summary of learning styles and implications for practice.

Thinking

Thinking involves many complex processes, such as concept formation, strategy learning, decision making and problem solving. All are involved in the construction of knowledge.

Of particular significance are general methods of thinking that improve learning across a variety of subject areas (Borich and Tombari, 1997). Such cognitive strategies include rehearsal (repeating to yourself the ideas you are reading or hearing), elaboration (linking what you are learning to a particular image, idea, or keyword, to relate the old and new learning), and memorisation strategies (clustering or *chunking* information according to some system that is meaningful to you). It is also possible to learn strategies for problem solving, both general and subject specific. This is particularly relevant for scientific thinking (Kuhn, 1989). Bransford and Steen (1984) created IDEAL, a problem-solving system that may be used in a variety of curriculum areas with students of varying ages. It involves five stages:

1   *I*dentify the problem
2   *D*efine the terms
3   *E*xplore possible strategies
4   *A*ct on the chosen strategy
5   *L*ook at the effects.

When we teach our students cognitive strategies for learning, they cannot apply them in a vacuum. We want them to use these strategies to gain *general knowledge*, knowledge useful for learning across a variety of tasks both in and out of school. However, as science teachers, we also want them to apply the strategies to the information content of the subject we are teaching. In other words, we want them to use them to acquire the facts, concepts, skills, procedures, theories and principles that make up science as a way of thinking and working, and science as a body of knowledge. This is *domain-specific knowledge* and, once acquired, it will allow students to think and work productively. Cognitive psychologists also classify knowledge as *declarative* and *procedural*. The former includes verbal information learned from listening to others (through lectures, books, television and so on) and is sometimes described as 'know what'. The latter is the 'know how' – knowledge of the actions and procedures required for carrying out tasks. I would argue that there is also a third category – 'know why' – which is concerned with explanatory knowledge or *understanding*. We will return to this below.

This conscious thinking about your own thinking is known as *metacognition*. However, knowing how to use cognitive strategies does not guarantee that your students will use them when needed. As teachers, we need to think about how we can support our students in learning, retaining and using these processes.

Task 7.1

Is there a difference between intelligence and the cognitive processes of thinking?

Make two lists: the characteristics of an 'intelligent' person and the characteristics of a 'good thinker'. How are they the same? How are they different?

A CONSTRUCTIVIST APPROACH

Today, we see potential to learn in all students, depending upon time, opportunity, motivation and support. This has several consequences for planning your teaching:

● your students need a rich learning environment to stimulate thinking and information processing;
● you need to be aware of individual differences in the learning potential of your students and variety in learning styles;
● the role of prior learning and how the brain processes information will be important.

Any approach to learning that identifies the integral role of prior knowledge in the construction of new knowledge and understanding may be termed *constructivist*. Theories of learning in science are currently dominated by constructivist perspectives in which the learners actively construct their own knowledge. Borich and Tobari (1997, p 177) define constructivism as an approach to learning within the cognitive perspective

> in which the learners are provided the opportunity to construct their own sense of what is being learned by building internal connections among the ideas and facts being taught.

They identify the characteristics of a constructivist teacher as someone who:

1   organises learning and instruction around key ideas;
2   acknowledges the importance of prior learning;
3   challenges the adequacy of the learner's prior knowledge;
4   provides for ambiguity and uncertainty;
5   teaches learners how to learn;
6   views learning as a joint cognitive venture;
7   assesses the learner's knowledge acquisition during the lesson.

The subject area in which by far the most research on constructivism has been carried out is science (see e.g. the work of Driver *et al.*, 1985; Shapiro, 1994). In the context of science, constructivists suggest that students may already have naive ideas about scientific phenomena before we begin teaching them. Meaningful learning can occur only through the development of existing knowledge and understanding, and not by simply imposing meaning from outside. Therefore, learners use their existing knowledge and understanding of the biophysical world to interpret new information in ways which make sense to them. Your teaching needs to start with the students' own ideas and you need to take these conceptions seriously. Research into students' ideas, what conceptions they hold at different ages, and the patterns of progression in those beliefs and ideas, is important. It can help you question assumptions about your students' learning, and guide your practice about what to do and why to do it.

This was emphasised by White (1988, p. 19) who stressed the crucial role of students' earlier experiences and prior knowledge:

> Learning is not the simple absorption of knowledge but the construction of meaning through the individual's relating things seen and heard to things already known. Learning is active – not passive.

Thus learning is often a process of examining and modifying existing ideas rather than simply absorbing new ones. This process is one in which the student goes through a sequence of steps: observing; searching; linking; checking; changing; and learning. The actions which occur in each of these stages are summarised in Figure 7.1.

As already mentioned, your students will bring with them ideas which they have formed in the everyday exploration of their world. They can be tenacious in their hold on these ideas despite being confronted with contrary evidence (Osborne and Freyberg, 1985). The Children's Learning in Science (CLIS) project is probably one of the most influential projects in this respect (see Driver, 1983; Driver et al., 1985; Scott, 1987). Led by project director Ros Driver, the key ideas behind the research were that learning is an active process and that knowledge must be constructed by the learner. A number of useful booklets summarised the findings in areas such as *energy*, *heat* and *elementary particles*. Underpinning the research is a generalised model for a constructivist teaching sequence, involving a set of stages:

- orientation (towards the new task or idea);
- eliciting ideas (about what is already known);
- restructuring ideas (supplementing or changing, as needed);
- applying ideas (in new contexts);
- reviewing changes in ideas (to raise awareness and check understanding).

Throughout, comparisons are made with previous ideas and understandings.

That learning in science involves changing ideas also helps to explain why telling students things or providing information in other ways (for example, through text) does not necessarily lead to learning in the sense of cognitive change in a required direction. If the information does not link with existing ideas the students will continue to use their own ideas to explain things for themselves, despite in some cases being able to recite the accepted knowledge. To know what, how, when, where and who does not always mean to understand why. This is what learning with understanding is about.

What seems to be particularly important in this approach is that adult support for students in the development of their thinking skills is valuable, with appropriate interventions to promote and extend students' understanding beyond the point they could have reached unaided. Vygotsky (1987) created a metaphor – the Zone of Proximal Development (ZPD) – to describe the range of skills and abilities bounded by what the learner can use independently and what he or she needs assistance in performing (from a teacher or other person). He emphasised the importance of social interaction and mediation in learning, and described 'joint cognitive ventures'. In science, this links to co-operative activity and group work.

Such support is sometimes referred to as mental scaffolding for learning. Scaffolding may be described as the process used by the teacher to enable the students to carry out a task, solve a problem or achieve a goal that would be beyond the student if not helped.

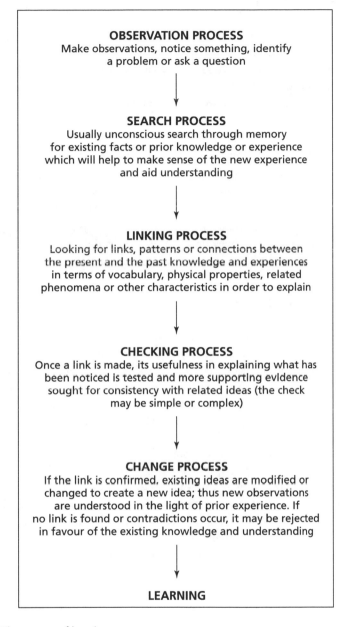

OBSERVATION PROCESS
Make observations, notice something, identify
a problem or ask a question

SEARCH PROCESS
Usually unconscious search through memory
for existing facts or prior knowledge or experience
which will help to make sense of the new experience
and aid understanding

LINKING PROCESS
Looking for links, patterns or connections between
the present and the past knowledge and experiences
in terms of vocabulary, physical properties, related
phenomena or other characteristics in order to explain

CHECKING PROCESS
Once a link is made, its usefulness in explaining what has
been noticed is tested and more supporting evidence
sought for consistency with related ideas (the check
may be simple or complex)

CHANGE PROCESS
If the link is confirmed, existing ideas are modified or
changed to create a new idea; thus new observations
are understood in the light of prior experience. If
no link is found or contradictions occur, it may be rejected
in favour of the existing knowledge and understanding

LEARNING

Figure 7.1 The process of learning

Scaffolds may be oral or textual, in the form of the social interaction that occurs between teacher and student or between student and student, and also between high-quality surrogate teachers, such as textual materials or computer software and the learner. The construction of effective scaffolding depends upon you, as a teacher, having:

- sensitivity to and skill in recognising what your students already know and understand;
- some awareness of the social and cultural context that influences each student's willingness and motivation to learn;
- knowledge and understanding of what constitutes appropriate learning experiences for the student;
- the ability to organise and deliver these elements.

Task 7.2

What does it mean to be 'good' at science?

Ask this question of the students in some of your classes. Find out what counts, for them, as important. Is it being able to answer your questions, carry out practical activities, get good marks on homework, do well at exams . . .?

Is there a difference between the year groups? Do Year 7 students have different views to Year 11 students? If so, why do you think this is the case?

PLANNING FOR LEARNING

Planning for learning therefore involves more than simply planning what set of science experiences should be offered to the students in your different classes. It requires you to identify the skills, knowledge and understanding they should develop, acquire or construct. This means you will need to be aware of how students learn generally, how they learn within your subject discipline, what other experiences they have had, and what your role or function will be in encouraging that learning. As John (1994, p. 11) suggested,

> Tasks can thus be seen as mechanisms by which teachers begin to develop cognitive activity in their pupils according to subject area. The completion of the tasks provides the teacher with evidence about both the extent of the learning and the efficacy of the task itself. Tasks are therefore selected because of their ability to promote learning in a manner which the teacher intends. In this sense they are highly personalised constructions which relate to the teacher's knowledge of his or her subject, classrooms and pedagogy.

One of the most thorough research studies of classroom tasks is that of Desforges (1985). He has shown that there are four main types of task which you can consider when planning learning experiences:

- incremental tasks to introduce new skills or ideas;
- restructuring tasks which require the student to invent or discover an idea;
- enrichment tasks which involve the student in applying familiar skills or ideas to new problems or situations;
- practice tasks which encourage the use of new skills in familiar problems or situations.

Learning in science should be a combination of both physical and mental activity, ranging from active participation in science experiments and investigations to more apparently passive activity such as observation and weighing evidence, where mental rather than physical activity is taking place. Ultimately, it is a process of making sense of information and evidence. This 'making sense' process is one of students trying to connect the new information to the existing knowledge and understanding they already possess. The necessary building on prior experiences does not always occur.

Hierarchically structured learning tasks which target the learning and behavioural objectives to be achieved can be useful, especially when specific facts and skills are desired. This seems to meet National Curriculum demands and allows lessons or activities to be planned and structured in a sequential and progressive way. In the past the emphasis has been on learning separate and quite often unrelated facts. Such facts were usually acquired by rote-learning. As already suggested, this does not mean that such facts, in the forms of laws, definitions or principles, are unimportant. They are important, but knowledge of them alone does not necessarily equate with understanding – knowing why things happen and being able to give explanations. The important point here is being able to connect the facts and ideas in order to develop understanding by building upon (but not necessarily accepting uncritically) prior knowledge and established ideas.

LEARNING WITH UNDERSTANDING

Generally, understanding is all about making mental connections between facts, concepts, ideas and procedures. It is that moment when the learner sees the light, grasps the point or gets the message! In science, these connections establish relationships between ideas, situations and events. They describe patterns in data, relate the stages in a natural process, and provide the reasons for particular sequences of actions.

We use the term *understanding* to refer to a variety of different mental activities. At some point in a science lesson there is the need to understand words (such as *transpiration* and *bond*) and sentences (such as *Can you compare the evidence so far so as to decide what you need to measure next?*). Here, understanding requires connections between the sounds and their meanings. In science there is also a need to understand situations, as when faced with grasping the feeding relationships in an ecosystem such as a freshwater pond. Particularly important in science is the need to understand the reason why there are fewer predators than prey, and the concepts of a food chain and a food web and the pyramid of numbers. This is often the reason why we teach science in the first place.

Research suggests that the ability to make mental connections is innate (Newton, 2000). However, your students may not always make the connections you want. They may not make connections at all or with sufficient precision unless you focus their attention on what matters and support their thinking. Making connections may be an innate ability but it can also be demanding. When it is, we have to reduce the demand to a level that the students can cope with and benefit from. Familiarity with many of the ideas we have to use has made some thinking easier for us as adults, but remember that your students have not had the advantage of this experience. This has to be considered when planning support for understanding. This will be returned to below.

According to Newton (2000) there are many different kinds of understanding, and in science some need our particular attention. These include:

- conceptual understanding;
- situational understanding;
- causal understanding;
- procedural understanding.

Conceptual understanding

This is what we expect when we say a student understands, for example, *electricity* or *respiration*. Each of these is a scientific concept and each involves other concepts. For example, the concept of *electricity* might be underpinned by the concepts of *current flow* and *voltage*. We would expect this to have meaning for students, to relate well to what they already know, and to link with particular instances of complete circuits and series and parallel circuits. The student would know what happens when things change in the circuit – add an extra battery, change to wire of a different resistance – and see links with what these changes might be made to do, such as illuminate a model or turn a small motor. The point is that components of the concept of *electricity* would be related to what already has meaning for the student; that is, to his or her prior knowledge. In turn, they would be related to each other to form a coherent whole.

Situational understanding

This kind of understanding could occur in both conceptual and procedural understanding. You set up some situation and the students must grasp what it amounts to and why it is significant. Suppose, for instance, you want to show the operation of the pin-hole camera. You set up a large cardboard box with a small hole in one wall of the box and grease-proof paper covering the opposite wall. You arrange it so that bright sunshine entering the window passes through the small hole. An inverted image of the geranium plant on the window-sill appears on the greaseproof screen. The majority of students will easily perceive the box, screen, pin-hole and plant and their relative positions. However, they also need to realise that the fact that the plant is a geranium is not important – any plant, indeed any object would do as long as it does not let light through. Similarly, that the box is cardboard is not of significance. What is significant is that the rays of light from the window enter the box and 'cross over' to produce the inverted image on the screen. They need to connect these observations mentally for an understanding of the situation before you, as a teacher, can move on to exploring the parallel situation of how light entering the eye behaves. Often, we as adults assume that the connections are obvious but they may not be for the students who see it for the first time. Furthermore, when such situations are described in school textbooks, the connections may be even more difficult to grasp. In this example, illustrators commonly draw in the paths of the rays of light as though they can be seen in order to help the readers. However, after such an illustration, what do students make of the real thing? We have to be sure that they understand situations as we intend them to because this is commonly how we present new phenomena to them.

Causal understanding

A causal event is when there is some change in a situation. While we want students to know that one thing leads to another, we often also want them to understand why. This means we want them to connect an initial situation with a final situation by a causal link. For example, when they dissolve sugar in water the crystals seem to disappear. If the solution is left for a long time in a warm place, the water disappears but the crystals reappear. Why? What is the cause? The students have to grasp the situation and the change, and bridge the gap between the two. Are their ideas well founded in some prior knowledge so that it makes some sort of sense to them? Causal links are particularly important in understanding the physical world and, often in simple terms, figure greatly in our teaching.

Procedural understanding

In science, we often expect students to be able to understand ways of doing things, particularly in connection with scientific enquiry. Remember that science as a process is both a way of working and a way of thinking. First, students have to comprehend the nature of ideas and evidence. They must then be aware of the strengths and limitations of procedural sequences. Finally, they may need to be able to carry out some of these procedures. But none of these means that the students know why they are doing them. Procedural understanding is when they know the reasons underpinning what they do. This is more than being able to remember the words you said, for example, giving the definition of a categoric variable. It requires them to know why it is important in this context, how it fits into each step of the mental or physical procedure and why the sequence is in the order it is. Again, like conceptual understanding, it should be under-pinned by and linked with well-founded knowledge.

If in science all that counted was giving the correct answer, then understanding would not matter. All your students would need to do would be to memorise the information and reproduce it on demand. But understanding is a valued goal in science teaching. The National Curriculum Programmes of Study, in setting out the expected standards of students' performance, emphasises: 'the skills, knowledge and understanding that students of different abilities and maturities are expected to have by the end of each key stage' (DfEE/QCA, 1999a, p. 7). This is because understanding has more to offer than memorisation. It can, as Newton (2000) suggests:

- satisfy needs, such as curiosity about why the world is the way it is, and help a student relate to the world;
- help students learn new material because it provides a framework to tie new information into;

- make learning durable and accessible – what is understood often lasts longer and is recalled more readily;
- make students' performances flexible – they are more likely to think productively in novel situations, solve problems and find new ways of doing things;
- help to manage information which is not well organised and which may sometimes be of doubtful quality, such as that offered by the Internet.

Therefore, what understanding has to offer is very significant. Ultimately, it enables the learner, whether child or adult, to make sense of the world and to make rational choices in life. Unfortunately, understanding is not always a central concern. Mitigating against it is the sheer quantity of National Curriculum content to be covered, the need to think of ways of making it understandable, the mental effort required by the students, and the impending examinations, whether internal or external. Nevertheless, understanding is so valuable that it is worth every effort. Teaching in ways that support understanding will make your job more interesting and more satisfying.

SUPPORTING UNDERSTANDING

The kind of understanding you want to foster shapes the kinds of mental or physical activity you will provide in your science lessons. You can do this in a variety of ways.

You might provide direct practical experience of some phenomenon, effect or event in order to help support students' conceptual understanding. The aim is to embed new knowledge firmly in firsthand observation and experience. However, it is not sufficient to provide experience and assume that concepts will develop adequately on their own. You will still need to support the process and monitor the quality of understanding that is constructed. Understanding in a practical activity can, and often does, involve conceptual, situational, event and procedural understanding. While our intention might be to focus on one of these, others often cannot be ignored. At times, you will draw on the students' prior experience to develop conceptual understanding. On other occasions, you will want to control that experience or provide new experiences, and you may choose to do that with practical, hands-on activity (Newton, 2000).

Science teaching within the National Curriculum also involves developing an understanding of scientific experimentation and investigation. Activities intended to explore or develop conceptual understanding may also lead to investigations and often involve a number of kinds of understanding, and, to be effective, all activities should be monitored. When developing investigative skills and understanding, attention is directed to an understanding of why the investigation takes the form it does. Note that some prior knowledge makes the experiments and investigations more likely to be a success. Sometimes, this prior knowledge will be based on informal, out-of-school experience. Sometimes it will be based on more formal exploration of the concepts of evidence. The students develop their own ideas about the biophysical world and how and why evidence can and should be used. The investigation allows them to test these ideas. Sometimes, you will have supplemented this informal experience with conceptual understanding and exploratory activities in earlier lessons. Together, these enable the students to make predictions for testing and to draw conclusions.

During the design of an experiment and its execution, or the use of evidence, the students will reveal their understanding of science through the procedures they adopt. Do they control variables and make a fair test? Can they explain why they do these things? How will their measurements provide the information they need to make decisions? To understand what, how and why they are doing things is the point of this exercise. As a bonus, the activity may also support the development of other kinds of understanding, such as conceptual understanding.

There is a tendency to think that only practical activity promotes understanding and to forget that understanding can be supported through other activity. One such activity is discussion. This may be between you and the class, you and a student, or among the students themselves. Discussion which involves explaining and giving reasons is particularly useful because it obliges the students to go under the surface, to develop their communication skills, and to justify what they think and say, to propose or conclude. Another activity can be reading about or listening to accounts from the history of science, provided that more than passive reading and listening is involved. Drawing and writing, too, are important because they make the students bring together half-formed under-standings and render them coherent. Do not assume that an understanding is well formed and secure because it has been shown in one context with prompting by you. Support it in other ways so that it develops. Understandings are not fixed; they may half-form, form and re-form at deeper or wider levels. Returning to an understanding from different directions is a useful way of supporting this development.

In all activity, practical or otherwise, it is important for the students' minds to be actively engaged as well as their hands. To ensure this, you will need to press for higher level thinking, going beyond the facts and descriptions of the science to what underpins it. This is where your understanding of the role of prior knowledge is important. It serves several, overlapping functions. Students draw on it to help them grasp what they are expected to know and understand. They then construct connections between the pieces of information but relate the new to what they know already. If they are successful in making a coherent structure and integrating it with their prior knowledge, the result is an understanding which could be deeply meaningful and long lasting.

MISCONCEPTIONS AND LEARNING IN SCIENCE

Students' prior knowledge is not confined to facts about the world. It also includes ideas and theories about how the world works. These help them understand the world and make predictions about it (often useful for scientific enquiry). As a teacher, you should not assume that your students' ideas about the world are always faulty and therefore will hinder learning. A lot of their prior experience may be adequate for the purposes you have in mind. Some may be simple and easy to rectify (for example, confusion often exists between producers and reflectors of light). Some erroneous ideas are less specific and may take a little more effort (for example, if the water is deep enough, anything will float). Other ideas may be deep-seated, well integrated and actually work in the student's world, but, scientifically, they are inadequate (for example, a student may believe that a continuous push is needed to maintain an object's motion. In the student's world, this is what experience teaches, and it predicts quite adequately the kind of action that is needed to keep a bicycle going along a level road, but in space a rocket's engine can be switched off and the rocket will continue to cruise along at the same speed unless it meets something else). Such ideas or misconceptions, as they are often called, can be difficult to overcome. You need to know, therefore, what students bring with them to the lesson. It will help you plan what to do next.

> **Task 7.3**
>
> Discuss with your mentor the kinds of misconceptions he or she has experienced with his or her classes. Draw up a list and then think about the strategies you might use to address them if they occur in your lessons.

There are various ways to find out what your students already know, understand and misunderstand. Begin with the direct approach.

- Ask questions: think of a recent event or relevant scenario and introduce it to the class, perhaps as a short anecdote to set the scene, and focus their minds on the topic in hand. Intersperse this with some exploratory questions relating to vocabulary, facts and understanding, making sure that you include the latter, but also be prepared to explore unexpected areas.
- Show a recording of a situation or event: ask the students to write an explanation and examine their explanations for clues about their underpinning ideas.
- Use concept mapping: give the class a list of words (facts, objects and ideas connected with the topic) and ask the students to draw connector arrows between them and write on the arrow the nature of the connection (as a phrase or a sentence). They may need to be shown what one is and how to construct it but, once learned, concept mapping may be used regularly for this purpose (and also as an indicator of developing and changing understanding). You should bear in mind that this form of assessment is rather rough and ready and you may need to ask the students to explain their maps.
- Use cartoon sequences: ask the students to draw a sequence of diagrams to show how they would do something or what is happening in a situation or event. This can reveal procedural and situational misunderstandings.
- Use an account of a practical task: ask the students to explain why a procedure/experiment does or does not work. In this approach, their naive theories can be revealed through their suggestions and explanations.

SCIENCE AND EXPLICIT RELEVANCE

It is easy to say that in science students should be mentally active and engaged in what they do, but how do we achieve this? First, younger students have a natural curiosity about the world which is to our advantage in science. Show them something new and they usually want to know more about it. Second, we can catch students' attention by observing what interests them and developing science exemplars from it.

Nevertheless, there are things that must be taught which may fall outside these opportunities. Yet there has to be some real reason why we are teaching this science to that class, so why not tell them? The point is that we should explain the relevance of science we are exploring to everyday life. Inevitably, the applications of science are what tend to come to mind. The vacuum cleaner, television and household lighting are what justifies teaching electricity. This is true in part, but there are other reasons for teaching about electricity and, if utility were to become the basis for the curriculum, it would be difficult to justify many topics in many subjects. Instead, we must look at why science is relevant in a broader sense.

Science is relevant because it satisfies human needs (Newton, 1989). These include:

- personal needs, such as curiosity, wanting to know why things are as they are, satisfaction at understanding something;
- utilitarian needs, what science has contributed to in the material world, generally relating to health, homes, transport, food and water supply, materials, exploration and communication;
- the need for a current world view, which is very different to, say, that of people in the Middle Ages or the Victorian period and which makes it difficult for us to relate closely to how people of earlier times felt.

How we make these explicit to our students helps them to understand why science is important to them. With younger students, the emphasis may be on concrete experience, doing science and being a scientist. The students are given opportunities to explore, test ideas, find out and talk about the scientific world. This satisfies personal needs such as those described above. The science is embedded in real world events that are meaningful to the learners. Older students will not, of course, cease to be curious, so this need should not be ignored. However, increasing maturity, knowledge and experience make other things possible. Case studies of scientists and activities related to their work may be used (with support from video and ICT materials here). Stereotypical images of the scientist as a bearded, bespectacled man in a white coat, working alone in a laboratory with bottles, flasks and chemicals, can develop early in the primary school, and be reinforced by cartoons on television and pictures in comics. Apart from being somewhat off the mark for much of science, it also gives the wrong message about opportunities for girls. Look for biographical stories about women and non-Western scientists to give some balance, and include information that tells of team work and scientific work outside the laboratory. This gives you a good lead in to discussing attitudes, values and beliefs in science.

Task 7.4

Discuss with your school mentor how science may be used to develop particular attitudes, values and beliefs.

What does each of the above terms mean for you in the context of planning your science teaching?

SUGGESTIONS FOR FURTHER READING

If you would like to explore more fully some of the issues touched upon in this chapter, the following books may be of interest to you.

Bennett, J. (2003) *Teaching and Learning Science: A Guide to Recent Research and its Applications*, London: Continuum.

In this book, Judith Bennett synthesises relevant research findings for the classroom practitioner, highlighting their implications for you. In particular, you should look at Chapter 2, 'Children's learning in science and the constructivist viewpoint' (pp. 21–49).

Borich, G.D. and Tombari, M.L. (1997, 2nd edn) *Educational Psychology: A Contemporary Approach*, New York: Longman.

If you are interested in exploring in more detail the different pedagogical perspectives discussed, this book gives an excellent overview of what you, as a teacher, need to know, with excellent examples drawn from practical classroom contexts and research.

Newton, D.P. (2000) *Teaching for Understanding: What it is and How to do it*, London: RoutledgeFalmer.

In this book, Douglas Newton brings together research findings and common sense, to provide a succinct summary of what counts as understanding in different domains and how teachers can support learners in their construction of understanding.

The sections on pp. 135–41 of this chapter are adapted, with permission, from chapters 9 and 10 of Newton, L.D. (2000), *Meeting the Standards in Primary Science*, London: RoutledgeFalmer. You should read the complete chapters for a fuller understanding.

8 Progression in Science Education

MARION JONES, LYNN D. NEWTON
AND ROS ROBERTS

INTRODUCTION

Having considered what we understand science and science education to be, we must now consider the reality of the science we are *required* to teach in secondary schools in England. We have a prescribed, centrally controlled curriculum, whether or not we agree with the content. The content of the current National Curriculum document has evolved through periodic revision from the original seventeen attainment targets (DES, 1989) to the four we have at present (DfES/QCA, 1999b). However, you must remember that this is the *minimum* requirement although, in reality, most schools struggle to cover this minimum. In theory you can include other aspects of science or ideas that will enable students to develop a better understanding. The provision of a Key Stage 3 science scheme of work by the QCA (QCA, 2000) has further guided schools down the line of prescription – what, and to some extent, how, to teach. The introduction of the Key Stage 3 Science Strategy in September 2002 (DfES, 2002) further reinforces what we must teach with suggestions of how to do so. This is discussed fully in Chapter 9.

In earlier chapters, we have considered the main ideas underpinning the four Programmes of Study and also how students learn science. We will now look at the concept of curriculum and students' learning in science and how these relate to the progression.

THE CURRICULUM FOR SCIENCE

The concept of curriculum in education is used in a variety of ways, from a very broad general term to encompass everything a school does to the very narrow specific term describing an educational activity designed for an individual student at a particular time in a particular area. Historically, schools have established curricula (content area courses) through which students progress with increasingly complex and precise learning experiences, often culminating in tests or examinations. This fits with the origin of the word *curriculum*, from the Latin *currere*, meaning 'the course to be run'.

When thinking about the curriculum for science there is a clear balance in the content between skills and procedural ideas to be developed and the body of knowledge to be acquired. You will need to offer a broad and balanced curriculum through which the students are constructing both procedural and conceptual understanding. Since all students are required to study science throughout their school lives, the programmes designed to achieve this must reflect a balance of the major components of science and also make provision for all students to have access to these components. The National Curriculum Order for Science selects Sc2: *Life Processes and Living Things*, Sc3: *Materials and their Properties* and Sc4: *Physical Processes* to represent the major components of conceptual knowledge, and defines the skills to be practised and procedural ideas to be developed in Sc1: *Scientific Enquiry*. Each should be given a fair and reasonable representation in activities. Through conscious planning, equal weighting must be given to the development of Sc1 skills and ideas as well as to the acquisition of concepts in science. This orientation is important for the way it manifests itself in the classroom situation and its consequences in terms of learning opportunities.

Teaching and learning cannot be divorced from the subject content. The nature of science as a subject itself imposes specific interpretations and particular demands for planning on the teacher. Certain areas of knowledge or experience need to be offered and experienced before others. The National Curriculum indicates that this is the case with its linear model of Level Descriptors. As Conner (1999) suggests in his discussion of progression: 'The introduction of the National Curriculum increased the importance of progression, since it assumes that it is possible to organise and sequence learning and therefore assign levels to students' achievements' (p. 141). However, he goes on to emphasise that such a hierarchical approach must not be seen as cast in concrete. Such a hierarchy of learning may not be appropriate for all learners in all curriculum areas at all times. In science we are not always progressing from simple to complex, from concrete to abstract, from easy to difficult. There may be cycles within each step of progress a student makes. Progression does not imply an automatic increase in demand of the learning tasks that are given to the students in line with their increasing ability to respond to similar tasks.

Theories of learning in science are currently dominated by constructivist perspectives in which the learners actively construct their own knowledge. Constructivists suggest that students may already have naive ideas about phenomena before we begin teaching them. Meaningful learning may occur only through the development of existing knowledge and understanding, and not by simply imposing meaning from outside. Therefore, learners use their existing knowledge to interpret new information in ways which make sense to them. Teaching needs to start with the students' own ideas, and teachers need to take their students' initial conceptions seriously. This has obvious implications when thinking about progression. Research into students' ideas, what ideas and conceptions they hold at different ages, and the patterns of progression in those beliefs and ideas is important. It can help you question assumptions about students' learning and guide your practice about what to do and why to do it.

PROGRESSION AND CONTINUITY

The word *progression* is one of the two overused buzz-words that are often run together: continuity and progression. They are often taken to mean the same thing or used in a mutually exclusive manner; that is, one ensures the other. This is not so. Put simply, continuity is in the mind of the teacher (it makes sense to the teacher to teach the content in a particular order) while progression is in the mind of the learner (they build up an understanding of increasingly more complex concepts). If the teacher has correctly identified the order of the teaching of these concepts, and provided learning experiences for the learner to become actively engaged in learning, then progression in understanding may occur. Simply ordering the concepts in a logical manner is not enough to *ensure* progression in learning; teaching and learning strategies have to be considered too.

There are two uses of the word *progression*. First, there is progression in relation to a course or programme of study planned for a group, such as a class or a year group, and covering a long period of time. The second use describes progression in planned experiences offered to individuals in order to develop particular skills, knowledge and understanding. The two are related although not interchangeable. Programmes of Study in science should support increasing levels of skill, knowledge and understanding. This is generally what is thought of as progression. Matching experiences to the needs of individuals in order to ensure this progression is generally believed to be both feasible and desirable, and yet it is no easy task.

There are certain assumptions that underpin matching and progression through learning experiences. First, the notion assumes that the level of demand of a learning experience can be assessed reasonably accurately. Second, it assumes that the level of development of students can be assessed with equal accuracy. Finally, there is the assumption that learning experiences can be designed that will match these two and, consequently, prove effective. However, the time and effort involved would seem to outweigh the outcomes, since students, contexts and subject matter all vary. Students do not come to new learning experiences with empty heads. Judgements about how meaningful and demanding any task is will depend upon knowledge of the whole learning situation, and the prior knowledge and experiences of the individual students. Their performance on activities will change according to contexts and emotions. Nor do students operate constantly at the same uniform level. Any prediction of their future performance can, at best, be no more than tentative, since it will be affected by numerous other factors, such as linguistic and mathematical demand, social interaction skills and general physical and emotional states. In other words, since such matching can only ever be loose and approximate, time and effort would seem to be better spent on more general and global strategies for individual, group and class progression.

A concept associated with progression is *continuity*. The school phases of a student's education are very varied. If what has been achieved at each stage is not to be lost, then links are needed between the stages to ensure continuity. Most schools will have structures in place to aid the transition from one phase of education to the next. These are often concerned with reducing students' worries about such transitions, but that alone does not bring about continuity.

Planning for learning in science requires that you will provide opportunities for progression in learning so that students can build understanding. This means that teachers must be aware of the progress students have already made and may be expected to make in their learning. What is their starting point? What prior knowledge, skills, understandings or experiences do the students bring with them? Where are they going? What do you, as their teacher, hope they will learn or achieve? What can you do to facilitate this development?

Learning, in the sense of developing understanding, is fundamental to the concept of progression. In the document *Science 5–16: a Statement of Policy* (DES, 1985), one of the ten criteria for good practice in science education is progression. It is defined as follows:

> courses being designed to give progressively deeper understanding and greater competence, not only within individual schools but also over the compulsory period as a whole, whatever the age of transfer between schools may be.
>
> (p. 10)

What goes on inside students' heads is the crucial issue. The important question is, What is *progressively deeper understanding*?

As mentioned above, progression and continuity are closely related. Indeed, they are often regarded as synonymous since the achievement of one often means the achievement of the other (Keogh and Naylor, 1993). However, continuity is teacher-focused and those involved, both within and between schools, share views about the curriculum content and the order of its delivery. On the other hand, progression is student-focused and relates to the forward movement through a sequence of learning targets designed to match needs and abilities. It is progression in learning by students.

Having established a centrally controlled National Curriculum for Science, the principle of continuity both within and between schools ought, in theory at least, to be achieved. Progression is more problematic since learning is more complex, involving at times regression as well as achievement. A teacher's selection of learning experiences for students must take such complexities into account. The meaning of the terms *understanding* and *competence* in the government's definition of progression will need to be defined and understood.

Implicit in the structure of the National Curriculum is a mechanistic model of learning which assumes a linear progression. It is also assumed that there is enough common ground between sequences in students' learning so that a hierarchical model is a useful way of recording attainment. As a consequence, it was considered possible to define Levels of Attainment and Level Descriptors. These assumptions are increasingly being tested and challenged (Hughes, 1996). One of the main themes explored by Hughes is that of students' understanding and the extent to which it progresses both within and across the subject areas. In his introduction, he states,

> The issue of progression has been made particularly salient by the ten-level scale underpinning the National Curriculum, and the associated need to draw up models of progression within each attainment target and each subject.
>
> (p. xv)

Research does indicate evidence of students becoming more knowledgeable within particular domains. For example, Simon *et al.* (1996) found progression in students' understanding in terms of their becoming more knowledgeable about forces. As part of the same research project, the work of Millar *et al.* (1996) also found evidence of learners becoming more knowledgeable about the nature of the domain of science investigation. They concluded that there was some progression in terms of students' understanding of how evidence is used in science, but, as Hughes pointed out, what is not clear from these findings is the nature of the relationship between these two kinds of knowledge. Does students' learning progress in a linear manner? In the work cited above, a linear and evenly spaced development was not apparent. Hughes concluded that:

> It is perhaps not surprising that this research has identified some clear areas of progression in students' understanding – one would, after all, expect learners to become more knowledgeable as they grow older. What is more surprising, however, are occasions when it appears that no real progression is taking place – or even where students' understanding appears to go backwards rather than forwards. There are at least two occasions . . . where the authors have pointed out what they consider to be significant gaps in key areas of students' knowledge or understanding.
>
> (p. 194)

Hughes also identified a common point emerging from all the studies, namely 'that there was often greater variation within particular age-ranges than across them' (p. 195).

HMI, in their surveys of schools in the early years of the National Curriculum, found that almost all schools visited had revised schemes of work to meet National Curriculum requirements (DES, 1991). The schemes included aims and objectives, teaching methods, resources, and interpretation at a general level of Programmes of Study and attainment targets. However, very few had identified the means by which progression was to be secured and achievement assessed and recorded at a more specific level. In an attempt to provide support for this, the QCA schemes of work were developed. They are not statutory. They have the status of guidance documents and their efficacy is yet to be determined.

It seems to be obvious that your planning should take account of the need for progression in skills, knowledge and understanding of the individual students. For this to happen there must be mutual recognition of the special responsibilities of each phase. There must also be appropriate channels of communication between schools to ensure that the work in science in the earlier years of schooling is acknowledged and built upon.

A genuine progression in terms of understanding and conceptual development is difficult to achieve (Pennell and Alexander, 1990). Conner (1999) concludes his report with a number of important messages about progression:

1   Progression is not necessarily age-related.
2   Not all learning is hierarchical in nature and some areas need to be revisited regularly in contrasting ways to ensure that the understanding is fully established.
3   Dialogue with students about their learning is essential. Putting their ideas into words provides evidence of their level of understanding.

For you as a teacher, reflection and evaluation are crucial steps in monitoring learning and making decisions about the next steps.

The principle of progression is not a simple case of planning what teachers teach with each class. This is a part of the process, but perhaps the lesser part. The real need is progression in what students learn, what they know, and what they can do and understand.

PROGRESSION AND SECONDARY SCHOOL SCIENCE

If we now consider the science content specified in the National Curriculum document, we can look for progression and continuity across the Key Stages.

Task 8.1

- From one of the Programmes of Study pick a topic (e.g. Sc2: nutrition; Sc3: changing materials; Sc4: electricity).
- Across the Key Stages identify the concepts covered in each key stage.
- Identify a hierarchy (what you need to understand before each new concept may be learned) – construct a concept map or spider diagram or flow chart.
- What have you discovered about the conceptual development required in each Key Stage? Is it equally weighted or does one Key Stage play a greater role?
- What have you learned about progression across all Key Stages?
- Did you identify any ideas that were missing from the National Curriculum but that you would need to include for students to develop an understanding?

In some education systems in other countries there is still emphasis on the rote learning of facts and skills. Even in this country, much of the criticism of the assessment system is targeted at the rote recall of facts required. It is recognised that such learning of facts is necessary at times with understanding developing later (think about how you learned atomic structure or the order of elements in the periodic table), but generally it is better to construct understanding alongside the remembering of facts (and ought to make remembering the facts associated with the assessment more meaningful).

So, to bring about progression in understanding we must consider:

- curriculum documents;
- key ideas contained within them;
- any missing concepts you consider essential to the construction of understanding;
- where the students are in their learning – what do they understand now?;
- how to develop concrete ideas into more abstract ones.

Task 8.2

Look at your representation of the conceptual hierarchy from Task 1 and isolate the Key Stage 3 section.

Your task is to break it down into manageable teaching units.

Construct a skeletal scheme of work putting the main ideas into a logical teaching order.

Find the matching QCA topic and compare the two.

What have you learned from this exercise?

Schemes of work

A scheme of work should be a useful working document with enough information in it to guide anyone through the topic. It should contain what is to be learned, with clear learning objectives identified for each lesson, and some suggestions of how to achieve those objectives. The author of the scheme of work will have worked out the conceptual progression throughout the topic so that the students can develop understanding as they go through. In a science department the production of schemes of work is usually a co-operative venture. This has many advantages in that a shared understanding and format emerges. Increasingly, hard-pressed departments will opt to adopt a published scheme, of which there are a number. This may seem to be a better option at the time, espe cially since many of them have been revised to incorporate the approved QCA scheme of work. However, it is the *process* of developing a scheme of work that is most useful to the science teacher, clarifying in your mind as the teacher exactly what the concepts are and how they translate into the learning objectives for each lesson. Hence the adoption of a published scheme may not be the better option in the long run for effective teaching and learning. The scheme of work may indicate possible learning activities but full details of activities will appear in the individual lesson plan.

The lesson plan

There is no single best lesson plan model. There are hundreds in circulation. Each initial teacher training programme for science is likely to provide different suggestions, and each school (or even each department within the school) may have a preferred lesson plan layout. It is the *process* of planning that is important. The hard copy plan is just the evidence that you have planned (and of course it acts as an *aide-mémoire* for the lesson).

So what should a lesson plan contain? Some people use an all-encompassing lesson plan pro forma as a check-list to make sure that they have considered every aspect of the lesson. With this in mind we list the things you need to consider:

- known factual information (e.g. date, time, class, numbers, set/band, room, topic, NC references);

- the key objectives (both learning and behavioural);
- the activities chosen to meet them (e.g. range, mental, written, practical);
- the resources needed (list everything; do not assume that each room has consumables);
- previous assessment (How do you know where to start this lesson?);
- safety issues (The risk assessment will vary with each class – what is fine for top set Y9 on a Monday morning may not be safe for bottom set Y9 on a Friday afternoon!);
- assessment opportunities (How will you know if your learning objective has been met?);
- Spiritual, moral, social and cultural (SMSC) opportunities;
- differentiation;
- links to literacy and numeracy (Do you have students with English as an additional language?);
- use of other educational professionals in the lesson (e.g. learning support assistants?);
- anything else that is relevant to your particular situation!

Many people like to turn a lesson plan into a paced script, with detailed timings and an account of what both the teacher and learner are doing. While this may be helpful to the beginning teacher, experience will show that timings are the first things to go astray in a plan. Such a detailed script may also become a strait-jacket if followed too rigorously. With this in mind you need to consider a plan B (and even plan C) for when the lesson does not go according to plan A for whatever reason. You will need to prepare extension work for those who finish early, alternative work to practical and so on.

PROGRESSION WITHIN SC1

Historically, Sc1 has been treated in a different way to the other science Programmes of Study, due partly to the fact that teacher assessment features largely at Key Stage 3 and for GCSE coursework. In many schools, therefore, investigations were only ever done in the context of assessment, rarely in the explicit teaching of the concepts involved. Schools that had analysed Sc1 in terms of progression and then incorporated it into schemes of work were very rare indeed. Currently, the Key Stage 3 strategy has highlighted the need for this progression both in scientific enquiry and thinking skills, and departments have to address this issue.

> **Task 8.3**
>
> Look at Sc1 across the four Key Stages and, just as you did before, identify one strand and trace it through (examples of strands could be obtaining and presenting evidence, considering evidence, planning, evaluation or ideas and evidence – these are suggested by the Key Stage 3 strategy). What should be taught in each year?

The difference with Sc1 is that having ordered the concepts to be taught, most departments do not construct a self-contained topic as we did with Sc2, Sc3 and Sc4 but have to integrate the teaching of Sc1 into the other three schemes of work. For example, you may decide that in Year 7 you will concentrate on developing an understanding of categoric data, two-column tables and bar charts, and in Year 8 you will move on to continuous data and line graphs. Thus in your schemes of work in Year 7 you will build in opportunities to collect categoric data and draw bar charts, and in Year 8 you will look for practical work to enable continuous data to be collected.

Task 8.4

Take the Key Stage 3 section of your chosen topic in Sc2, Sc3 or Sc4 identified in Task 2 and put alongside it the Key Stage 3 section of Sc1 identified in Task 3.

Can you 'match' the progression in both? Can you think of activities that would deliver the learning objective for Sc1 as well as that from your topic?

PROGRESSION IN OTHER AREAS

In addition to considering how to develop an understanding of the key areas of science in secondary education, the science teacher also has a responsibility to include in his or her planning how to promote learning in a number of areas such as spiritual, moral, social and cultural development (SMSC), key skills and thinking skills. These areas are not mutually exclusive and one activity in science can meet various learning objectives from different areas. For example, a Sc1 investigation set in the context of Sc2, Sc3 or Sc4 could cover the following:

- application of number (key skill);
- drawing conclusions based on observation and evidence (moral development);
- engaging in the process of scientific enquiry (thinking skill);
- using ICT in science (key skill);
- Sc1 concepts;
- Sc2, Sc3 or Sc4 concepts.

Most schools will have literacy, numeracy and ICT policies in place to guide you as to the progression in these areas across the school.

SUGGESTIONS FOR FURTHER READING

If you would like to explore further some of the issues touched upon in this chapter, the following books should be of interest to you.

Gott, R. and Duggan, S. (1995) *Investigative Work in the Science Curriculum*, Oxford: Oxford University Press

Hughes, M. (ed.) (1996) *Progression in Learning*, Clevedon: Multilingual Matters

Monk, M. and Dillon, J. (eds) (1995), *Learning to Teach Science: Activities for Student Teachers and Mentors*, London: Falmer Press

Sang, D. and Wood-Robinson, V. (2002) *Teaching Secondary Scientific Enquiry*, London: ASE/John Murray

Wellington, J. (2000) *Teaching and Learning in Secondary Science*, London: Routledge

9 The KS3 Science Strategy

AHMED HUSSAIN AND LYNN D. NEWTON

INTRODUCTION

Imagine a view taken from the Hubble Telescope showing the development of a new galaxy, millions of light-years away from Earth. Such a view generates awe and wonder for most observers. Science, through technology, can bring such images into our homes. Science also takes us out into space in the real sense. Scientific advances have not only placed astronauts on the Moon, but have also enabled us to approach the possibility of a manned mission to Mars. The impact of science on our lives, and indeed our society, is immense. Scientific advances provide the electricity we use, the cars we drive and the health care we enjoy. But these recent achievements have not occurred by chance. They are the result of the endeavours of people who have been stimulated and enthused by science throughout their lives.

The media are a significant vehicle for translating the impact of science on society in today's world from 'science speak' to 'public speak'. For example, an article in *Nature* (15 February 2001) describes the breakthroughs in the human genome project. *The Mirror*, almost six months earlier (27 June 2000), had provided its version: 'It's one small piece of man . . . one giant leap for mankind – joy as scientists crack DNA code of life.' Both articles document the sequencing of the human genome project, another huge advance in science that may have immense ramifications for health care. However, the same discoveries also make possible the manipulation of genetic material within organisms; from genetic engineering to cloning. Thus, we are educating future citizens who will influence how science impacts upon society. We want citizens who are scientifically literate, who can interact with the scientific issues and evidence, and then construct informed attitudes and opinions.

We would hazard a guess that those scientists involved in the operation of the Hubble Telescope, planning the manned mission to Mars or 'cracking' the DNA code demonstrated an interest in the scientific world in which they lived during their early school years. Hopefully, the awe and wonder that was generated there was enhanced and developed throughout their later formal education. While this opportunity for such continuity may not always have existed in the past, the National Curriculum has made it possible today. Continuity in the experiences between primary and secondary school science is fundamental if we are to generate the able scientists who can create theories, construct solutions and use fantastic ideas to explore and extend our biophysical world. This is at the heart of the KS3 science strategy.

The capabilities fostered in the primary school with science at Key Stages 1 and 2 must be built upon and enhanced at Key Stages 3 and 4. This highlights the importance in continuity between KS2 and KS3 science. Teachers of KS2 science have a responsibility to ensure that students are prepared for what they encounter at KS3. Teachers of KS3 science have a responsibility to identify what KS2 students have experienced in terms of science education so as to build on it.

KS3 SCIENCE AND THE SIMILARITIES AND DIFFERENCES TO KS2

So what does KS3 science look like? In fact, it should be recognisable in that it shares lots of similarities with KS2 science (as it should, if we have a truly progressive National Curriculum). There is the programme of study prescribed by the National Curriculum with the four sections within a spiralling curriculum. Below is a summary which identifies the development and expansion from KS2 to KS3.

Sc1 Scientific enquiry

- Ideas and evidence are expanded to incorporate interplay between empirical questions, evidence and scientific explanation.
- Investigative skills are enhanced by introducing the notion of variables, data collection, and expanding on the range of scientific equipment and means of presenting data.
- Consider evidence; identify relationships.

Sc2 Life processes and living things

- Build established knowledge of humans as organisms by introducing the role of enzymes in the digestion and absorption of food.
- Extend the idea of the chemical basis of respiration.
- Reproduction is expanded to include all the plumbing and foetal development.
- Knowledge of plants is built upon and expanded to introduce photosynthesis and plant nutrition.
- Variation and inheritance are introduced.
- Feeding relationships are expanded to incorporate the notion of energy being transferred between trophic levels.
- Cells and cell function are introduced.

Sc3 Materials and their properties

- Particle theory is introduced to explain states of matter.
- Introduce the properties of elements and consider how they combine during chemical reactions.
- Geological changes are introduced; rock cycle.
- Physical changes are developed; conservation of mass.
- The nature of chemical reactions is greatly expanded; equations and conservation of mass.
- Behaviour of metals, acid and bases.

Sc4 Physical processes

- Simple electrical circuits are expanded to include parallel circuits and voltage.
- Magnetism is introduced; electromagnetism.
- Expand upon existing knowledge of forces by introducing concepts such as speed, unbalanced forces, turning effect and pressure.
- Expand upon existing knowledge of light; refraction and colour.
- Introduce the role of the ear in perceiving sound.
- Introduce the solar system and satellites in relation to the Earth and beyond.
- Energy resources, energy transfer and conservation of energy are introduced.

The National Curriculum levels continue to apply with the idea being that students will rise through the levels so that there is a shift from Levels 2–5 at KS2 to Levels 3–7 at KS3, with most students obtaining Level 5 or above.

THE NATIONAL KS3 SCIENCE STRATEGY

The KS3 Science strategy evolved from the *Key Stage 3: Strategy for Strengthening Standards* (DfES, 2001) and was introduced in September 2002. The aim is to strengthen or raise standards in science through engaging, challenging and inspirational lessons. It is suggested that the lessons be based on the non-statutory DfES/QCA schemes of work, and the support materials reflect this.

To this end, the KS3 science strategy does what the National Curriculum Order for Science does not do: it extends from *what* to teach into *how* to teach it. It was developed to address the ambitious targets set by the government; that is, that by 2004, 70 per cent of students would achieve at Level 5 in science, and by 2007, 80 per cent will achieve at Level 5. To fulfil this, the government has asked school departments to audit teaching and learning standards and to encourage staff to make use of the KS3 science strategy framework, continuing professional development (CPD) courses, transition strategies, mentoring opportunities and booster classes for students.

The framework developed by the DfES has the purpose of:

- sharing best practice;
- ensuring scientific enquiry is integrated with knowledge and understanding;
- settting out yearly teaching objectives;
- setting high and consistent targets for student achievement.

Continuity between knowledge, skills and understanding developed at KS2 is essential, building on what students should know at KS2 in scientific enquiry (Sc1) and substantive content (Sc2–4).

Key scientific ideas have been identified that build upon knowledge, skills and understanding developed during KS2. Central to this is the notion that *Sc1: Scientific Enquiry* is to be regarded as equally important. Such enquiry should link practical experience with key scientific ideas and should be integrated into most lessons. Students should be asked to reflect on evidence supporting scientific interpretations.

Scientific enquiry

This is central to helping students appreciate how scientific ideas develop and providing the skills and processes needed for scientific enquiry. It helps students to interpret and weigh the advantages and disadvantages of evidence. Scientific enquiry must be incorporated into substantive contexts. What is meant by scientific enquiry is:

- test ideas experimentally;
- develop practical skills;
- carry out investigative fieldwork;
- employ collaborative approaches to solving problems;
- appreciate the importance of experimental evidence.

Types of scientific enquiry include pattern-seeking (correlations), using first- or secondhand sources of information, identification and classification, using and evaluating scientific procedures, fair tests and control of variables, and the use of models and analogies. The aim is to support the students in making the skills and processes of enquiry explicit, in carrying out whole investigations and in plannning for different types of enquiry.

Task 9.1	Look at the National Curriculum Order for Science.

What are the expectations of what Year 6 students should understand about scientific enquiry? Compare them with the expectations of Year 7, listed above.

By Year 6, students should be able to conduct systematic investigations to plan and carry out a fair test, read data from tables and graphs, and communicate ideas using scientific language, diagrams, charts and graphs. Students should also be able to identify patterns in results and to locate anomalous data, draw conclusions consistent with evidence and support further predictions, and understand that scientific work creatively combines observations and evidence to generate new ideas and scientific knowledge.

In Year 7 students will build upon and expand understanding of scientific enquiry by:

- considering the work of early scientists;
- planning, obtaining and presenting evidence;
- considering safety precautions and selecting appropriate equipment;
- describing and evaluating results and considering the limitations of data;
- carrying out more complex investigations (with uncontrolled variables);
- considering the advantages and disadvantages of scientific advances;
- improving enquiry through more accurate and numerous recordings.

The key scientific ideas

Five ideas within science have been identified: cells, interdependence, particles, forces and energy. The knowledge and understanding to be developed throughout KS3 follows a sequence that builds on prior knowledge and is flexible enough to permit cross-curricular links. Progression is an important principle, while misconceptions must be addressed so that students abandon flawed, preconceived ideas. The use of models and analogies is also important.

1   *Cells*
     The concept of cells is new at KS3. By Year 6, students should have an appreciation of life processes such as growth, reproduction or nutrition. In Year 7, the main idea is introduced that cells are the building blocks of life in plants and animals. The specialisation of cells in multi-cellular organisms to form tissues and organs, the occurrence of life processes such as photosynthesis and respiration in cells and the links with energy (photosynthesis and respiration) and particles (digestion) is developed.

2   *Interdependence*
     The Earth is not composed of discrete parts but is a continuous and holistic environment. Thus there is great interaction between the biological and the physical world. By Year 6 students should be able to identify links between life processes and the environment, classify organisms, consider feeding relationships and discuss adaptive strategies. In Year 7, students build on classification by discussing shared characteristics, variation (which is new), feeding relationships, communities and succession, natural and artificial selection, and the importance of plants. Again, there are links with energy through trophic levels, entropy and energy flow.

3   *Particles*

Particle theory of matter is an idea that helps explain the behaviour of materials. By the end of Year 6 materials are grouped as solids, liquids and gases, and notions of evaporation and condensation are discussed. Materials have been sorted according to physical properties and simple chemical changes have been explored. In Year 7, particle theory is introduced and used to explain physical phenomena such as diffusions, gas pressure, expansion and changes of state. The knowledge of atoms, molecules and elements is used to explain compounds and mixtures, and to establish the use of formulae and word equations. Again, there are links with both cells and energy.

4   *Forces*

Motion depends on the sum of forces acting on an object. By the end of KS2, students should have explored and be able to describe pushes and pulls as forces and to develop some ideas on friction, weight and the use of the convention of arrows to describe forces. In Year 7, the notion of forces possessing magnitude and direction is introduced, and ideas of friction (in both liquids and gases [air]), weight and balanced/unbalanced forced are expanded. New is the idea of the turning effect of forces, pressure and the link to astronomy through the position and movement of the planets. Links with particles and energy transfer in biological and physical systems are made.

5   *Energy*

This is an abstract idea which is difficult to define, but is powerful scientifically due to its ubiquitous involvement in physical and biological phenomena. It is not studied explicitly at KS2 but, given that students at this level have been introduced to light, sound, electricity and, sometimes, heat and temperature, it would be naive to propose that they will have not constructed some idea of what energy comprises. In Year 7 they must explore the scientific notion of energy and get to grips with the idea that it cannot be used up but is transformed from one form into another during physical, biological and chemical interactions. Contexts frequently used are transfer of thermal energy by conduction, convection and radiation, energy transfer in Earth cycles (the water cycle) and exploration of energy resources (electricity generation). It is used to underpin explanations of electrical current, light and sound, and links are made to forces, cells and interdependence.

THE KS3 STRATGEY AND ISSUES OF TEACHING AND LEARNING

By now you should appreciate the need for continuity in expectations and teaching approaches between KS2 and KS3. This means avoiding unnecessary repetition and duplication, and also ensuring broad and balanced coverage of science content. Progression is a stepwise development of scientific concepts and techniques between one year group and another. It depends on planning which provides learning experiences that challenge students, with scientific enquiry being seen as important in the link between KS2 and

KS3. At the end of KS2, 87 per cent of students obtain a Level 4 or greater, yet the evidence is that at KS3 some 85,000 students (28 per cent) of students do not progress further. The KS3 science strategy aims to address this problem. The framework prescribes yearly teaching objectives that students should experience and learn each year. The idea is that it should support learning and be used for planning and assessment, and thereby raise standards. Teaching results in higher standards when teachers have high expectations and clear objectives. Their lessons should be well paced with challenging oral and mental work, interesting contexts and examples, and non-routine problems. Differentiation and effective questioning are important in this process.

Planning

Planning can raise standards if long-term (schemes of work), medium-term (module) and short-term (lesson) planning is carried out collaboratively by the teaching team. At the individual level, you must consider how each lesson fulfils the yearly teaching objectives, identify the key scientific terminology, create a relevant starter activity which will be developed in the main part of lesson and reinforce the learning in the plenary session. Relevant and effective homework needs to be set.

Timing and activities

It is recommended that at least three hours a week be set aside for science lessons or 12 per cent of the teaching week. The teaching should be direct and interactive, and include a range of activities and approaches:

- directing or telling
- demonstrating
- explaining and illustrating
- investigating
- consolidating
- reflecting and evaluating.

The lesson

An effective lesson will possess a tight structure with clear objectives and high expectations, and comprise a starter and a summary or plenary session. The main learning activity must possess appropriate learning tasks that promote interest and challenge. Frequent use of informal assessment is considered important for guiding learning. Extended discussions are viewed as important in enabling students to appreciate the views of others. Models and analogies are seen as being important for developing an understanding of abstract concepts.

A typical lesson would comprise:

- a 5 to 10-minute starter activity (to set the scene and provide a mental warm-up);
- a 25 to 40-minute main activity (to build on the starter, interactive teaching/probing questions throughout, specific skills taught);
- a 5 to 10-minute plenary (to round off the lesson, consider progress made and application of idea learned).

There may be loops within a lesson, revisiting tasks and ideas, and the main activity needs to be flexible. At times, students may work individually, in pairs or as a whole group.

The use of ICT

ICT is used to promote the learning of the individual or the whole class, not only to contribute to the aims and objectives of the ICT curriculum. As a tool in science, ICT may be used to reflect on the world of science through access to vast quantities of information and skills. All lead to questioning, observing, measuring, recording, interpreting and presenting data.

Assessment

Assessment raises standards when students understand and take part in assessing their own work through self-evaluation. Teachers can use the students' contributions to assess strengths and weaknesses and for target setting. Assessment includes observations of students at work, discussion and oral questioning, written tasks and homework and occasional tests. Attainment is recorded in a meaningful way.

Assessment should involve data collected from KS2, such as personal records, targets and interventions, which can assist at KS3. A clean slate approach may be an ideal but realistically it is too slow. You will need to be able to challenge all students in their learning as quickly as possible. The minimum evidence used is often the KS2 SAT results and associated projections forward to KS3. You should record and use such assessment records, as they can provide immediate impact for both teacher and student.

To help students improve, there are three levels of assessment at which you should work:

1   *Short term*: formative and informal; part of every lesson, continuous or at plenary, or at intervals such as homework; checks mental skills and recall; used to promote learning and adjust planning; checks whether or not objectives were met; data may not need recording.

2   *Medium term*: for gathering new information and not simply reaffirming what is already known; may review a unit of work or a half-term programme; used to set new targets; cross-references to yearly teaching objectives; record the data.

3   *Long term*: summative in form and made against National Curriculum Attainment Target Levels on 'best–fit' basis; allows comparison of individual progress against descriptors and school, local or national targets; used to report to parents and relevant others; end-of-year tests good example of long-term assessment; useful to break down NC levels (e.g. high 4).

Inclusion

Science can engage and inspire all students. Each student must be included in every lesson through appropriate activities and interactions. Inclusion is closely related to planning (for example, you may use learning objectives for Year 8 students with low-achieving Year 9 students). The classroom climate should permit all students to contribute to the science experiences offered, with appropriate support to enhance progress.

The planning of your lessons must include differentiation, to take into account the need for inclusion. Varying strategies, such as questioning, use of group work so that students learn from their peers, adaptation of recording and written work requirements (larger print, structural steps or adapted) and varied practical tasks with adjusted equipment may all be used. Gender differences should be accounted for and the gifted and talented students should be challenged with appropriate supplementary or extension activities. You need to target support early and remember that it may be necessary to have additional lessons or withdraw a group for separate work. In addition, think about aiding literacy (vocabulary lists) and numeracy (alternative presentations). Capitalise on the visual and active elements of science and arrange access to specialist equipment.

A good working relationship with your school's SENCO (special educational needs co-ordinator) is necessary to provide you with assistance to maximise effective strategies. With some SEN students (for example, students who are statemented or who have profound needs) you could work back from existing schemes of work to KS2 but set tasks and information in a context suitable for a teenager.

Behavioural issues may be overcome if students are motivated by well-structured lessons with pace, especially with oral work. Plan for the use of support staff and technicians, and negotiate roles in lessons.

Leadership and management

It is believed that higher standards are promoted by high-quality leadership and management. Leadership should come from the Head of Department who, with high expectations, oversees organised schemes of work that promote progression, discusses the KS3 strategy, sets departmental targets, and monitors resources and accommodation. Audits should identify strengths and areas for development, share best practice, and disseminate training monitor implementation.

SOME PROBLEMS IDENTIFIED IN THE KS3 SCIENCE STRATEGY

A number of issues have been raised in connection with the KS3 science strategy. For example:

- Isn't it just good practice anyway?
- A tremendous range of costly materials have been produced. Could the money be better spent?
- The key scientific ideas may be questioned along with yearly teaching objectives. Are they coherent and do they fit in with educational research?
- There is a very high emphasis on the DfES/QCA scheme of work for science at KS3. Are these the best models or are they too prescriptive?
- Scientific enquiry is perceived as a mixture of skills and processes, as opposed to a body of knowledge or understanding. Is this appropriate?

Task 9.2

Look at the range of materials for the Key Stage 3 strategy for science – they should be available in your university library or placement school.

With the above questions in mind, how do you feel about the strategy?

We believe that an appreciation of both KS2 science and the KS3 science strategy is vital for teachers of science in both Key Stages if we are to facilitate the transition of students between Key Stages. The more efficient the transition, the better our students' science education is enhanced. Indeed, it may be argued that students are entitled to this. Teachers must endeavour to facilitate the transition from primary to secondary school. We want students who are going to be inspired by the awe and wonder of science, who wish to embrace science as a subject and become the future scientists or scientifically literate citizens our society depends upon. We need, therefore, to provide our students with the understanding and skills necessary to succeed at the next stage of their formal education.

SUGGESTIONS FOR FURTHER READING

If you would like to explore further some of the issues touched upon in this chapter, the following books should be of interest to you.

Hollins, M. and Whitby, V. (2001) *Progression in Primary Science: A Guide to the Nature and Practice of Science in Key Stages 1 and 2*, London: David Fulton
   If you are particularly interested in what comes before secondary science teaching and learning, this book is worth looking at to give you a feel for the primary science experience.

Mannion, K., Brodie, M., Needham, R. and Bullough, A. (2003) *Transforming Teaching and Learning in Key Stage 3 Science*, Exeter: Learning Matters
This book provides thorough and detailed guidance on the new framework for teaching science, links ideas with practical examples and suggests sources of professional support and development.

A range of documents (support files and resource packs) have been produced by the DfES to help you to teach KS3 Science. You should ask to look at these materials when you are in schools.

10 Motivating Students in Science

DOUGLAS NEWTON

INTRODUCTION

Does motivation matter? Most teachers prefer students who want to take part and learn science. They say that this kind of learner is motivated. Some teachers believe that motivation is entirely the student's responsibility. When planning lessons, they think about explanations and questions, the equipment they need and what the homework will be: all basic ingredients of a good plan. Then they meet real students. You can give all your time to planning the perfect lesson, but if it ignores motivation, you will be lucky if you get away with it. Student motivation has to underpin your plan. If you disregard it, all your planning and organisation can count for nothing – so, yes, motivation matters.

You want students who want to learn science. What can you do about it? You can:

- reward the students yourself;
- design your lessons so that the reward comes from the doing and learning of science;
- behave in ways that make students inclined to learn.

I will describe each of these in turn.

AN APPLE FOR THE STUDENT

In the workplace, people are generally rewarded with money. It is an effective way of inducing people to work but not one you are likely to use in the classroom. Material rewards have their problems. First, there are limits to what a teacher might reasonably and rightly give. Second, there is a danger that students will take part only if the reward is available. Third, such rewards tend to promote the view that things are only worth doing for tangible, material gains. This gets in the way of finding that science may be worth doing because the doing itself is rewarding. For these reasons, motivation of this kind is often confined to praise and similar types of affirmation (gold stars, good grades and reports, and examination certificates) and the promise of good things to come (career and employment success).

However, in the workplace the other side of the reward coin is the docking of pay for poor work or lateness. In school, there are other sanctions which serve as punishments and they can motivate students. Some teachers rely on the threat of punishment to keep students on task. This is not a good, long-term strategy. To maintain the threat, you have to police the classroom continually, which can be exhausting and stressful. Lessons like this are hardly a pleasure for you or the student. You probably want your students to like science but, instead, they associate it with threat and punishment. You may, of course, have students who have set their minds totally against school and learning, who disrupt the learning of others and do not allow you to try to motivate them. If your best lesson fails to turn things around then you will have to use your school's general procedures for dealing with such students.

Rewards and punishments of this kind may be appropriate at times but they have their limitations. The doing and learning of science itself, however, can be rewarding. If you can make science enjoyable, your students are more likely to like science, look forward to your lessons and learn.[1]

SCIENCE HAS ITS OWN REWARDS

Science has its own rewards but what are they? Here are some of the rewards that could come from your science lessons:

- feelings associated with mental stimulation and physical activity that relieve boredom;
- interest and enjoyment;
- satisfaction of curiosity;
- feeling of having some control over events (autonomy or self-determination);
- relating to others.

Having done some science and learned something, other rewards can follow, such as:

- a feeling of success, accomplishment, of a goal being achieved;
- feelings associated with greater levels of skill, competence, personal effectiveness and seeing structure in the world;
- a feeling that doing science is personally important, that it has relevance and relates to the real world outside the classroom, enabling us to function effectively in it.

The problem is: What kind of lesson is likely to provide such rewards? Few lessons will be able to provide rewards all the time, and students are different, so what rewards one may not reward another. You will need to study your students, experiment to find out what works and build variety into your lessons. Here are three short clips to illustrate how science can make certain rewards available.

Life processes and living things

The human circulatory system and composition and functions of blood are taught at this level. Instead of releasing a flood of factual information on your students, you could begin by asking why Valentine cards have hearts on them. At one time, the heart was thought to be the seat of emotions. For many centuries, what the heart really did was anyone's guess. For instance, some doctors thought the heart made blood, then squeezed it to the extremities where it was consumed. A doctor called William Harvey was the first to get it right, not by sitting in a chair and thinking about it, but by observing hearts at work and measuring what they did. He found valves in veins that let the blood flow only one way, back to the heart. (You could demonstrate the valve action in veins by sliding your finger along a prominent one in your arm.) The arteries, Harvey found, took blood away from the heart. He then measured the amount of blood the heart squeezed out and found it was more than it could possibly make. He concluded that the heart was a pump that sent blood around the body and back again, repeatedly. He was still left with a problem. The ends of the arteries split into thinner and thinner tubes, then seemed to disappear. They did not seem to join up with the veins. How could the blood circulate if there was no connection between arteries and veins? This was a real problem for his theory but he suggested that the tubes split repeatedly and became so fine that they could not be seen. Out of sight, they became veins, joined up again and returned the blood back to the heart. Later, someone with a fairly good microscope was able to show he was right. From here, you could ask what the students think blood does. Beginning with their ideas, you fill in the picture and ask them to test and explain the effect of exercise on pulse rate. You conclude with a conversation about blood transfusions and some blood diseases and their effects (using caution and sensitivity). You ask the students to prepare an account of the session, either as a written and illustrated account drawing on textbooks and class work, or as an A4 poster for display, or as a comic strip showing 'an hour in the life of a heart'.

This approach gets away from a dry diet of facts by putting people back into the science and presenting it as a story of authentic scientific enquiry. The practical relevance to people is made explicit and the students are allowed some control by being given a choice in how they will prepare and present their accounts. An opportunity for some active involvement is provided in what can be, for obvious reasons, an activity-free lesson.

Materials and their properties

Iron is a rather reactive substance but students at Key Stages 3 and 4 seldom think of it in that way. For them, iron (or, rather, steel) is a boring, ubiquitous metal. To begin a lesson with 'Today, we are going to look at iron' would hardly set things on fire but that is exactly what iron can do. It is not unusual to find iron cannon-balls, encrusted with sand, in shipwrecks. I was reading the other day about such a cannon-ball that, when the sand was knocked off, glowed red hot and burned its way through a table top (*New Scientist*, 2002, no. 2342). Other cannon-balls have been known to become hot and burst. Why should an old, iron cannon-ball behave like this? To cut a long story short, we would probably show the students how wire wool, with its open, loose structure, burns readily. This would, in due course, lead back to the cannon-ball. The ball begins to rust and expands as it does so because rust takes up more space than pure iron. The ball slowly becomes encrusted and this keeps out oxygen. Decaying organic matter now reduces the rust to iron. The ball, however, has expanded, so what results is a bigger cannonball made from the same amount of iron. This means it has a very loose, pumice-like structure (its density being half of what it was), rather like the wire wool. When it is brought to the surface, the area in contact with the air is very large and much of the ball rusts quickly. Rusting gives off heat, so it becomes hot and burns through the table.

Why could the cannon-ball story make a difference? First, it introduces novelty, something unusual, unexpected or surprising. Iron is no longer that rather boring material we take for granted. Novelty attracts people's attention and breaks up the monotony of an otherwise unchanging routine. Second, it presents the topic in the form of a puzzle, not necessarily one you expect students to solve without help but it makes them ask, 'Why?'. Third, it reveals your own interest in science, 'I was reading the other day . . .'. This can entice students to share your interest (see 'Enthusiasm' (below), where this is described in more detail). Fourth, it takes iron outside the laboratory and into the world of people. It is not just another substance in a detached world of chemistry in a list of pointless things to be learned. However, note that there was no attempt to make a difference at the expense of the science. Attention was not gained by acting like a clown or by talking about last night's football match. It came from the properties of iron.

Physical processes

Energy transfer and its conservation are important, not least because of its relevance to energy resources. It is relatively easy to talk about laboratory examples but to do so risks leaving the subject detached from the world that matters to the students. There is a paint, recently invented in China, that will help keep a house cool in the summer and warm in the winter. When the temperature falls below 20C, the paint absorbs heat from the Sun. If it rises above 20C, it begins to reflect the Sun's heat. It does this by changing colour. The trick was to find substances for the paint that change at the right temperature and to the right colour. The inventors have found that their paint can raise the temperature in a house by 4C in winter and can reduce it by 8C in summer. This could reduce the use of fossil fuels (*New Scientist*, 2001, no. 2287). The point is that science can often be related to everyday life. In this case, you might tell the students about the paint and illustrate how some substances change colour when heated using cobalt chloride paper that turns from pink to blue. But what colours would we want the paint to be? Which absorbs heat best? Which reflects heat best? This could obviously lead to a practical investigation but the problem need not end there. A black house, for instance, might absorb heat from the sun on a cold day but what would happen on a cold night? Is black still the best colour? What would the ideal paint do?

Why could the paint story make a difference? First, it points to the practical utility of science in informing technology. (Practical utility is often an easy justification for what we teach in science but try not to make it your only one. Some topics are not easy to justify in this way. Take, for instance, mitosis and meiosis. Their potential relevance to the lives of the students can seem rather weak and remote.) Second, it ties the science to the real world and to the real concerns of people. Third, it adds to the purpose of the practical activity.

What do these have in common?

What do these examples have in common? They take science out of the laboratory and tie it to the real world and the lives of people. At the same time, they attempt to satisfy the mental needs of students by stimulating interest and curiosity. If students see a topic as pointless, it generally means that they do not see what is in it for them, not even interest. You can overcome this by relating the topic to people. We tend to assume that students see the relevance of science but this is not always the case. Complaints such as, 'Why do we have to do this?', 'What's the point of learning that?', are signals that the relevance of your lessons is passing them by.

Remember that students are not all the same

You give a lesson one year and it works well. The next year, with a different class, it falls flat. The two sets of students probably have different needs and find different approaches rewarding. There is nothing earth-shattering in that. You have to get to know your students and tune your lessons to provide more of the rewards to which they respond. Some differences between students, however, can have complex consequences. For example, ensuring your students will experience success seems, instinctively, to be a good thing. After all, there can be little that is more demotivating than repeated failure. You have to pitch it right. Make the work too easy and the students see little achievement in it. Make it too hard and they always fail. However, there is more to it than this. Some students attribute failure to lack of effort or persistence on their part. This is within their control. They believe that if they make more effort, concentrate more, put in more time, are more persistent, success will follow. For these students, success is achievable. Other students habitually attribute failure to innate and unalterable deficiencies in their mental abilities. Any success they do have they attribute to the simplicity of the task. In other words, success and failure are out of their control. There is nothing they can do about it. Such students can be difficult to motivate. They will tell you that they did badly in the test because they are not as able as the others – or words to that effect. These students need to learn that effort pays off. You should avoid attributing failure to lack of ability and associate it with behaviours and actions that are within the students' control, such as effort, time, planning, and learning strategies. Competition is another example where students respond in different ways. Some respond well and achieve more while others do not. The point is that students may vary in their response to your lesson: one size does not always fit all. Allow for that in your planning by including a variety of rewarding opportunities.

TEACHERS BEHAVING WELL

As well as providing incentives and opportunities for science lessons to be rewarding, there is what *you* do when you teach the lesson. Your behaviour affects others both consciously and unconsciously. Enthusiasm, humour and immediacy behaviours, for instance, can draw students towards the topic and incline them to engage in it. I will say a few words about each behaviour.

Enthusiasm

Enthusiasm in a teacher is generally seen as a good quality. Studies in the USA and the UK have shown that headteachers rated enthusiasm very highly when interviewing and judging teachers. Older learners even see enthusiasm as making up for a teacher's shortcomings. This is because enthusiasm can arouse interest and make students more inclined to take part. For example, the enthusiasm of the Victorian scientist Michael Faraday

> sometimes carried him to the point of ecstasy when he expatiated on the beauty of nature. . . . His body then took motion from his mind; his hair streamed out from his head, his hands were full of nervous action. . . . His audience took fire with him, and every face was flushed . . . each hearer for the time shared his zeal and his delight.
>
> (Williams, 1965, pp. 333–4)

Your enthusiasm can also improve your students' achievements. This may be because enthusiasm elicits attention and more attentive students often learn more. But simply feeling enthusiastic is not what counts. When headteachers look for an enthusiastic teacher, they want one who shows enthusiasm because that is what produces greater on-task behaviour on the part of students. Even false enthusiasm can be effective. It seems that students are not always good at distinguishing between that and the real thing. Real or false, take care not to go too far so that your behaviour attracts ridicule. Faraday's ecstasy may be too much for you and your class. Enthusiasm needs to be seen but, as is so often the case, moderation is probably a good thing. The following is an example of a teacher introducing a pinch of enthusiasm into a lesson about microbes.

> Do you all remember why they're called microbes? It's obvious isn't it? It's because you need a microscope to see them. Well, I just read the other day about this bacterium – Wow! It's enormous! It's *half a millimetre* long! Just think about it! That means you could see it just with the naked eye, just lying there. You'd only

need twenty of them to make a centimetre of bugs! It's the world's biggest bacterium! Fortunately, it doesn't infect us. It lives in a fish's gut. It wouldn't take many of them to feel full. [If this enthusiasm has made you curious, this rod-like bacterium is *Epulopiscium fishelsoni*, discovered by Linn Montgomery in 1985 in fish in the Red Sea.]

Humour

Teachers seen as effective by their students consistently use humour more than those who are not perceived in that way. Humour can be a form of sharing and can bring students closer. It can also make the science memorable. For instance, after more decades than I care to recall, I still remember calculating the pressure exerted by an elephant's foot and a stiletto-heeled shoe, and then being asked which I preferred to dance with, an elephant or a woman. Of course, the calculations led me to say the elephant, only to be told dryly that there is more to life than physics. The humour took away the tedium of the calculation, caught our attention again and made us more inclined to engage with the next task. But take care with humour. You need to know your class reasonably well. Too much, and the students will remember the jokes and not the science. They will come to your lesson for the vaudeville act and not to learn, and class management could also become a problem.

Immediacy behaviours

Immediacy behaviours include, for instance, proximity, the use of gestures, variations in tone of voice, looking at the class, smiling, relaxed posture and moving among the class. In effect, they can help to make you and the group a cohesive unit working towards a shared goal. They have been found to be associated with greater learning. To a certain degree, actions such as these are unconscious. You do them while you teach and without thinking. Setting about to develop these behaviours may make them obviously artificial or extreme. You will probably find that you do these things naturally to some extent, so continue with that. With a new class, you may be inhibited until you get to know them better. That, too, is appropriate. Only a few teachers find it difficult to show immediacy behaviours. If you think that this applies to you and you believe it matters, then you should ask another teacher to observe and advise you.

The effects of enthusiasm, humour and immediacy behaviours can be short-lived if your lesson is a bad one. These three behaviours are not substitutes for good lesson planning but they can add something to a good lesson.

PLANNING FOR MOTIVATION

When planning your lesson, motivation matters. If you plan your lesson so that it can satisfy some mental need, it stands a chance of being rewarding for the student. You may be able to provide legitimate external rewards but always aim to interest, stimulate curiosity, provide opportunities to develop competence and self-esteem, and allow the students to experience some success. Do not leave the students' grasp of the relevance of the science to chance. Talk about it with them. Enthusiasm will help, as, at times, will humour. Building a cohesive group with a shared goal and developing the students' belief that learning is possible and worthwhile takes time but is important. On occasions, you may be able to add to that by allowing students some freedom in how they work. None of these events happen by accident. They have to be thought about before a lesson and built into your lesson plans. Remember that what works with one student may not work with another, but when you find something that works with most, remember it and use it again. The following is a list which brings together the main ideas.

Motivating students in science lessons; some points to consider

- *Relevance*: Ask yourself: Why is this topic important? Be prepared for, 'Why do we have to do this: it's boring!' Plan to make the relevance of the science explicit by talking about it with the students at the outset. Avoid gender bias in your choice of examples. Relate the science to the real world: try to include 'authentic' science with the 'school' science, and ask if there are 'world of work' connections you might draw on (personal relevance, practical relevance, societal relevance).
- *External*: Are there any appropriate external rewards (material rewards)? Take care not to rely on these rewards excessively or exclusively. Try to make the subject itself provide the rewards.
- *Internal*: Have you read, seen or can you do something that is novel, or sets the scene for a puzzle or problem? Look for something that will interest both genders. Can you centre your lesson on it or draw your lesson from it (interest, curiosity)? Give your students clear learning targets they can achieve in the lesson (self-esteem, self-worth, success, competence). Can you provide alternative ways of learning in this lesson (self-determination, different ways of learning)? Vary how you do things (mental stimulation, physical activity, working with others).
- *Delivery*: Use simple language whenever you can (effective communication means you stand a chance of making contact with their minds). Show some enthusiasm (attraction of students to the topic, mood changing). Use humour and immediacy behaviours but with care (variety, mood-changing, affiliation).

MOTIVATING STUDENTS

Even when you successfully motivate your students so that they engage in science willingly and happily, there is a moral dilemma to consider. Inducing compliance in someone else amounts to controlling him or her. Ideally, we do not seek to control students but want them to comply because they see the point of it. In the classroom, of course, students come to you with ideas and beliefs about science, school and learning that can make this an impossible short-term goal. Nevertheless, we should not forget that education aims to prepare students to see value in learning and take responsibility for it themselves.

Finally, people are complex and not everything is within your control. You may not be able to motivate every student in every part of every lesson. However, over time, you should be able to build up a feeling amongst your students that your lessons are worthwhile.

Task 10.1

Plan your motivational strategy for the following topics. You should begin with the one that is most familiar to you and progress to the least familiar. You could use the vignettes as models and the above planning routine as a guide. Be prepared to do a little research to find good starting points.

Life processes and living things
KS3: the role of the lung structure in gas exchange
KS4: evolution

Materials and their properties
KS3: the weathering of rocks
KS4: the periodic table

Physical processes
KS3: light travels in a straight line
KS4: radioactivity

NOTE

1   For those who wish to read more about this topic, providing incentives and material rewards is called *extrinsic motivation*; using the rewards the subject itself can provide is known as *intrinsic motivation*.

SUGGESTIONS FOR FURTHER READING

If you would like to explore further some of the issues touched upon in this chapter, the following books should be of interest to you.

ASE website http://www.ase.org.uk/publish/secondary/index.html
The Association for Science Education produces resources that you can use in your lessons to help motivate the students. Begin by looking at the range of SATIS materials (Science and Technology in Society), such as *SATIS 8–14*, the *SATIS 14–19 ATLAS* and the SATIS-style units in books such as *Science in Space (14–16 years)* and the package *Power Challenge*.

Cowley, S. (2001) *Getting the Buggers to Behave*, London: Continuum
Behaviour management and motivating students to learn are not the same but they are related. Those who feel they cannot begin to motivate students because of their behaviour may find this useful.

Galloway, D., Rogers, C., Armstrong, D., Leo, E. with Jackson, C. (2004) 'Ways of understanding motivation', in H. Daniels and A. Edwards, (eds) *The RoutledgeFalmer Reader in Psychology of Education*, London: RouteldgeFalmer, Ch. 5, pp. 89–105
   This chapter explains why motivating students is a complex matter.

Newton, D.P. (1988) *Making Science Education Relevant*, London: Kogan Page
   This book describes the theory and practice of making the relevance of science explicit. It has a number of examples of lessons.

Newton, D.P. (2000) *Teaching for Understanding*, London: RoutledgeFalmer
   This book describes a variety of strategies for supporting understanding in science.

11 Key Skills in Secondary Science

ALAN BRENNAN

INTRODUCTION

The National Strategies for English, Mathematics and Science have all emphasised the principles of:

- *Expectations* – establishing high expectations for all students and setting challenging targets for them to achieve.
- *Progression* – strengthening the transition from KS2 to KS3 and ensuring progression in teaching and learning across KS3.
- *Engagement* – promoting approaches to teaching and learning that engage and motivate students and demand their active participation.
- *Transformation* – strengthening teaching and learning through a programme of professional development and practical support.

In this chapter, I hope to be able to support these aims in a practical (though, of necessity, limited) way, emphasising the holistic nature of teaching and the need to integrate, seamlessly, the individual skills mentioned into lessons. Such lessons can then be built up to form a challenging, engaging and diverse scheme of work. In looking at the diversity of learning/teaching experiences, it is important to be aware of current developments in teaching, especially those involving 'brain-based' learning, such as accelerated learning programmes. Remember that practice by doing, teaching others and the immediate use of the learning are most effective at helping students to retain the information and/or skills.

Students need to practise skills, receive constructive, critical feedback and undertake personal reflection on their performance. All of these, and the necessary monitoring and intervention, need to be planned broadly into schemes of work and specifically into lessons. There must be a logical progression in the work, allowing students to improve as they gain knowledge, skills and understanding by being challenged with more difficult ideas and tasks.

The areas in which skills need to be developed include literacy, numeracy, information and communication technology, thinking, practical activity and personal development. The government has highlighted the same key skills but categorised them slightly differently:

1   Effective communication
2   Application of number
3   Information technology
4   Working with others
5   Improving own learning and performance
6   Problem solving

(QCA, 1999, p. 8)

Although these skills are considered in isolation in this chapter, it is important to appreciate that students encounter them embedded in the lesson and as part of a larger scheme of work. When looking at developing these skills, it is important to take this holistic approach in planning and delivery.

A possible approach to thinking about and developing these key skills involves the following cycle:

- know where the students are;
- know where you want the students to progress to (and beyond);
- construct the appropriate learning experiences;
- monitor and intervene in the learning as necessary;
- review the whole experience.

The first point is especially important in secondary teaching as students will arrive in Year 7 with, possibly, a variety of learning experiences and expertise. It is important to consolidate and build on these experiences and to remove redundant work to ensure a rapid transition to a challenging learning scheme. In later years in secondary education, it is still important to ensure a firm base on which to construct the upcoming work.

Enquiries are a comparatively new area, encompassing investigative work, and could be a major focus for the development of skills in all areas.

Finally, as a practising teacher and not an educationalist, I hope to give this chapter a practical bias. I want to help you to rapidly integrate the teaching of key skills into your lesson plans and schemes of work. What is described here should 'just be part of what you do' and not a major issue. Teaching, in my experience, is a very fluid process, and teachers need to have a basic structured approach to their work which allows them to rapidly adjust not only to the needs of their students, but also to the demands placed upon themselves inside and outside of the school environment.

LITERACY SKILLS

> Students should be taught to express themselves clearly in both speech and writing, and to develop reading skills. They should be taught to use grammatically correct sentences and to spell and punctuate in order to communicate effectively in written English.
>
> (SCAA, 1997)

Students need to become proficient in both writing and speaking. They need to be able to access, assess and reflect on scientific issues and to be able to make informed, sensible comment. They need to develop a vocabulary they can use in conversation, discussions and presentations and have clear ideas that are the result of the collection and critical appraisal of information in various forms. Students must be willing to listen to others, consider other opinions and be willing to revise their own ideas.

Five individual areas can be highlighted and emphasised through teaching to provide the basics for the higher skills mentioned above. These are vocabulary, speaking, listening, reading and writing. It is important to emphasise that often more than one area may be covered at one time. As a teacher, you must find or create opportunities to allow your students to use these skills in an integrated way and at a higher level of thinking and working. Some practical ways you might do this follow for each of these areas.

1 Vocabulary (words, spelling, usage and meaning)

You should have access to a number of dictionaries (e.g. *Oxford Junior Dictionary*; *Science Dictionary*) for use by students and possibly an *ACE Spelling Dictionary* for use by less able students. Do not be afraid to check your own spelling in front of the students; we all go blank at times!

You must be prepared to challenge confusion with words and their incorrect usage (e.g. students who confuse melt and dissolve, heat and temperature, flower and plant). In addition, many words have both everyday and specific scientific meanings (e.g. weight, boil, force). Focus on 'Keywords'. You can do this in a number of ways:

- *Lists* – for every topic the keywords need to be listed and any additional ones added depending on particular circumstances.
- *Word walls* – keywords may be displayed on sections of laboratory or classroom walls, in the backs of student exercise books or on A4 word walls (Figure 11.1).
- *Vocabulary books* – keywords may be written into specific vocabulary books (students are used to doing this from their primary school days).
- *Spelling* – on encountering new or difficult words, students should be taught strategies to help them to spell correctly and remember (e.g. *look, cover, spell, check*).
- *A4 whiteboards* – ask students to write keywords and hold for rapid checking, reinforcing correct spelling.
- *Meaning checkers* – keyword lists where students can provide their own meanings and check them against dictionary versions, self-evaluating in the process (Table 11.1).

HEALTH

A	B	C	D	E
F	G	H	IJ	KL
M	N	O	P	QR
S	T	UV	W	XYZ

Figure 11.1 Example of a word wall chart for work on health

Table 11.1 Example of a meaning checker

Words	What do you think they mean?	Definition from book	Marks out of ten for your own meaning
Acid			
Alkali			
Litmus			
Acid rain			
Neutral			
Neutralising			
Distilled			
Indicator			

- *Word puzzles* – students enjoy these but they must be used for a purpose; they are often very useful at beginnings and endings of lessons:

  - anagrams – especially if fun (e.g. nocrab (carbon), livers (silver), earth (heart))
  - matching exercises (e.g. word to picture, word to definition)
  - using keywords to make other words (e.g. photosynthesis makes toy, snot, this)
  - categories – such as the board game Scategories, a fun activity
  - word searches – use sparingly; a fun activity extended by matching keywords to definitions
  - crosswords – higher level as these involve understanding as well as spelling keywords.

- *Correcting mistakes* – spelling and other mistakes in prepared passages; correcting own and partner's/peers' work.

2 Speaking

Students need to use language in order to communicate information and ideas effectively. Situations need to be engineered where students actively engage in conversation with both their peers and the teacher. When developing these activities you need to think about:

- student familiarity with the subject matter;
- the type of subject matter (facts/descriptions/experiences/issues/opinions);
- the length of time involved in speaking;
- if students will initiate the speaking or respond.

Once again, there are a number of strategies you can use to promote high-quality discussion.

- *Pictures, drawings and diagrams* – may be used to focus students' attention and identify key structures. They can be asked to describe what they see (for example, when shown a picture of a pedal bin and a side view through the bin, students can be asked to describe the mechanism that lifts the lid). Describing, explaining and interpreting pictures, drawings and diagrams may also be used to develop students' higher level thinking skills.
- *Video clips* – (with their sound track removed) can be useful in stimulating discussion and drawing out explanations.
- *Short texts* – may also be used to support explanation and interpretation. Extracts from poetry and fiction may be used as a starting point for such discussion. This relates to reading, discussed below.
- *Concept cartoons* – a scientific idea or concept is presented in the form of a cartoon, usually with a question and several possible solutions/explanations (only one of which is scientifically correct) given in speech bubbles by the various characters in the cartoon (Naylor and Keogh, 2000).

- *Presentations* – summaries of factual research, investigations (whole or parts of), summarising topics, presented to other groups/classes.
- *Concept/mind maps* – individual. Group or whole class analysis and/or synthesis of ideas related to a concept or idea; may be done by using the overhead projector (OHTs), in poster form or using commercial software such as *Inspiration*.
- *Drama and role play* – dramatic re-enactments of events or debates on contemporary issues with individuals/groups taking on specific roles (e.g. the MMR debate; the greenhouse effect; the discovery of vaccines).
- *Simulation followed by debriefing* – useful for supporting understanding of systems and interactions (e.g. electrolysis, kinetic theatre, from ATLAS publications).
- *Jigsaw activities* – pictorial representations or word format summaries of ideas and events that are presented in a mixed segmented style to be reassembled (e.g. food chains and feeding relationships; life cycles).

It is important to note that the way such resources are used is very important. While such activities can be fun when used properly and judiciously, overuse or inappropriate use will devalue their worth. It is also important to relate the science activities to students' everyday experiences and to make this relevance explicit.

3 Listening

The difficulties students will encounter when listening and which must be taken into account when planning are as follows:

- the complexity of language
- the nature of the ideas and concepts involved
- the length of the passage of speech
- the speed and clarity of speech
- the number of speakers
- background noise and other distractions
- the number of non-verbal clues
- the amount of repetition
- the amount of redundant language.

Possible activities to improve students' listening skills include the following:

- *Identifying sounds* – a tape of everyday sounds can be made and played to students who listen and identify as many as they are able.
- *Listening to peers* – encouraging students to listen to other students reading and explaining prepared passages, topic summaries, presentations, debates, jigsaw activities, loop cards, use of poetry, song lyrics, aural puzzles.
- *Listening to story tapes* – these can be commercially produced or made by you as the teacher for the classes/topics you are teaching (e.g. making recordings of students performing plays).

- *Listening to music* – many relevant songs have been written over the past forty years which can engage students and form a base for other related activities. Examples of relevant songs include the following:

  - 'Philadelphia' – Bruce Springsteen (AIDS)
  - 'The Earth Song' – Michael Jackson (environment)
  - 'Protect and Survive' – Runrig (environment)
  - 'Silent Spring' – Richard Grainger (environment)
  - 'Neptune' – The Poozies (environment)
  - 'The Elements' – Tom Lehrer (elements).

4 Reading

Reading may be undertaken as a solitary activity, as part of small supportive groups or in a whole class context. All variations should be used for the additional benefits which accrue from their use.

When choosing a piece of text it is necessary to ensure that it matches the abilities of the students as well as addressing the specific scientific content. Teachers should consider the following potential difficulties for students:

- length and layout of text;
- presence of accompanying visual clues;
- repetition of keywords and ideas;
- amount of redundant language;
- relevance and familiarity to the student (e.g. everyday situations);
- complexity of the language (words, sentence structure).

Textbooks have increasingly attempted to address these issues and to provide relevant activities. Some publishers have produced in-depth science readers to (e.g. the *Nature of Science* and the *Livewire Real Lives* series), while others have produced reading materials which present information in engaging contexts with attention-grabbing facts and amusing illustrations (e.g. *Horrible Science* series). Poetry is often a quick way of incorporating reading which can be fun (see, for example, some of the work of Michael Rosen) but also very succinct. Reading science materials can also be a fun activity and should be encouraged.

In order to read to acquire knowledge and understanding, a number of sub-skills are important and can be developed. These are as follows:

- *skimming* – fast reading to extract information or the essence of a piece of writing;
- *sequencing* – putting events and ideas into logical order;
- *extracting information* – can be used in a variety of ways (e.g. collecting and arranging information into a table; labelling diagrams from text; annotating diagrams from text);
- *criticism* – proofreading and criticising text(s);

- *modelling* – reading and use of glossary, index;
- *question writing* –individually or in small groups based on a section of text.

5 Writing

When writing yourself, explain to the students the decisions you are making about the style and content. Perhaps you could ask them to tell you what to write following a reading or discussion activity. Before engaging students in a writing activity designed to improve and develop their writing competencies, teachers should consider the following:

- the amount of writing envisaged;
- the amount of help with structure and spelling to be provided;
- the style of written responses (e.g. sentences, bullet points);
- the level/type of support to be offered.

An open-ended piece of writing will be daunting for students unless they have support and are provided with the necessary sub-skills to be able to meet the challenge. Students can be supported by being given discrete activities which build towards a complete independent piece of prose. For example, you could use:

- rewriting false statements
- cloze procedure
- turning pictures into words
- annotating diagrams
- bullet-pointing
- creative writing (e.g stories and poetry, letters, newspaper articles)
- writing frameworks
- practical write-ups
- visual/written sequencing activities (e.g. instructions for making a cup of tea).

Writing up investigations is the standard (and often the only) creative writing activity asked of students in secondary science. Clear guidelines on what is expected from them in their research and the acceptable quality of presentation is important. Students should be shown, also, the importance of imaginative thinking in the development of scientific ideas and be provided with regular opportunities for extended imaginative writing. Typical exercises involve imagining what it would be like to be 'ingested, digested and egested' and to 'travel' around the water cycle. Collaborative writing should also be considered, since it has benefits arising from peer-teaching.

I have considered these five aspects of literacy separately but you must be aware that students do not experience them in isolation. It is important for these skills to be focused on for their development but they need to be integrated and used in a holistic way.

Task 11.1

1 Collect the keywords from one of the QCA KS3 Topics. Look through the scheme of work and add any other words which you feel might need to be considered. An example has been done for you for QCA 7A Cells.

Keywords	Additional words
organ tissue cell membrane cyctoplasm nucleus chloroplast vacuole wall	microscope magnification neurone respiration (and other MRSGREN words) mitochondrion (most able) body system words, e.g. digestive, nervous

2 Collect together three or four of the most up-to-date textbooks for KS3 or individual years within KS3. Analyse their support for literacy under the heading used in this section of the chapter (i.e. vocabulary, speaking, listening, reading and writing).
3 Choose a QCA KS3 unit and highlight where you could possibly address the development of speaking skills.
4 Perform a search of newspapers and periodicals to collect a set of cartoons/photographs which may be used to illuminate students' understanding.
5 Produce an overview of which literacy skills you expect Y7 students to have and which need developing. Take one of the QCA topics for each year of KS3 and put in place specific literacy activities to develop literacy skills in a progressive manner.

	Vocabulary	Speaking	Listening	Reading	Writing
Y7					
Y8					
Y9					

NUMERACY SKILLS

Students need the ability to process and evaluate numerical data. School policy with regard to numeracy (as well as access to the National Curriculum descriptions and levels) should be made available during planning. You should be looking to support the school's policy and to ensure a transfer of skills into the scientific domain.

From the teacher's point of view, my experience is that we are still inconsistent in our use of terminology. The particular example which springs to mind involves the use of the terms *bar chart*, *bar graph* and *histogram*. There have been attempts to standardise practice but there still seems to be some confusion. These problems need to be addressed in KS2 as well as KS3 so that there is consistency.

The introduction of the Numeracy Hour has impacted on both primary and secondary education, and has valued a diversity of correct responses to the same problem. This means that you have to be flexible and allow for alternative explanations/methods in the correct solution to mathematical problems.

Finally, in science, we often look for a level of mathematical ability beyond that which the students have been taught in maths. This is particularly true when we are doing investigative work. You must take this into consideration in your planning and be prepared to provide the necessary support for your students. Students should be supported in being able to perform the following:

1   *Basic computation*:

- addition, subtraction, multiplication, division;
- systematic counting with progression to pattern recognition and hypothesising;
- proportion and scale (important in examining organisms and when dealing with microscopic contexts for the work);
- percentages;
- decimals;
- averages (means, modes).

2   *Data presentation*: All the following ways of displaying data may be incorporated in practical activities (i.e. taught in context). In addition, where extra practice is necessary, discrete activities to practise and assess them may be written. The use of ICT to support students can also be beneficial (see the ICT section). Specific things to think about include the following:

- tables;
- pictograms;
- bar charts (the term *bar graph* should not be used; useful for the display of discrete/discontinuous variables; gaps should be left between each vertical bar);
- histograms (for the display of continuous variables; no gaps are left between each vertical bar);
- line graphs (for continuous variables, points are plotted and joined by lines of best fit).

3   *Data analysis*: real (collected by the students or from a media source) or created data (designed for a specific task) may be used. The students need to develop the following skills:

- pattern recognition – positive, negative and no correlation;
- precision – how accurate are the results?
- reliability – how sure can you be of the precision of your results?
- averages, modes and means – modes and means are easy but how do you really adequately describe what an average is?

Task 11.2

Take one strand of the QCA KS3 scheme of work (e.g. Sc4 strand) and construct a scheme for the progressive development of data presentation skills during the key stage.

Take this one step further by writing up the practical activities which support your scheme.

INFORMATION AND COMMUNICATION TECHNOLOGY

ICT is an exciting tool with which to support students' learning in science and to transform aspects of teaching and learning. Developing students' ICT skills rests on the optimal use of the school's resources and upon the whole school approach to ICT. You must ensure you have an up-to-date knowledge of students' capabilities and experiences so that ICT challenges do not swamp their support of scientific learning. A variety of strategies/approaches may have to be adopted by the teacher, ranging from whole class teaching, through small group work and into individual work.

ICT not only includes the use of computer technology but also of audio and photography, both still and video. ICT is an area that has seen and will continue to experience rapid change. You need to be aware of the ICT skills possessed by many KS2 students and their increasing familiarity with the use of digital still and video images. Our students bring these widely varying levels of skills to KS3 and these must be recognised and built on. Students should not be allowed to stagnate. In addition, the increasingly widespread use of interactive whiteboards requires imaginative and creative planning to maximise their impact and optimal use.

- *Audio* – Little use seems to be made of tape or digital recording in lessons. This is an area where, with a little imagination, parts of the actual lesson could be used to examine, highlight and review a whole host of students' ideas and contributions. This could boost the confidence of students.
- *Digital still photography* – The ease of taking and downloading digital still images makes the use of digital cameras in class an exciting prospect. You can catch the students in action and incorporate the images in future review and consolidation.

The work could become much more personal and meaningful. In addition, students can record the lesson visually with the resultant recall of more information.

- *Video photography* – Most members of staff and students are not in the position to be able to use digital video to support teaching and learning but this will soon change. Being able to review and revisit work at the end of a topic or term by reference to the actual events could provide an important focus for teaching and learning. In addition, the development of a range of video clips for projection would assist in those situations where practical work was too dangerous, difficult to observe or occurred rapidly.

- *Computers* – Teachers and students may use ICT in a variety of ways. The most obvious is as a source of information, with reference CD-ROMS available for most aspects of Sc1, Sc2, Sc3 and Sc4, and myriad references on the internet. In addition, specific use may be made of word processing and desk-top publishing, the digital projector for presentations, databases and spreadsheets, presentation packages, probes for sensing and data logging, control and simulation packages, video microscopes and, most recently, interactive whiteboards.

The use of ICT in secondary science is discussed fully in Chapter 12.

PRACTICAL SKILLS

The range of practical skills required of students is well documented (see Chapter 3) and has, in the past, led to practical skills being taught as individual items. Today the tendency is to teach practical skills in context, when they are needed. An awareness of skill levels is needed before planning practical work into schemes of work and, as in other skill areas, a meaningful progression needs to be established.

1   *Measuring skill* – distance; volume; time; temperature; mass.
2   *Describing* (see Literacy) – organisms; observation of events (e.g. chemical reactions); imaginary situations (e.g. being a red blood cell);
3   *Apparatus* – choice; handling; use (e.g. glassware; electrical equipment; microscopes).
4   *Safe use of chemicals* – weighing; carrying; mixing; disposal.

Most departmental handbooks will cover (3) and (4). With respect to (1), it is worthwhile, in departments that have these skills integral to their schemes, to spend some time analysing when and where these skills are met.

| Task 11.3 | Use your scheme of work for Y7 to analyse the coverage of measuring skills. What conclusions can you draw and what actions do your conclusions suggest you should take? |

CONCLUSION

In this chapter, I have tried to provide some practical ideas for the integration of key skills into science lessons. The current emphasis on lesson structure, with well-thought-out starter and plenary sessions, is supported by this chapter's contents, as is the importance of science in being a creative, imaginative and visual subject with a long, rich history to draw upon. I hope, also, that the value of scientific enquiry (Sc1) as set out in the National Curriculum is apparent and that it may be used as a wonderful tool for the development of all of these skills and more. At its best, it involves the following:

- the posing of interesting questions based on experience;
- exploration of the question through research (e.g. books, the internet) and practical investigations;
- collation of materials obtained above;
- problem-solving;
- analysis and synthesis of the information;
- presentation of the analysis/synthesis;
- peer review of the work.

The areas outlined above and the activities given to make them more concrete should not be viewed in isolation. Indeed, these skills, along with personal and thinking skills, are being exercised continuously in an integrated, holistic way. Skills should be integral to each lesson and to the entire scheme of work. Skills are not isolated, and several are often addressed by one activity. Furthermore, science is generally a collaborative experience in which many ideas contribute towards our overall understanding. Imagination has played a major role in the development of many ideas and will continue to do so.

Students can be helped to develop all the necessary skills, in whatever areas, through guidance and the provision of a well-thought-out, progressive scheme of work providing a variety of learning experiences. The responsibility of the teacher is to take such a scheme and personalise it for the students in their charge.

SUGGESTIONS FOR FURTHER READING

If you would like to explore further some of the issues touched upon in this chapter, the following books should be of help to you.

Frost, R. (1994) *The IT in Secondary Book*, Hatfield: ASE
This book provides an excellent overview of the use of ICT in science education.

Sutton, C. (1992) *Words, Science and Learning*, Buckingham: Open University Press
Sutton provides a thoughtful discussion on the importance of language and communication in the context of science and gives pointers for encouraging effective communication through science.

Watts, M. (1998) *Creative Trespass*, Hatfield: ASE
Creativity is a current buzz-word in education. Mike Watts' book provides an interesting starting point for science teachers' thinking about what it means.

12 ICT and Secondary Science

SUE BETTS

INTRODUCTION

This chapter is about using ICT in teaching and learning science in the secondary school. The ideas under discussion are given in Figure 12.1. The chapter could be regarded as a taster for further reading. The ideas presented here are not original; nor is it possible to discuss all the issues surrounding this topic. Consequently, you are strongly advised to refer to the reading material suggested at the end of the chapter to gain a fuller picture.

THE POTENTIAL OF ICT: LEARNING EXPERIENCES IN SCIENCE

Imagine you are preparing to teach a science lesson to a Year 10 class. What you are going to teach is likely to depend at least on the students' prior knowledge of the topic, the scheme of work and national curricula, so setting some achievable objectives for your students for this lesson is not too difficult. How you are going to give students the best opportunities to achieve those objectives requires more thought. What sorts of learning experiences will you design and what ways do you intend to work with your students? Will ICT play a part? Whatever way you decide to tackle your lesson, the desired result is high quality in learning in science. This can mean high standards in, for example:

- understanding science concepts and acquisition of science knowledge;
- being able to use this understanding and knowledge flexibly in a variety of situations;
- understanding the nature of evidence in relation to the construction of scientific knowledge.

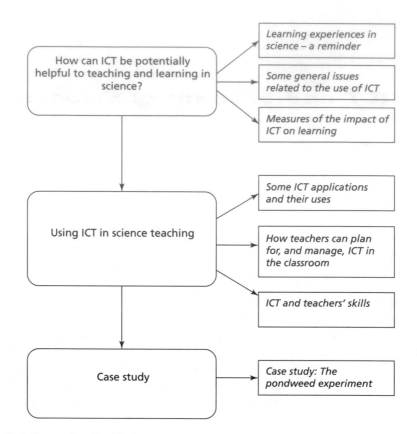

Figure 12.1 Ideas explored in this chapter

Evidence of high standards in skills developed could include an ability to:

- devise and safely carry out investigative and other practical work;
- communicate ideas using appropriate methods;
- work independently and collaboratively with others.

(Association for Science Education (ASE), 2002)

You will recall that learning outcomes in general are affected by a number of factors. For example, they are related to characteristics of the teacher, the learner and the task (Figure 12.2).

Your students need to be motivated to learn. Ideally they need to want to learn for reasons of interest, curiosity and challenge. Well motivated students are concerned with understanding phenomena, with giving reasons and explanations. As a result they respond positively to tasks, and become mentally engaged in them. The trick is to know some of the practices of teachers and learners and the nature of tasks in science lessons that are likely to bring about this kind of situation and maximise learning. Some ideas are given in Figure 12.3.

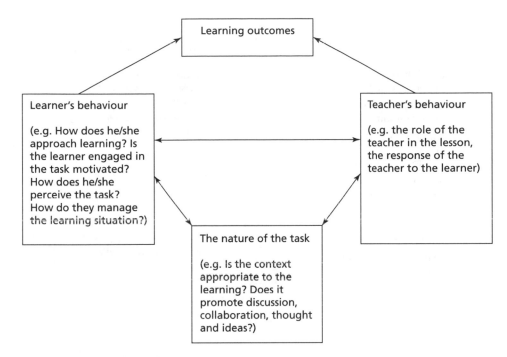

Figure 12.2 Factors affecting learning

A better understanding of science concepts or ideas could be the result of giving students the opportunity to link practical experience (e.g. investigating and measuring, or interpreting results) with scientific ideas (e.g. developing and evaluating explanations with their teachers or peers) in an interesting appropriate context. Understanding is necessary for students to use their learning of science in a variety of situations. The experiences you provide for your students, how you use them with students and how they interact with them and with you are crucial to learning in science. Of course, ICT is not necessary for any of this, but it is a multi-faceted resource with the potential to have an impact on learning in many of the ways described above. You may well consider using ICT when you are preparing for your lesson. So how can ICT help?

Task 12.1

Make a list of as many different ways that ICT can help you prepare and teach science as you can think of. Put it to one side to return to later, when you have finished reading this chapter. Then compare your list with the ideas raised here.

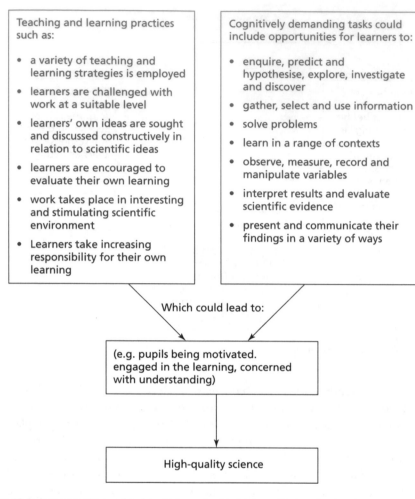

Figure 12.3 Some practices and tasks which can lead to high-quality learning in science

Source: Adapted from Association for Science Education (ASE), 2002

GENERAL ISSUES TO DO WITH ICT

There are several ways in which ICT may be viewed in relation to teaching and learning. One way of viewing the use of ICT is to see it as a tool for learning (Somekh and Davis, 1998). 'Tool' in this context refers to an intellectual tool, rather than a physical object that we use for a practical task, though its use is similar in that it often makes things easier. For example, variables in a spreadsheet may be linked by formulae to represent, say, how the stopping distance of a car depends on the speed of travel, or the driver's thinking distance and braking distance (Newton and Rogers, 2001, p. 95) Learners can explore how changing some of the variables affects the stopping distance, then provide explanations. They could develop such a model by adding or altering data to indicate a wet road.

Learners are using the computer as a tool to explore a situation, or to predict and hypothesise without an actual experiment taking place. Freed from time-consuming calculations now carried out by the computer – the physical tool associated with the intellectual tool – students can discuss concepts or ideas with the teacher, possibly leading to a better understanding of the principles or concepts involved.

From another perspective ICT can take over some of the work of the teacher (Newton, 2000). For example, ICT can provide knowledge and information structured in a variety of ways, support understanding and interact with students. Multimedia can offer particularly powerful opportunities for learning in these respects (Collins *et al.*, 1997). For example students can explore patterns in the properties of metals and non-metals, or develop their understanding of the functions of organs in the body by navigating pathways through material, based on their responses to questions or through the choices they make. Students' attention can be directed to what matters in the learning, leading to better understanding. All this means that there are fewer demands on the teacher, that teachers have more time to communicate with students usefully, or become what has been described as 'enablers of quality experiences' (Somekh and Davies, 1998). In turn, in this situation, the students can exert some control or autonomy over their learning.

Both the above views of the use of ICT in science may mean that the major role of the teacher in the lesson is that of 'expert guide'. There are features of ICT, or of ways of using ICT, that depend on how well the teacher uses this role. ICT can contribute to learning experiences in environments where tasks are exploratory. Such lessons can involve using ICT in whole class discussions, or students working in groups, for example, as they might do in conventional practical work. Research literature tells us that the use of collaborative group work (small group work where students are allowed to explore phenomena together) gives more space and time for students to engage in sustained discussion. However, students often need practice and the teacher's guidance in this kind of group work.

One useful feature of ICT is that it can save time and perform tasks for us that would otherwise be labour-intensive, such as carrying out complex calculations or plotting graphs. In theory, this leaves time and space for students to get to grips with the purpose of the activity. How this time benefit is used affects how well students learn. It is then that the teacher's skills in using ICT with students are paramount.

Of course, the nature of the software may be such that a student can use it *entirely* independently. Then the computer could be regarded as a tutor. Students' responses can be monitored to ascertain their prior knowledge. Subsequent knowledge or activities can be structured in a way that suits students. Such tutors imply that one student is totally engaged by the programme, and that it caters for their specific learning needs on a one-computer-to-one-student basis. On the other hand, there is a view that such tutors may have the effect of narrowing students' learning, since it is likely that not all types of learner are catered for. Their usefulness to learners depends on the quality of the software. Modern integrated learning systems are sophisticated examples. However, the use of such software means that there is little opportunity for social interaction between teacher and students or among the students themselves.

MEASURES OF THE IMPACT OF ICT ON LEARNING

Before you think further about choosing to use ICT for your lesson you will probably read some research studies about the effects of ICT on teaching and learning. *The ImpacT Report* (Watson, 1993) involved studies made on the impact of ICT learning on more than 2000 students in primary and secondary schools in England and Wales. Many developments in ICT have occurred since that time but there are some useful points that are still relevant today. In this study, comparisons were made between classes that used ICT for learning and those that did not in English, mathematics and science. The general conclusion of *The ImpacT Report* was that ICT did make a contribution to learning but that the contribution was not consistent across subjects or age groups. In science, several case studies in various topics were carried out. The summary of findings from these indicates that computers were generally beneficial to motivation and concentration and interest in the topics studied. Another study, the Plait Report (Gardner *et al.*, 1993), where 235 students in nine schools were given their own portable computers for a year, also noted students' increased motivation. Both reports also highlighted the problems encountered by teachers in making effective use of ICT in the classroom. For example:

- there was concern over how to teach some parts of the science curriculum with ICT. Teachers were not used to styles of teaching which involved students collaborating, and tended to use ICT as an add-on to lessons, rather than as a means of learning involving interaction among students or students and teachers;
- the skills and confidence in using ICT of the teachers mattered.

They suggested that new techniques of teaching were needed, and that there should be regular use of ICT in lessons.

The effects of home computers on students, and the greater access to computers which has arisen in the years since these two reports were published, are evident in the preliminary findings of a second, more recent study called the *ImpacT2 Report* (forthcoming). This is a major longitudinal study (1999–2002) involving sixty schools in England. Its aims include identifying the impact of networked technologies on learning. At the time of writing this report is still in preparation, but interim reports suggest that:

- the integration of ICT into subject teaching depends upon teacher confidence and skills and varies widely within a school;
- many teachers commented on how ICT changes the teaching process and in particular the role of the teacher.

If you now think that using ICT is a possibility for the lesson you are preparing, you have to consider *which* applications and software you will use and *how* you will use it with the students in your class.

SOME ICT APPLICATIONS AND THEIR USES

The intention here is merely to *summarise* the main features of ICT available for use in science teaching, and to point to some ways they may be used in teaching and learning. More comprehensive accounts may be found in the suggested reading material at the end of this chapter. It is in the interest of the reader to find out more about the possibilities of each kind of application by trying it out him or herself.

The main uses of ICT for secondary science involving computers are as follows:

- simulations and modelling;
- data-logging;
- databases and spreadsheets;
- publishing and presentation of software information sources (e.g. the Internet or CD-ROM and datafiles).

Modelling

Computer models provide a means of better understanding a situation. An argument put forward by some authors in favour of using models in science is that scientists and researchers frequently use models. They are a means of investigating abstract ideas, or simplifying complex situations, or predicting data and explaining a situation. Results from experiments may be compared with a model and the model evaluated. An important feature of modelling for students at school is to be able to set up a model using formulae, which are then used to calculate new data so that they can explore a situation or investigate what might happen in certain circumstances.

For example, on work about nutrition or movement, a spreadsheet could be set up showing the activities of individual students over twenty-four hours (NCET, 1994). A list of energy requirements for each activity and the duration of activities are listed. The total energy required for each activity can be entered onto the spreadsheet. The student's resulting individual energy needs can then be totalled for that period (Figure 12.4).

Thus a model of activities and total energy requirements can be set up. Variables are the activities, and the time for which the activity is carried out. Formulae involved are those that calculate the energy needed for the time spent on each activity, and for twenty-four hours' worth of activity. At one level this kind of model could be used to ask questions or make predictions. What happens if I play football for two hours or have only six hours' sleep? What effect does this have on my total energy requirements? How does an athlete compare with a computer operator? At another level, there may be questions about whether everyone uses the same amount of energy when they run. The model could be refined or altered to account for a person's age. Subsequent work could involve comparing students' daily intake of the nutritional elements of food with that recommended, and also with the energy needs described by the model, and then evaluating how well the model compares with the experiment.

Models may be built using formulae embedded in data-logging and graphing programmes (e.g. modelling radioactive decay series) (Newton and Rogers, 2001, p. 101).

Activity	Energy used	Time	Energy total
	(kJ per hour)	(hours)	(kJ)
Sleeping	250	8 hrs	???
Watching TV	300 kJ	2 hrs	300 × 2 = 600 kJ
Studying	350		
Washing up	800		
Walking	800		
Walking upstairs	2400		
Running	3200		
Swimming	4800	¹/₂ hour	
Totals			

Figure 12.4 A model of energy needs (after NCET (now BECTA), 1994, p. 17)

Here the formulae are used continuously to calculate the amount of an unstable isotope left as it decays. A disadvantage of modelling seems to be that, if students do not altogether understand the possible relationships between the variables, they are not always capable of building a realistic model. At Key Stage 3, manipulating variables in a simulation where the relationship between variables is fixed might be a first step before modelling is used.

Simulations

Simulations are specific modelling tools which have their own set of formulae embedded in them. They may be used by learners to control factors that affect a particular situation. Simulations can represent physical systems or make visible difficult concepts through associated graphics.

Simulations can be, for example, direct representations of laboratory activities, of industrial processes or of the behaviour of ideal gases or frictionless surfaces. Simulations can provide models of the effect of temperature on the energy of particles illustrating an aspect of the kinetic theory of matter, or the balance of life in a pond. Simulations are limited to how well the formulae represent the situation, and how good the graphics are.

Using simulations means that the management and organisation of experiments for students is simpler. The cost of equipment and consumables is reduced. Students can be safe while doing experiments that would otherwise be difficult in the laboratory and much time is saved compared with that needed to set up and carry out experiments. One disadvantage is that the users can manipulate only those variables that are built into the model.

Data-logging and graphing tools

Data-loggers are measuring and calculating tools that extend our senses. Observations that are usually too fast or too slow, too small or too large may be easily carried out. Data-loggers are used with sensors that detect variables such as light intensity, temperature, angle of rotation, voltage, pH, or oxygen concentration. The data-logger converts it into an electrical signal that can then be displayed graphically on a computer screen (Figure 12.5).

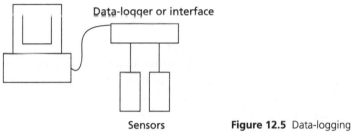

Figure 12.5 Data-logging

There are various ways of using data-loggers and sensors. Graphical representation of data can be produced while the experiment is in progress, for example, in measuring the temperature of a liquid as it cools over a period of time. Data can also be collected remotely, stored by the data-logger and reviewed later, for example when measuring the variation of plant growth according to light level using data sampled regularly over a number of days. Single measurements may be made at the discretion of the user, or the data collection can be delayed until a certain time or event occurs. Data-loggers assist in recording presentation and analysis of results.

Frequently the use of data-logging in the classroom involves the immediate production of a graph from data collected by sampling regularly and at short time intervals. Graph plotting 'by hand' may occupy much of a student's attention and time so that the focus of the activity can be lost. In theory, where graphs are produced by the computer from data-logging, students can better focus on the meaning of the graph and there is an immediate link between the investigation or experiment (e.g. Barton, 1997). However, the waiting time while the computer is logging can lead to children being off-task (Rogers and Wild, 1994) unless the teacher uses this time well.

Other benefits of 'real-time' graphs produced by data-loggers from experiments have been suggested.

- Using data-logging can help students link concrete practical experiences with theoretical ideas in science. For example, temperature sensors may be used to investigate the evaporation of, say, methylated spirit and water (Newton and Rogers, 2001). Tissue wrapped around each sensor is soaked in one of the liquids and allowed to cool. The cooling curves that are produced immediately could be discussed in terms of the behaviour of particles in matter.

- As a graph is produced, it can promote predicted questions (*What might happen next?*) that can be helpful for progression (Newton, 1997). For example, at Key Stage 3 (12–13 years) students compare results with predictions. They might read values from the graph, or describe variables, say, in two positions on the graph in terms of what is actually happening in the experiment. At Key Stage 4 (14–16 years) they need to find relationships between variables or notice that particular graph shapes arise from the relationships. If the trends in data can easily be practised qualitatively at Key Stage 3 by using ICT, then this can help with further analysis at Key Stage 4.

Spreadsheets

Spreadsheets are useful calculating tools that have a wide use in science activities. They are useful in presenting results in various forms, and in sorting data. Their features enable students to look in detail at graphical data, to investigate relationships between variables or to consider cause and effect. For example, students can enter data from field activities in collecting numbers of plants in various habitats and use bar charts to explain trends. They could analyse or explore data presented graphically from an investigation about pressure and volume of a gas. Spreadsheets can also facilitate both independent and collaborative group work, in the same way as graphical interpretation. Students are usually familiar with the basic structure and working of spreadsheets, so, for example, it is likely to take only a short time to remind students how to insert new formulae for subsequent calculation into the spreadsheet.

Sources of information

CD-ROMs, databases, the Internet and the National Grid for Learning and Virtual Teacher Centres are now offering access to unlimited information and links with numerous scientific sources. A focus on being selective in choosing sources of information, questioning its value and checking its accuracy are important features of how information sources are used in the science classroom. Using these sources encourages interaction and collaboration among students. This in turn means that teachers will not be 'in control' in the traditional sense which reinforces the idea that the teacher's role is now more one of motivator, counsellor or guide in many situations (Wellington, 1985).

Multimedia are CD-ROMs that store information and a huge range of stimuli in the form of text, images, videos and sounds. A variety of paths through the media is available which means students can choose which path to follow and revisit parts of the programme if necessary, a feature which enables students to interact with the multimedia resource to some extent. Through the use of multimedia, students of science have access to information, events, materials, processes and sounds, often outside the range of what is possible in the laboratory. Multimedia can be mentally engaging through their interactivity, though how well students learn from this depends on how well the multimedia are structured and designed. The technical expertise of the student with the piece of software is also important. Some consider learning experiences to be limited when students are working individually rather than benefiting from the social interactions taking place in group activity.

The Internet enables stores of information such as those on CD-ROMs to be accessed through networking. One great advantage is access to what is sometimes called 'real-time' data, such as current weather information, or satellite pictures or information from telescopes. Since the information that can be accessed using the Internet is so huge, at a variety of levels and is often being changed, teachers need to research the sites being used for themselves beforehand.

Databases are software that stores information including words, images, videos and sounds in an organised way so that it may be retrieved or interrogated. Students can also make databases themselves, either by entering information into a pre-prepared structure, or by learning the sorts of questions that need to be asked to create a 'key'.

Desktop publishing and word-processing programmes

These packages help students to present their work and communicate their findings. Producing attractive and carefully presented work where students have to focus on what the work is saying may contribute to their understanding of the material. Being accurate is a scientific skill worth practising. What is written and the kinds of presentation selected depend on the task. There are too many to describe here but obviously reporting experimental work, describing observations, presenting a case for discussion or giving an explanation are examples. Reluctant writers are often encouraged by the results of their efforts with publishing programmes. The use of templates means that various kinds of support to presentation may be given. Group presentations can give rise to much useful discussion. Because there are so many features associated with these programmes, students can become concerned with the way the material looks rather than focusing on the clarity of meaning, so the teacher's emphasis during the lesson should be on the lesson objectives.

Images, video and photographs

ICT animations, video and sound can assist teachers in illustrating and explaining science concepts. Digital cameras are a useful tool for providing immediate images which may be more memorable than a written description later for some learners. They can integrate the real world with school science, which may be a step towards 'authentic' learning. For example, digital cameras may be used for sequencing events such as the stages of their investigation or to capture images of the behaviour of animals, or images of plants in an environmental area where they cannot be collected. Sounds and images of all varieties, moving or still, may be used in multimedia authoring. Microscopes, which may be used with the computer and screen, can provide a useful means for teacher discussion with groups or with the class.

PLANNING AND MANAGING THE USE OF ICT IN LESSONS

The previous section illustrates some of the features of ICT available for learners, but increases in learning afforded by the use of ICT are likely to depend largely on how the teacher uses ICT both in the classroom and for his or her own professional use. From the teacher's perspective, many factors can affect the way you use ICT with students. Moseley and Higgins (1999) report that: 'what a teacher does in the classroom and the way the pupils react to these actions or behaviours influences what they learn' (p. 14). The characteristics of high-quality learning, and classroom practices that contribute to it, referred to above, are also likely to influence how you use ICT. Of course, the resources available also influence teachers' choices. It is not the intention here to discuss these, save to say that currently your plans for the use of ICT with students in science may depend on the nature of those resources.

Task 12.2

What useful ICT resources could be made available to teachers of science and what are their main uses? Make a list, such as the one begun below.

Resource	Use
School computer suite	Access to the Internet, CD-ROMs, whole class use

---

The Teacher Training Agency notes the following:

> At the heart of the ITT National Curriculum for the use of ICT in subject teaching are *three key principles* which trainees need to know, understand and be able to apply.

> 1   Decisions about when, when not and how to use ICT in science lessons should be based on whether *the use of ICT supports good practice in teaching the subject.* If it does not it should not be used.
> 2   In planning and in teaching, decisions about when, when not and how to use ICT in a particular lesson or sequence of lessons *must be directly related to the teaching and learning objectives in hand.*

3   The use of ICT should allow the trainee or the pupil *to achieve something that could not be achieved without it*; or allow the trainee *to teach*, or the pupils to learn *something more effectively and efficiently* than they could otherwise; *or both*.

(TTA, 1999, p. 3)

These principles should underpin your teaching in science where ICT is used.

Another document, the current Key Stage 3 strategy, also has a framework of requirements for the use of ICT in science teaching for students of this age (DfES, 2002). The main aim of the strategy is to raise standards by strengthening teaching and learning, developing cross-curricular skills and helping students who come into Year 7 below Level 4 to make faster progress. The framework for teaching science at Key Stage 3 emphasises that ICT should promote better learning in science. It should reflect the current world of science where science makes use of many ICT-controlled analytical tools, for example, in the sequencing of the human genome. The strategy provides some ideas for the ways ICT can be used with students at Key Stage 3. One or two points in relation to planning and assessment both for Key Stage 3 and Key Stage 4 students are worthy of further comment.

Planning and assessment

You need to be clear about the functions of ICT which make it useful for your lesson objectives, as well as how to use it effectively to support students' learning in science. It is also important to judge whether the ICT you use is pitched at the right level for your group of students. For example, information gained from the Internet or from a CD-ROM on, say, functions and structure of cells in the body may be extremely detailed, or complex language may be used. Some students will find difficulty selecting and interpreting relevant information from such material. Depending on the interactivity of the software, you would be wise to suggest routes through the material, or provide question sheets with a glossary requiring students to focus on specific areas of the information, depending on the objectives of the lesson. This means that there is less likelihood of students reproducing quantities of information without selecting and analysing it.

It is necessary to give careful consideration to the software you are going to use for a particular purpose and to guard against using ICT because a programme is attractive or available, or to use it as an add-on to your lesson. In a 'revision' lesson, for example, unless the software emphasises precisely the concepts or elements of learning that you have planned to review, consolidating earlier learning may be more easily and effectively carried out using other means. At the same time, for some students (e.g. those with a physical disability), ICT can be a practical support to learning. Handling and reading a thermometer may be more difficult for some than reviewing a graph of temperatures produced with a data-logger and temperature sensor.

You may consider that ICT can be a more efficient and effective way of supporting learning than carrying out a difficult or time-consuming conventional experiment. At the same time you would like students to either experience the 'real' experiment' or have the opportunity to use the equipment involved. You then have to consider whether both methods could be used in the lesson; one method could possibly be used as a demonstration with whole class discussion. The arrangements you have for the access and use of ICT can affect your choice here. Frequently parallel ICT and non-ICT activities are carried out by groups of students. One benefit is that students can see the advantages of using ICT for that purpose. On the other hand, if similar objectives are set for all groups in the class and ICT is used as an 'alternative activity' with one group, depending on the lesson concerned, this could lead to the ICT group having a better understanding of the topic. The result could be that this group is ready to move on more quickly than the rest of the class. For example, animations such as those used to explain changes of state in terms of the particulate nature of matter provide useful mental models, which can be manipulated by the student and with discussion with the teacher, to provide a link between experience and theory. If this is a group activity, where other groups are using books, worksheets or other means, students may have different rates or depths of learning, so that lesson plans need to be flexible enough to accommodate this.

In assessing students where ICT is used in science lessons, it is important to focus on how well students have learned in relation to the science objectives set rather than their efficiency in using ICT, or on the presentation of work alone. To do this you could plan key questions to ask during interventions to ensure that objectives are met (e.g. 'Why do you think the graph is flatter where melting is taking place?'). You should ensure that you plan time for discussion with students. In this way you can assess how well students have focused on the salient scientific points when they are searching for information, or if they are better able to explain the ideas behind a theory, or interpret a graph through using ICT. At the same time effective work using ICT in science can often build on work done in ICT lessons, improving students' ICT capability. New contexts provide an opportunity for students to hone their ICT skills. For example, students may learn how data-logging software could be used to examine parts of a graph in detail, or to overlay graphs for comparison.

Managing the classroom with ICT activities

It has been mentioned that one benefit of using ICT is that it often leaves students with more time for reflection. Your role will be to ensure that this time is used most effectively. Students who have greater time to focus on the meaning of results, for example, often need other resources to provide them with information or explanations whether it be the teacher, books, the Internet, or other means. Some students need more; they require prompts or other carefully structured arrangements to move them forward, and to check that they are making maximum effort. If students are in groups, using a 'jigsaw' technique where students in a group each have to complete part of a task, or find out selected information, which can then be assembled as a whole, ensures that each member of the group participates.

Where ICT is used as a demonstration, the quality of the questions and discussion is fundamental to students' learning. The skills of the teacher in focusing on those parts of learning in science which are well demonstrated by using ICT are also vital. For example, a common practical activity is for students to investigate the factors that affect the rate of a chemical reaction such as the reaction of hydrochloric acid with sodium thiosulphate. This activity may also be carried out using a light sensor and data-logger (e.g. TTA, 1999, p. 38). A light sensor records the amount of light transmitted through the solution as colloidal sulphur is produced during the course of the reaction. Students looking at the instantly produced graph can watch the progress of the reaction. From the graph, the teacher can discuss with the students how long it takes for the reaction to start, when it finishes, how the rate changes, and how rate could be measured. Students could be asked to predict what would happen if different concentrations of reactants were used, and later could be introduced to the idea of how collisions between particles are related to reaction rate.

It has been mentioned that students are becoming familiar with the common management systems for many ICT applications, which means they can find their way around an application more easily these days. However, in a class of thirty students this cannot be assumed, and flexibility has to be built into the lesson for some students. Briefing sheets on the use of a programme, or tutoring of a group by one student in the group who is familiar with the use of ICT, can help.

Bearing all that has been said in mind, a possible model for the use of ICT in the science classroom based on constructivist ideas and taking into account some of the factors that are likely to contribute to high-quality learning is shown in Figure 12.6.

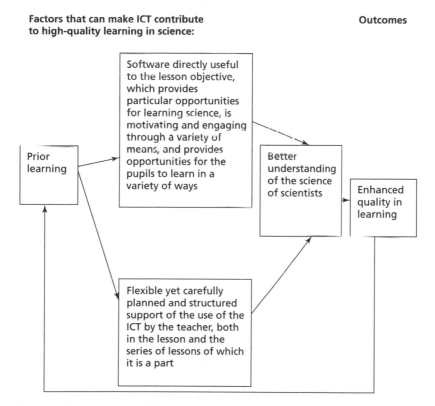

Figure 12.6 A model for the use of ICT in the science classroom

ICT AND TEACHERS' SKILLS

ICT can provide valuable support to your teaching. Careful evaluation of software enables you to be certain of your reasons for choosing ICT in planning teaching and assessment. You should develop competence and confidence in using ICT for various purposes (e.g. TTA, 1999, pp. 17–27). For your own professional development, you should be familiar with the latest research and inspection evidence in relation to the use of ICT in science education. The rate of developments in ICT and consequently its possible application to teaching science is so great that 'keeping up' can be difficult unless you consciously set aside time to talk with other groups of teachers or contact virtual teacher centres, for example. A list of useful sources is given at the end of this chapter. (You will soon find that, for some of the latest 'tricks of the trade' in the skills of using computers, students are a very good source of help!)

CASE STUDY

The following case study illustrates an occasion when using ICT supported learning effectively for the students concerned and those lesson's objectives. It is not meant as a guide, but more as an illustration of why the teacher chose to use ICT, how he or she used it with students and the added value it provided for learning. The study includes background notes on the lesson, how the key requirements for trainee teachers for the use of ICT in teaching science are met (summarised in **bold type**) followed by a commentary on the lesson.

Case study: The Pondweed Experiment

Background notes

The lesson was carried out with a mixed ability Year 9 group. Students were aware of the habitats of a variety of plants and knew of the main factors involved in photosynthesis. The general learning objective of the series of lessons was as follows:

- to learn how some organisms are adapted to survive daily and seasonal changes in their habitats (National Curriculum – DfEE/QCA, 1999a (KS3, Sc2, 5c)).

The learning objective for this lesson was as follows:

- to investigate the effects of varying light intensity and temperature on Canadian pondweed (*Elodea canadensis*) and to write a report on this.

Students were used to working either in groups or as a whole class in science. They were familiar with safety rules for practical work. The work involving ICT was carried out in a laboratory where a single computer, a data projector and a large screen were used. The steps in the lesson were as follows:

1   An interactive whole class session exploring students' prior knowledge of photosynthesis and how students thought water plants photosynthesised.
2   Students carried out the practical activity involving finding the effects of light intensity on pondweed. The teacher judged that students would have time to find out how much oxygen was given off in two positions of the lamp.
3   Both the effect of light intensity and temperature on the pondweed would be investigated using a demonstration to the whole class with ICT.

KEY ISSUES

- **Know when ICT is beneficial to teaching objectives and when it is not, and the implications of the functions of computers for learning in science.**
- **How to choose the most appropriate ICT for teaching objectives and be able to say why you have chosen it.**

The teacher chose to use an interactive simulation, which allowed students to vary light intensity or temperature on pondweed. The oxygen given off by the pondweed was shown as bubbles collected in a syringe that could be easily manipulated on screen so that the amount given off was measured on a scale. The practical equipment used in varying light intensity involved similar equipment to that depicted by the computer program, except that on the computer the amount of oxygen was measured by counting the number of bubbles given off per minute. The program provided an easily manipulated model which allowed more focused thought than was possible during the practical activity. The use of ICT needed minimal preparation by the teacher and all students had witnessed pondweed giving off what they assumed was oxygen.

The teacher's reason for using ICT was that she judged that the use of the simulation enabled students to quickly and easily look at a much wider range of effects of changes in light intensity, and also of temperature, than was possible practically. Any effects of these changes on the plant could be discussed, these two factors contributing to students' understanding of how pondweed is adapted to suit its environment. They could deepen their knowledge of photosynthesis and of how plants survive in a watery environment. At the same time, the teacher thought it best to give the students the opportunity to see the effects of light on pondweed as a living plant, and to collect 'real data' and have the experience of manipulating the equipment. Students could link specific practical experiences to generalisations about how pondweed has adapted to its environment if practical experiences and ICT were used. She estimated that students would be able to use two positions of the lamp in the time available to measure the rate at which bubbles of oxygen were produced for each.

KEY ISSUES

- Identify various features in planning (e.g. organisation of the lesson) or key questions to be used in interventions, specific contribution of students with special educational needs.
- Effective organisation of classroom ICT resources to meet learning objectives in science.

The teacher chose mixed ability groups for the practical experiment to ensure that each group comprised students with a variety of ICT skills. She made clear, through a briefing sheet, her expectations for the practical session. The teacher allocated certain tasks to members of each group, and ensured that each member of the group had a record of results. She had previously prepared a recording sheet to save time. In the demonstration session the teacher used a data projector so that all the students could see the screen. She was familiar with the simulation, for example, with the limits of light intensity and temperature available, and how to enlarge the syringe so that the scale could be read easily. The teacher planned to involve as many students as possible in the demonstration. The teacher had also prepared key questions for the whole class session such as 'Do you think there will be a limit to the amount of oxygen produced? Where is the carbon dioxide needed for photosynthesis?'

KEY ISSUES

- How to monitor and assess teaching band students' learning in science when using ICT and to evaluate the contribution that ICT has made to science

The teacher was able to assess students through the use of observation and through later written questions, which she discussed with students in groups.

- How to contribute to the development of students' ICT capability

Although students' ICT skills were not directly needed during this lesson, they were able to assess the use of a model for representing a situation that is difficult and time consuming to perform in the laboratory.

Commentary

During the initial session the teacher checked that students realised that water plants still need carbon dioxide for photosynthesis and asked students where they thought the carbon dioxide was coming from for photosynthesis. She also asked students what they thought happens to light and temperature levels in water during the day, taking the opportunity to find out if students were aware of the range of temperatures that might be expected. Towards the end of the session the teacher explained what data she expected students to have recorded and how to use the equipment. She discussed with students why a heat shield was needed which helped students to realise the importance of manipulating only one variable at a time. Students then carried out the practical task. After the practical equipment had been cleared away, the class gathered around the data projector with their results and notebooks. The teacher demonstrated to the students how the simulation worked, including the options of enlarging the syringe so that the measurements could be seen. She then asked for two suggestions of positions of the lamp, and asked students to record in their notebooks both the position and the corresponding volumes of oxygen produced as measured on the screen syringe as the lamp was moved. (The teacher learned a great deal about the efficiency with which these Year 8 students could accurately read scales at this point!) She then asked students to write down predictions of the amount of oxygen produced for several more positions, referring to their results from practical measurements. If possible, students were to draw a sketch graph of the position of the lamp against the volume of oxygen produced. She then moved the lamp on screen to some of these positions, taking care at this point to keep to positions she knew would increase the volume of oxygen produced. Students could soon see that increased oxygen production was the result of increased light intensity, and hence that the nearer to the light the plant was, the better chance it had of photosynthesising and surviving. The teacher then allowed the students to choose a wider range of positions of the lamp in the simulation. Because the simulation was easy to manipulate, the teacher was able to develop important ideas with the students.

- The students also noticed that extreme light intensity did not produce the expected increases in oxygen, and wondered about the availability of carbon dioxide to the plants. This led to the idea of limiting factors.
- The teacher took the chance to ask the students whether they thought light would travel through water easily. Students eventually realised that light penetrates into water for relatively short distances, and related this to the changes in light intensity during the day and to the idea of the plant being adapted to its habitat as near to the surface as possible.

The teacher then turned to changes in temperature. As before, she asked for predictions that could then be easily tested using the simulation. There was much interest again when it was found that there was an optimum temperature. The teacher took the opportunity to discuss with the students whether temperature variations might affect carbon dioxide levels in the water, and the effects this could have on plants in ponds, lakes and rivers. Students recognised that a number of factors influenced the rate of photosynthesis in plants.

The students enjoyed the practical work, even though collecting results was frustrating at times due to the difficult nature of the experiment. They found the simulation interesting. The speed and ease with which the simulation could be manipulated meant that students were able to examine two variables. The use of ICT in this situation was a focus for much discussion about the effects of changing the variables in the experiment, and the response of the plant to changing external conditions. Had there been enough equipment, the teacher could have given all students experience of using ICT.

CONCLUSION

This chapter has focused on how ICT can be viewed and used in supporting teachers and learners to achieve high quality learning in science. The main categories of ICT involving computers currently used in schools in science and ways that they can be used with students effectively have been summarised. Cautions, such as making sure you focus on the achievement of students in relation to the science objectives set for your lesson, and not just on their competence in using ICT have been noted. There is reference to the ways in which teachers can use ICT themselves to enhance their teaching. A case study has illustrated the use of ICT in science.

SUGGESTIONS FOR FURTHER READING

If you would like to explore further some of the issues touched upon in this chapter, the following books should be of interest to you.

Frost, R. (1997) *The IT in Secondary Science Book*, Written and produced by the author
This is a compendium of practical ideas for using ICT in science with worksheets and information for teachers. Roger Frost's materials are available from: R. Frost, Fowlmere Road, Foxton, Cambridge CB2 6RT or visit his website: www.rogerfrost.com

Newton, L.R. and Rogers, L. (2001) *Teaching Science with ICT*, London: Continuum
This is a thorough account of relevant issues surrounding the use of ICT in science with practical examples for enriching teaching and learning.

Somekh, B. and Davis, N. (1998) *Using Information Technology Effectively in Teaching and Learning*, London: Routledge
The first chapter of this book is a discussion about the effects that ICT can have on learning.

13 Assessing and Monitoring Progress in Secondary Science

JUDITH DOBSON

INTRODUCTION

Assessment is a very complex, integral part of teaching and learning. Without assessment, we would not be able to judge the effectiveness of our teaching or the extent to which pupils have learned and understood the work we have set. The notion that teachers should check on the effectiveness of their teaching is as evident as it is important. Prior to the National Curriculum, much of the checking involved written or verbal tests to find out what pupils could remember of the work covered. The National Curriculum for England introduced the idea of quality assurance into the education process through monitoring progress and assessment. *Monitoring* is the regular checking of the progress of pupils. It is often an informal process such as marking homework, talking to the pupils in lessons, question-and answer sessions, short written exercises and so on. *Assessment* is the more formal process of gathering evidence so as to judge achievement as well as progress.

The process of assessment must:

- establish clear and measurable outcomes for pupils' learning;
- systematically collect, analyse and interpret evidence to determine the extent to which achievement matches expectations;
- use the data acquired to promote more effective learning.

The National Curriculum for England provides some guidance on assessment through attainment targets and associated level descriptions. The Qualifications and Curriculum Authority (QCA) has provided interpretation through Standard Assessment Tests (SATs), optional tests for Year 7 and Year 8 and General Certificate of Secondary Education (GCSE) examinations.

There are many types of assessment, each with a specific role to play in the overall education of our pupils. They fall into two main categories: assessment *of* learning and assessment *for* learning.

ASSESSMENT OF LEARNING

Assessment of learning usually takes place at the end of a unit or year or Key Stage, or when a pupil is leaving school. It is therefore used to make judgements about a pupil's *performance* in relation to the National Standards. Assessment of learning is often a snapshot of small parts of the whole picture, as it were, taken at one particular time. Key Stages 2 and 3 Standard Assessment Tests (SATs) are imposed externally by the Assessment and Qualifications Authority (AQA) and by an Examination Board at Key Stage 4. With this type of assessment there is always the possibility of seeing the unexpected. For example, a pupil may, by pure good luck, have revised exactly the content of the questions set, and therefore gain a higher grade than the teacher expected. The grade given by the teacher is known as the teacher assessment (TA). This form of assessment provides information about progress and achievement of the individual for themselves, parents, teachers, and a range of other people including governors, OfSTED and the local education authority.

The basis for teacher assessment is in the level descriptions, found at the back of the Science National Curriculum document. A numerical value is often given (e.g. Level 4), and in order to ensure that all teachers are consistent in the levels they give, there needs to be some standardisation about these levels, through standardisation and moderation meetings. The purpose of these meetings is to ensure quality assurance, both within a department and within neighbouring schools to justify the meaning of each level. Teacher assessment is also used for management purposes regarding setting or other organisational groupings.

ASSESSMENT FOR LEARNING

Formative assessment or *teacher assessment (TA)* is ongoing throughout the pupil's science education. It happens all the time in the classroom or laboratory. It should assist and support the pupil to know where he or she is in relation to the National Curriculum and contributes to an ever-changing picture built up over time. This type of assessment involves both the pupil and the teacher in a process of reflection and review about progress. It is integral to normal work, so it involves marking written or practical work: marking tests or commenting on longer projects. There is, however, the danger of seeing the expected. Work carried out in class, written up and then marked would show an understanding of that work only, and not, in general, allow the pupil to demonstrate any further knowledge or greater understanding of the principles involved. The Qualifications Curriculum Authority (QCA) states that formative assessment, or assessment for learning, is:

- embedded in the teaching and learning process of which it is an essential part;
- shares learning goals with pupils;
- helps pupils to know and recognise the standards to aim for;
- provides feedback which leads pupils to identify what they should do next to improve;
- has a commitment that every pupil can improve;

- involves both teacher and pupils reviewing and reflecting on pupils' performance and progress;
- involves pupils in self-assessment.

(Taken from the QCA website)

Diagnostic assessment is used to identify strengths and weaknesses of a pupil's work. It may take the form of a test, a practical activity or a written report. What is certainly required is a comprehensive written response, which will be of benefit to the pupil, rather than comments such as:

- 7/10 good.
- A fair attempt.

Such comments are rather sketchy, without any guidance as to what they actually mean. Something along the following lines gives more meaning for the pupil:

> I enjoyed reading your account which showed good understanding of the circulatory system. Your comments about the role of the heart were clear, but you could have given more detail about the role of the bicuspid and tricuspid valves. You clearly understand the differences between arteries and veins. Have you thought about including diagrams to show what you mean?

This type of comment gives far more insight into the sound areas of knowledge and understanding, and also suggests some areas for further improvement.

Evaluative assessment should assist you, as the teacher, to evaluate your teaching and learning programme, and is the key to the assessment cycle.

There is yet another type of assessment, which I have already mentioned, and this is *self-assessment*. Particularly at Key Stages 3 and 4, this process is very beneficial, since pupils can judge their own work against a given set of criteria. Many primary schools introduce self-assessment to their pupils, and by secondary school this form of assessment is commonplace. Pupils can see for themselves how they are improving and which areas they need to work on in the future.

An example of the criteria given for self-assessment for sections of Sc1 scientific enquiry might be along the following lines:

- During the study of Sc4 Physical Process, 3g Hearing, the pupils are asked to devise an investigation to show that people have different audible ranges.
- It has previously been planned into the scheme of work that this investigation will assess the pupils' ability to *plan* an investigation.
- A criteria sheet is given to each pupil so that they can assess their own planning ability. This might resemble the one shown in Figure 13.1.

A similar self-assessment exercise for practical skills Year 7 Key Stage 3 might be a drawing of a test-tube with different sections marked out for pupils to date once they feel confident that they can use a piece of apparatus properly and safely (see Figure 13.2). You, as the teacher, can then check at an appropriate time that the pupil is able to use the apparatus listed.

Self-assessment No: .... Name: .... Form: .... Date: ....

Investigative skills

[KS3, Sc1, 2a] I am able to use my own scientific knowledge and understanding to turn ideas into a form that can be investigated, and to decide on an appropriate approach.

Please highlight the statements that **you** feel are best suited to you.

Section 1:
- I am able to think of questions to ask for myself.
- I am able to think of questions to ask when I work in a group.
- I find it very hard to think of any questions.
- I would like some extra help from the teacher.

Section 2:
- I understand the science needed to do this investigation.
- I **think** I understand the science needed for this investigation.
- I am not very sure about the science needed for this investigation and I would like more help from my teacher.

Section 3:
- I can continue to plan this investigation for myself.
- I can continue to plan this investigation if I work in a group.
- I cannot continue to plan this investigation.*

*If you have highlighted this statement, put your hand up NOW and talk to your teacher.

My comments about this planning task.

Figure 13.1 Example of a self-assessment form for Year 7 (Key Stage 3)

WHAT TO ASSESS

As mentioned above, assessment is an integral part of teaching and learning. It is vitally important that it is planned into the pupils' learning experiences, and not as a bolt-on extra at the end of a topic or learning package. In order to do this, we must carry out the following:

```
Self-assessment No: ……….  Name: ……………………….  Form: ………  Date: …………

Investigative skills
I can use the following:

        A microscope…………………  ☐

        A Bunsen burner……………  ☐

        A measuring
        cylinder……………………  ☐

        A pipette………………………  ☐

        A burette…………………  ☐

My comments about my investigation skills.
```

Figure 13.2 Example of a self-assessment form for Year 7 confidence in using scientific equipment

- identify learning outcomes;
- identify contexts;
- identify learning activities;
- identify assessment opportunities in the learning activities.

At the end of each Key Stage we are required to study the level descriptors which are intended to describe the range of performances that a pupil, working at a particular level, might be expected to possess or exhibit. In other words, they are descriptions of a pupil rather than of an individual piece of work.

In order to build up a description of a pupil, information needs to be gathered over the course of the Key Stage. This evidence provides information about what the pupil can do/knows and understands, and what he or she needs to do in order to move on to the next stage of learning. It also enables you, as the teacher, to evaluate the effectiveness of your teaching. Hence we need to identify specific learning outcomes when planning each section of work. Such outcomes are related to the programmes of study at Key Stage 3 or the examination syllabus at Key Stage 4, and indicate what pupils should be able to do as a result of successful learning experiences. Level descriptions found in the attainment targets allow us to judge where any set of learning outcomes map into the National Curriculum levels. For example, the level description for the attainment target for Level 5 of *Sc2: Life Processes and Living Things* states:

> Pupils demonstrate an increasing knowledge and understanding of life processes and living things drawn from the Key Stage 2 or Key Stage 3 programme of study. They describe the main functions of organs of the human body [e.g. the heart at Key Stage 2, stomach at Key Stage 3], and of the plant [e.g. the stamen at Key Stage 2, root hairs at Key Stage 3]. They explain how these functions are essential to the organism. They describe the main stages of the life cycles of humans and flowering plants and point out similarities. They recognize that there is a great variety of living things and understand the importance of classification. They explain that different organisms are found in different habitats because of differences in environmental factors [e.g. the availability of light and water].
>
> (DfEE/QCA, 1999b, p. 77)

This level could apply to either Key Stage 2 or Key Stage 3. We are given examples to help us understand the depth of knowledge and understanding required for the different Key Stages. However, Level 6 clearly states that: 'Pupils use knowledge and understanding drawn from the Key Stage 3 programme of study' (p. 77). It is therefore very clear that it is not envisaged that pupils could attain Level 6 at Key Stage 2. Indeed, although it has been possible for this level to be awarded at Key Stage 2, in reality, very few pupils managed to achieve this level. From 2003, due to changes in the SATs, it will not be possible to get a Level 6, and therefore, for the majority of pupils, their Key Stage 3 work will be pitched at levels 5 or 6 in Year 7.

HOW TO ASSESS

Each school will have its own systems, which ensure that their assessment judgements are consistent in the form of various policies (e.g. marking and assessment policy). Record-keeping systems should be capable of providing information about what pupils have done, be able to inform planning and to make summative judgements at the end of the Key Stage.

Any assessment system used in schools should be:

- Fully understood by pupils and teachers; it should also be accessible to parents and other interested parties.

- Reliable and valid.
- Positive.
- Easy to use.
- Compatible with external requirements (e.g. National Curriculum, examination boards).

An assessment scheme cannot be enforced in isolation. It must be compatible with the departmental scheme, the school system and the requirements of the external examining agencies. It is therefore of vital importance that you read and understand the necessary documentation for your school. It will also be necessary to differentiate your lessons according to ability groups, so that assessment style can be matched to ability. In other words, a child with learning difficulties may not be able to manage a written test, but could quite happily use a tape-recorder to orally answer simplified verbal questions. You will have to consider all pupils in each class that you teach, in order to give equal opportunities not only for written and practical work, but also for assessment.

Task 13.1

Collect together all relevant policies for your school (i.e. marking and assessment, record keeping).

Compare these with the Science Department policies.

- What are the common features?
- Are there any vital discrepancies?
- Are assessment criteria built into the scheme of work for the different year groups?
- How is the assessment scheme used to inform future teaching and learning?
- What guidance are you given for writing reports?

By now, you are probably wondering, *How on earth do I do all this assessment when I have X number of classes with approximately thirty pupils in each class?* There is no clear-cut answer to this question, except that it is impossible to assess everyone at once. We therefore have to allow for assessments taking place at different times, within different topics and with different groups of pupils. In order to allow equal opportunities for all, lessons need to be differentiated to take into account the various ability levels within a particular class. Bearing this in mind, science lessons should be suited to all abilities in such a way that allows the highest standards to be maintained by the most able pupils, but still catering for those pupils who are unable to achieve those standards. This will then provide the broad and balanced science for all set out in the 1985 science policy statement (DES, 1985).

METHODS OF ASSESSMENT

Assessment at KS3

Due to an ever-evolving National Curriculum and the assessment arrangements for this, it is likely that requirements will change on an annual basis. Indeed, from 2003, due to the introduction of the science strand of the Key Stage 3 strategy, the Standard Assessment Tasks include more questions to assess Sc1 (scientific enquiry). Questions may be in the context of any of the science attainment targets and there may also be discrete Sc1 questions. The QCA tells us that questions in the tests may ask pupils to describe:

- how an investigation could be carried out;
- what factors need to be controlled;
- what factors need to be measured;
- whether the outcome can be predicted;
- how the results are going to be presented;
- what the results show and whether they match the prediction (QCA, 2002).

Pupils are also expected to be able to explain the outcome and whether the evidence collected is significant, reliable and valid (QCA, 2002). It is therefore of vital importance that you keep up to date with the most recent publications from the Qualifications and Curriculum Authority (QCA).

Teachers are required to assess the four areas of science, namely:

Sc1   Scientific enquiry;
Sc2   Life and living processes;
Sc3   Materials and their properties;
Sc4   Physical processes.

At the end of May, teachers must be able to state the level of performance in each of the given areas. To do this, a range of work for each pupil from Years 7 to 9 needs to be matched against the level descriptors found at the back of the National Curriculum Science document. For each of the four areas of science, the level is assigned by the 'best fit' rule. This involves reading the statement for each level and deciding which level is appropriate to the pupil you are assessing. It often helps if the appropriate statements are high-lighted for each level and then you can see clearly the 'best fit'. At no stage is any part of a level descriptor a hurdle to be overcome.

Many schools, both primary and secondary, now have a portfolio of work which shows clearly the type of work needed to attain, say, Sc3, Level 6. The levels are agreed by all staff involved through discussion, moderation and agreement. The work is then annotated to show the characteristics that make the work appropriate to that particular level. This evidence may then be used to help you justify levels when reporting to parents, for school governors, OFSTED inspectors, the audit agency, or anyone else who may require the necessary information. No matter how your school functions, you should keep a record of why you have selected these samples of work. The teacher assessment levels are equally weighted and the average level is reported at the end of Key Stage 3.

In May, the statutory tests are set by the QCA. These are two papers, each of one hour's duration, covering tiers of levels 3 to 6 or 5 to 7. The teacher decides which tier best fits the pupil. There is also currently an extension paper for Level 8 and exceptional performance. However, these ceased to be available from 2003, as many teachers found that this was not the best way to assess their most able pupils. Their place was taken by a range of ways to assess the most able and gifted pupils. These included:

- a range of tasks that teachers may use to support their teacher assessment judgements;
- early entry for the end of Key Stage tests if the pupil has completed the Programme of Study for that Key Stage and is about to move into the next Programme of Study;
- taking an optional end-of-year test early;
- the opportunity for pupils on an accelerated programme to take the tests for the end of the next Key Stage.

(QCA, 2002)

Any pupil working below Level 3 (in science) has teacher assessment only. The QCA will also be producing optional tasks for pupils working below the level of the tests. These tasks will be designed to support teachers in making their teacher assessment decisions, and will usually be available on the QCA website from March of the relevant year.

Task 13.2

Collect a sample of work from Year 9 pupils in your school. (It is not necessary to collect from one pupil, but this would help.)

Study the work and then use the level descriptors to give an overall level for the 'pupil'. Use a highlighter pen to cover all the areas you see in the work, and at the end of the process assign a level for each science area.

How does this compare with the school's perception of the various levels?

Does the school have a portfolio of work? If so, compare your perceptions of a certain level with the portfolio, and then discuss your findings with a colleague.

Assessment at KS4

Assessment of Key Stage 4 is by teacher assessment only for Sc1 and by GCSE examination for Sc2 to 4. Other course work, up to a maximum of 20 per cent, may also be used for teacher assessment, depending on the examination board. Every science course must have a terminal examination, which will account for 80 per cent of the final mark for non-modular courses and at least 50 per cent of the final mark for modular courses. This is summarised in Table 13.1.

Table 13.1 Summary of the model for Key Stage 4 assessment

Scheme of assessment	Available suites	Available grades	Written paper	Course work	Additional features
General Certificate of Secondary Education (GCSE) Candidates must offer:	*Science:*	Tier F: G–C Tier H: D–A*	3 papers of 1.5 hours each:	Course work – 4 skills areas:	Assessment objectives for coursework:
1 Double award or 2 Single award or 3 Three separate sciences including biology or biology (human)	Double award (Modular A) Single award (Modular A) Double award B (co-ordinated) Single award B (co-ordinated) Biology Chemistry Physics Biology (human)		Paper 1 covers Sc2 Paper 2 covers Sc3 Paper3 covers Sc4 Each paper 26.67 per cent of total mark (80 per cent on written paper)	P – Planning O – Obtaining evidence A – Analysing and consistency E – Evaluating	AO3 Investigative skills Assessment objectives for written papers: AO1 Knowledge and understanding (16.67 per cent) each paper AO2 Appliance of knowledge and understanding, analysis and evaluation (10 per cent) each paper

Assessing Science 1

The basic principles of assessment such as using a combination of observation, oral and written techniques are used to assess Science 1. You will need to study the National Curriculum carefully to see what assessment is required and to use sample material from the QCA to help at Key Stage 3, and from the examination boards at Key Stage 4. The main difference between *practical* science and scientific enquiry is that practical science involves following instructions supplied by the teacher, but investigative work means that the pupils follow their own plans. This does not mean that they are left entirely to their own devices. They need guidance and support, and this, in turn, has implications for you, the teacher, with regard to allocation of time, the number of pupils doing investigations and general overall lesson planning. It is envisaged that by the end of Key Stage 4, pupils should be confident to carry out their own investigations from beginning to end, without any guidance or support. There will always be those pupils, however, who will never achieve this level of independence.

Task 13.3

Collect together as many examples of practical activities as you can from your school's science scheme of work.

1 Analyse them to see if they are practical or investigative.
2 If they are practical, can you think of ways in which you could make them investigational?
3 How does the department assess these activities?
4 Can you think of some investigations that would fit into the scheme of work? (They should be integrated into the scheme, not bolt-on extras at the end of a topic.)

KEEPING ACCURATE RECORDS

As you carry out your assessments, no matter which form they take, you will need to keep accurate records to help you when it comes to writing reports for parents and pupils. Your mark book needs to be organised so that you can write comments about each pupil in some kind of shorthand, which you can easily follow. It is important that each time you include something for a particular pupil, you clearly date it and give it some kind of title so that you can cross-reference with your lesson plan. In this way, you can easily track if a particular pupil constantly fails to hand in homework or perhaps tries to avoid written tests. You can also keep a record of behaviour issues if appropriate. The school will also have particular record-keeping systems which you must complete, but details in your mark book should make this much easier for you.

OUTCOMES FROM ASSESSMENT

What happens once you have completed your assessments for a particular pupil, group of pupils or class? Apart from writing reports or giving feedback to pupils and parents at parents' meetings, your assessments should contribute to the following:

- improved planning;
- effective teaching;
- focused learning;
- secure understanding (for the pupils);

leading to:

- enhanced achievement.

In other words, you will be able to make clear judgements about how well your teaching is impacting on learning and to make changes accordingly. You will be able to use SAT results and GCSE results for the school as a guide, not only for your own teaching, but also for that of colleagues. The whole cycle is one of ongoing change, evolving with the pupils and national initiatives.

To conclude, assessment is something that you must work at constantly in order to give the pupils the best teaching and learning opportunities possible. Some issues will be imposed upon you by the school and by law; other issues are for you decide. As you get to know the individuals in the classes you teach, the assessment process will become easier. You will build a picture of each pupil through written work, practical work, oral and written tests, and you will be able to report on the positive aspects of their work, whatever they are, regardless of ability. A summary of all the contributing factors towards effective assessment is shown in Figure 13.3.

SUGGESTIONS FOR FURTHER READING

All QCA publications for the current year, either via the website or documents sent directly to schools: www.qca.org.uk
This will keep you fully informed about test dates, any changes to the system or the types of questions set, and general background information about assessment.

The relevant examination syllabus for your school, so that you are fully aware of the content and assessment issues.

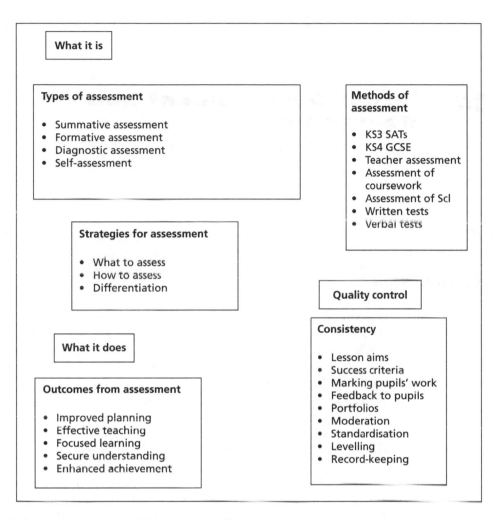

Figure 13.3 Assessment and the monitoring of progress at Key Stages 3 and 4

14 Career Development and Moving On

LYNN D. NEWTON AND FRANK SAMBELL

INTRODUCTION

The successful completion of a training programme leading to qualified teacher status is the first step in your career as a teacher. Throughout your training you will have developed and enhanced your skills and knowledge to become an effective teacher but your success as a teacher will be influenced by experience. Every student is different and a teacher needs many strategies for teaching. Experience counts.

Teachers need more than initial training and practical experience. It is important to keep up to date in science education and to keep in touch with national initiatives. Science is a dynamic subject which changes over time and you need to be aware of key developments. Currently, the Key Stage 3 strategy is the major development, and all teachers of secondary science should be actively involved in the programme. The strategy subsumes work for students with special educational needs and those identified as gifted and talented. Science teaching has been closely involved in the development of thinking skills through the Cognitive Acceleration through Science Education (CASE) project. Both of these have already been mentioned.

There are many sources of support for continuing professional development (CPD). In-school subject-specific in-service education for teachers (INSET) will address the needs of a relatively small group and will be sharply focused on school- and department-related issues. Other providers of INSET include your local higher education institution, the local education authority (LEA), your regional branch of the Association for Science Education (ASE) and the Consortium of Local Education Authorities for the Provision of Science Services (CLEAPSS). They have a wider audience of science teachers but still offer focused themes. Often in secondary schools, individuals within the science team are asked to support the head of department by taking specific responsibility for an initiative; for example, to be the KS3 science coordinator or the teacher in charge of ICT in science. You would then attend relevant regional and national meetings on your particular area of responsibility and be expected to disseminate the information to colleagues and plan for implementation as appropriate.

There is another important dimension to CPD, and that is working towards a higher degree. Research in education can, and should, make significant contributions to our understanding of how our students learn and how we, as teachers, can support them in this process. As a teacher your first duty is to the students you teach. CPD should have a significant but realistic demand on your time and energy.

THE ROLE OF THE HEAD OF DEPARTMENT

One significant development in your career may be having responsibility for science in a school. Schools, large and small, are complex organisations. It is the responsibility of the head teacher and the governing body (or managers) to ensure that each student has access to an appropriate curriculum. For most schools (all state schools and some independent schools) this means providing coverage of the National Curriculum. In addition, schools may provide opportunities in curriculum areas outside the National Curriculum.

For the head teacher and governing body (or managers), this is a major logistical exercise even at a basic level of provision. Ensuring that teaching and learning are effective and that the ten National Curriculum subjects are appropriately integrated with any non-statutory provision is a challenge for the school management team. It is increasingly the case that head teachers seek contributions from all staff and governors before making major changes to the curriculum. The day-to-day running of the school is the responsibility of the head teacher who generally delegates responsibility for one or more curriculum areas to an experienced member of staff. The extent of the authority of a teacher for a curriculum area depends on the head teacher's judgement, but it can involve executive decision-making and financial management.

The job title accompanying responsibility for a curriculum area varies from school to school. In a primary school the titles *subject coordinator* and *curriculum leader* are common. In the secondary phase, *head of department* and *head of faculty* are often used. Whatever the title, the tasks are similar from subject to subject and from phase to phase. There is no standard format for a job description but there are common features from school to school. A job description will reflect the school's vision of the post and will indicate *what* is to be done. The post-holder will have to decide *how* the job is to be done. First and foremost the head of science is a teacher and the job description will identify the teaching duties of the post. The additional responsibilities will indicate that the head of department should provide *professional leadership* and *management* for the subject.

Figure 14.1 shows the major areas of responsibility for the head of department with a brief indication of what these entail. The roles of leader and manager become clear.

SOURCES OF INFORMATION AND SUPPORT

You should not see yourself as working alone and without support. As well as school and university staff who can help and advise you on matters to do with teaching secondary science, there are various materials and resources that can help you in your role. What follows is a summary of those most readily available but, inevitably, the list cannot be

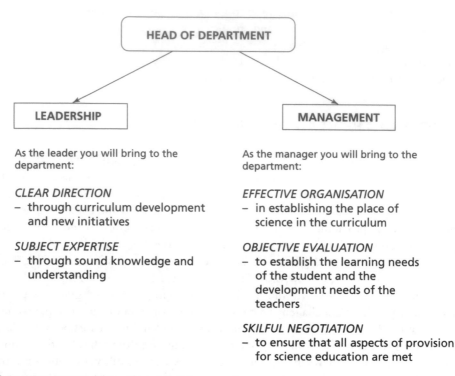

Figure 14.1 Responsibilities of a head of department

complete. Commercially produced schemes and textbooks, for example, have not been included, although we recognise that some provide very good support materials which you can use to turn ideas into reality. They also give structure to planning and assessment. Here we will list details of some support materials we feel you should be aware of. You may also come across free resources in unusual places which may help you and your colleagues. For example, many of the large superstores produce leaflets for customers which describe how they are being energy-efficient or environmentally friendly. You should also write to as many publishers, suppliers and other contacts as possible, asking to be placed on their mailing lists for catalogues and other information.

ASSOCIATIONS

While you do not have to be a member of a science group or association, you will find that this is a good way to keep informed and share ideas. The following are some examples.

Association for Science Education (ASE)

The ASE has a long history of support for science teaching in secondary schools. It publishes the *School Science Review* (*SSR*) three times a year to share ideas, usually written by teachers and other science education professionals, about the teaching of school science. It also regularly publishes *Education in Science*, the in-house magazine for disseminating information about the activities of the ASE. The ASE also produces a range of books and guidance materials for teachers, which are advertised in the *SSR* and may be purchased at a 10 per cent discount by members. The association also organises local and national meetings, and runs an advice and support system. There are different categories of membership; teachers can subscribe as individuals, or schools can take out a group subscription.

British Association for the Advancement of Science (BAAS)

The British Association aims to support and promote science at all levels. It holds an annual festival of science, open to schools, other institutions and the general public, and produces *SCAN*, a science awareness newsletter. At the school level, the BAAS supports the BAYS club scheme (British Association for Young Scientists) for 8- to 18-year-olds, organising science challenges, and awarding bronze, silver and gold level certificates. The BAAS also holds a national database of speakers on science and technology, called Talking Science Plus.

Earth Science Teachers' Association (ESTA)

The ESTA publishes journals for teachers at both primary and secondary school levels, containing ideas and information related particularly to aspects of geology, and organises in-service meetings and conferences. There are special rates for members buying rock and mineral samples, books, maps and postcards.

Consortium of Local Education Authorities for the Provision of Science Services (CLEAPSS)

There is one other organisation which you should know about: CLEAPSS. About 95 per cent of all local education authorities in England, Wales and Northern Ireland are members of CLEAPSS, and it is also possible for schools and colleges to join independently. Its aim is to support the teaching of practical science and technology through a range of publications and also the provision of in-service courses. It is particularly helpful with advice on resources and equipment, and health and safety issues. Check whether or not your own LEA is a member, and if so make sure you are on the mailing list for the publications and information.

JOURNALS AND PROFESSIONAL MAGAZINES

There are a number of journals and professional magazines which you should try to look at on a regular basis, both for ideas and to keep yourself informed. Most should be available through your local university library, although you could become a member of the organisation that produces them and then you would receive your own copy.

Education in Chemistry (EiC)

This is a professional journal for teachers, published by the Institute of Chemistry four times a year. It is aimed at secondary science teachers.

International Journal for Science Education (IJSE)

This is a leading journal, published four times a year, which brings together the latest research in science education from around the world. It should be of interest to science teachers who wish to go beyond their immediate role and to keep up with developments in science education for their own benefit.

Journal of Biological Education (JBE)

This is a professional journal for secondary science teachers, published by the Institute of Biology four times a year.

Physics Education (PE)

This is a professional journal for teachers, published by the Institute of Physics four times a year, and again, as with *EiC* and *JBE*, is aimed at secondary science teachers.

SOME SUPPLIERS

The list of possible suppliers of science resources and equipment is enormous, and some schools are restricted by their LEAs to purchasing from particular ones. However, if you do have a choice it is worth shopping around, because prices can vary tremendously. Probably the most familiar will be Griffin and Philip Harris. Some unusual ones you might look at include the following.

Insect Lore

This firm provides resources related to studying the natural world (CD-ROMs, books, videos, posters, kits, puppets, and other materials). A catalogue is available.

Northamptonshire Inspection and Advisory Service (NIAS)

The science centre provides schools with a range of resources, both kits and textual materials, to support the teaching of science in schools. Produced by advisory teams for their own schools, the materials are closely tied to the needs of schools and have often been prepared in consultation with school staff.

Pictorial Charts Educational Trust (PCET)

PCET provides wallcharts and illustrated materials to support the teaching of science; extensive range and high quality.

Small-Life Supplies

This firm supplies a range of living things for the classroom that are both easy to keep and safe to use. It also supplies cages, books, tapes, posters and foodstuffs. An illustrated talk service is also available. A catalogue is available on request.

Technology Teaching Systems (TTS)

Despite its misleading name, TTS provides a full range of resources for teaching science. A catalogue is available giving full details.

INDUSTRY, ENTERPRISE AND OTHER LINKS

Various official documents encourage schools to enhance their links with industry and business, and to maximise the value of such links.

British Kidney Patient Association

A teaching resources pack is available which includes a ten-minute video, classroom poster, teacher's guide and photocopiable sheets for use in the classroom and at home. It is aimed at 9 to 14-year-olds. The pack is free but a charge is made to cover package and postage.

British Nuclear Fuels Ltd (BNFL)

BNFL produces video materials, booklets and posters, resource packs and other materials to support school science teaching. Visits to power stations and energy centres can also be arranged with the education officers. A free catalogue is available.

The Chemical Industry Education Centre (CIEC)

The CIEC at the University of York works with teachers and industrialists to write teaching materials which make science and technology experiences explicitly relevant to primary and secondary students. Units usually contains teachers' notes, background information and photocopiable activity sheets. A catalogue is available on request.

Institution of Electrical Engineers

The Institute produces a range of resources to support school science. Topic packs and video materials focus on supporting the teaching of electricity, energy and control.

Royal Society for the Protection of Birds (RSPB)

The RSPB has a network of education officers around the country who will visit schools and give talks on topics related to birds. Teaching resource materials are also available and schools as well as individuals may apply for membership.

The School Curriculum Industry Partnership (SCIP)

SCIP is an organisation which aims to promote partnership between education and industry, and to support the education of students between the ages of 5 and 19 years.

Standing Conference on Schools' Science and Technology (SCSST)

This is the organisation which runs the SATROs (the science and technology regional organisation partnerships between education, business and industry), from which very useful resource materials may be purchased (e.g. electrical components such as bulbs and wires). Each centre usually produces its own list of supplies available to schools. SCSST also organises the CREST Awards for creativity in science and technology (with the British Association for the Advancement of Science).

Understanding British Industry (UBI)

The UBI provides information on businesses and organisations which offer information, support and links with schools. Teacher placement schemes are also included.

INTERACTIVE SCIENCE AND TECHNOLOGY CENTRES (ISTCS)

ISTCs are fashionable, being one way to take science and technology to the wider public and aimed at changing people's perceptions of and attitudes towards science and technology. Their essence is their hands-on approach, which enables sensory interaction, and interests and motivates all those involved. As with museums, a preliminary visit by the science coordinator is advisable to assess how it may be used, to make contact and see what kind of support is available during visits. There are ISTCs based in most of our large cities, and some of the more well known are listed below.

- *Discovery Dome*
  c/o Science Projects,
  Turnham Green,
  Terrace Mews,
  London W1 1QU

- *Glasgow Dome of Discovery*
  South Rotunda,
  100 Govan Road,
  Glasgow G51 1JS

- *Light on Science*
  Birmingham Museum
  of Science and Industry,
  Newhall Street,
  Birmingham B3 1RX

- *Technology Testbed*
  National Museums and Galleries
  on Merseyside,
  Large Objects Collection,
  Princes Dock,
  Pier Head,
  Liverpool L3 0AA

- *The Exploratory*
  The Old Station,
  Temple Meads,
  Bristol BS8 1QU

- *Launch Pad*
  Science Museum,
  Exhibition Road,
  London SW7 2DD

- *Science Factory*
  Newcastle Museum of
  Science and Engineering,
  Blandford Street,
  Newcastle upon Tyne NE1 4JA

- *Xperiment!*
  Greater Manchester Museum of
  Science and Industry,
  Castlefield,
  Manchester M3 4JP

HELP FROM ICT

Organisations such as the ASE and the National Council for Educational Technology (NCET – see below) provide information, publications and teaching materials. ASE runs regional meetings and conferences, often including IT in its programme. NCET produces leaflets and information packages on hardware and software. It has also commissioned a series of television programmes on the use of IT in schools.

Fifty-three local education authorities also have SEMERC centres – computer centres offering training, advice and support in all areas of computer use in school. Many of the centres also supply SEMERC software to their local schools, often at a discount. Further information and a catalogue are available.

WEBSITES

The number of websites that may be of use to you is enormous. Some websites that you may find useful include the following:

Association for Science Education:	http://www.ase.org.uk
BBC Education:	http://www.bbc.co.uk/education/schools/science.html
British Association:	http://www.britassoc.org.uk
British Library:	http://www.portico.bl.uk
Channel Four:	http://www.channel4.com/schools
Institute of Biology:	http://www.iob.org
Institute of Chemistry:	http://www.ioc.org
Institute of Physics:	http://www.iop.org
Meteorological Office:	http://www.meto.govt.uk
NCET's Science Curriculum IT Support Project:	http://www.ncet.org.uk/science/scindex.html
Natural History Museum:	http://www.nhm.ac.uk
Schools Online Science:	http://www.shu.ac.uk/schools/sci/sol/contents.html
Science and Plants for Schools at Homerton College:	http://www-saps.plantsci.cam.ac.uk
Science Consortium:	http://www.cpd4teachers.co.uk
Students' and Teachers' Educational Materials (STEM) Project at the Science Museum:	http://www.nmsi.ac.uk/education/stem
Wellcome Trust:	http://www.wellcome.ac.uk

References

Adey, P. S., Shayer, M. and Yates, C. (1995) *Thinking Science: The Curriculum Materials of the CASE Project*, London: Nelson.

Association for Science Education (ASE) (2002) *Policy Statement: Quality in Science Education*, http://www.ase.org.uk/policy/qualpolf.html

Bacon, F. (1605) 'The advancement of learning', in A.R. Hall (1954) *The Scientific Revolution 1500–1800: The Formation of the Modern Scientific Attitude*, London: Longmans Green & Co.

Baird, J.R. (1986) 'Improving learning through enhanced metacognition: a classroom study', *European Journal of Science Education*, **8**, pp. 263–282.

Barton, R. (1997) 'How do computers affect graphical interpretation?', *School Science Review*, **79** (287), pp. 55–60.

Bennett, J. (2003) *Teaching and Learning Science: A Guide to Recent Research and its Applications*, London: Continuum.

Black, P. (1993) 'The purpose of science education', in R. Hull (ed.) *ASE Secondary Science Teachers' Handbook*, Hemel Hempstead: Simon & Schuster Education.

Blagg, N., Bellinger, M. and Gardner, R. (1988) *The Somerset Thinking Skills Course*, London: Nigel Blagg Associates.

Bloom, B. (1981) *All Our Children Learning*, New York: Pergamon Press.

Borich, G.D. and Tombari, M.L. (1997) *Educational Psychology: A Contemporary Approach* (2nd edn), New York: Longman.

Boujaoude, S. (2002) 'Balance of scientific literacy themes in science curricula: the case of Lebanon', *International Journal of Science Education*, **24** (2), pp. 139–156.

Bransford, J.D. and Steen, B. (1984) *The IDEAL Problem Solver*, New York: Freeman.

Bruner, J.S. (1966) *Toward a Theory of Instruction*, New York: Norton.

Carr M., Barker, M., Bell, B., Biddulph, F., Jones, A., Kirkwood, V., Pearson, J. and Symington, D. (1994) 'The constructivist paradigm and some implications for science content and pedagogy', in P. Fensham, R.F. Gunstone and R.T. White (eds) *The Content of Science: A Constructivist Approach to its Teaching and Learning*, London: Falmer Press.

Claxton, G. (1991) *Educating the Enquiring Mind: The Challenge for School Science*, London: Harvester Wheatsheaf.

Collins, J., Hammond, M. and Wellington, J. (1997) *Teaching and Learning with Multimedia*, London, New York and Toronto: Routledge.

Conner, C. (1999) 'Two steps forward, one step back: progression in children's learning', *Primary File*, **36**, pp. 141–144.

Crook, C. (1994) *Computers and the Collaborative Experience of Learning*, London: Routledge.

Darwin, C. (1859) 'Origin of the species and by means of natural selection, or the preservation of favoured races in the struggle for life', in A. Desmond and J. Moore (1991) *Darwin*, London: Penguin Books.

Davis, N., Desforges, C., Jessel, J., Somekh, B.,Taylor, C. and Vaughan, G. (1998) 'Can quality in learning be enhanced through the use of IT?', in B. Somekh and N. Davis (eds) *Using Information Technology Effectively in Teaching and Learning*, London: Routledge.

DeHart Hurd, P. (2002) 'Modernizing science education', *Journal of Research in Science Education*, **39** (1), pp. 3–9.

Department for Education and Employment (DFEE) (1995) *Science in the National Curriculum*, London: HMSO.

Department for Education and Employment (DfEE) (1997) *[Circular 10/97] Consultation on Teaching: High Status, High Standards [Circular 4/98] Requirements for Courses of Initial Teacher Training*, London: HMSO.

Department for Education and Employment (DfEE) (1998) *Teaching: High Status, High Standards [Circular 4/98] Requirements for Courses of Initial Teacher Training*, London: HMSO.

Department for Education and Employment/Qualifications and Curriculum Authority (DfEE/QCA) (1999a) *The National Curriculum: Handbook for Secondary Teachers in England*, London: HMSO.

Department for Education and Employment/Qualifications and Curriculum Authority (DfEE/QCA) (1999b) *Science – The National Curriculum for England*, London: HMSO.

Department of Education and Science (DES) (1985) *Science 5–16: A Statement of Policy*, London: HMSO/Welsh Office.

Department of Education and Science (DES) (1989) *Science in the National Curriculum (The Orders)*, London: HMSO/Welsh Office.

Department of Education and Science (DES) (1990) *National Curriculum Orders [Circular 3/90]*, London: HMSO.

Department of Education and Science (DES) (1991) *Science in the National Curriculum (The 1991 Orders)*, London: HMSO/Welsh Office.

Department for Education and Skills (DfES) (2001) *Key Stage 3: Strategy for Strengthening Standards*, London: DfES.

Department for Education and Skills (DfES) (2002) *Key Stage 3 National Strategy, Framework for Teaching Science: Years 7,8, and 9*, London: DfES/QCA or via http//www.standards.dfes.gov.uk/keystage3/strands/publications

Department for Education and Skills (DfES) (2003) *Teaching and Learning in Secondary Schools: Pilot –Unit 10: Learning Styles*, London: DfES.

Department for Education and Skills/Teacher Training Agency (DfES/TTA) (2002a) *Qualifying to Teach: Professional Standards for Qualified Teacher Status [Circular 02/02]*, London: TTA/HMSO.

Department for Education and Skills/Teacher Training Agency (DfES/TTA) (2002b) *Handbook to Accompany the Standards for the Award of Qualified Teacher Status (QTS) and the Requirements for the Provision of Initial Teacher Training (ITT)*, London: TTA/HMSO.

Desforges, C. (1985) 'Matching tasks to children', in N. Bennett and C. Desforges (eds) *Recent Advances in Classroom Research*, Edinburgh: Scottish Academic Press.

Driver, R. (1983) *The Student as Scientist?*, Milton Keynes: Open University Press.

Driver, R., Guesne, E. and Tiberghien, A. (1985) *Children's Ideas in Science*, Milton Keynes: Open University Press.

Driver, R., Leach, J., Millar, R. and Scott, P. (1996) *Young People's Images of Science*, Milton Keynes: Open University Press.

Driver, R., Squires, A., Rushworth, P. and Wood-Robinson, V. (2000) *Making Sense of Secondary Science*, London: Routledge.

Dunne, D. (1998) 'The place of science in the curriculum', in M. Ratcliffe (ed.) *ASE Guide to Secondary Science Education*, Cheltenham: Stanley Thornes.

Edwards, D. and Mercer, N. (1987) *Common Knowledge: The Development of Understanding in the Classroom*, London: Routledge.

Fensham, P.J., Gunstone, R.F. and White, R.T. (1994) 'Science content and constructivist views of learning and teaching', In P. Fensham, R.F. Gunstone and R.T. White (eds) *The Content of Science: A Constructivist Approach to its Teaching and Learning*, London: Falmer Press.

Feynman, R. P. (1998) *The Meaning of it All*, London: Penguin Books.

Fitz-Gibbon, C.T. (1996) *Monitoring Education: Indicators, Quality and Effectiveness*, London: Cassell.

Gardner, H. (1993) *Multiple Intelligences: The Theory in Practice*, New York: Basic Books.

Gardner, J., Morrison, H. and Jarman, R. (1993) *Learning with Portable Computers*, Belfast: School of Education, Queen's University of Belfast.

Gott, R. and Duggan, S. (1995) *Investigative Work in the Science Curriculum*, Oxford: Oxford University Press.

Gott, R. and Duggan, S. (1998) 'Understanding scientific evidence – why it matters and how it can be taught', in M. Ratcliffe (ed.) *ASE Guide to Secondary Science Education*, Hatfield: ASE.

Gott, R. and Mashiter, J. (1991) 'Practical work in science – a task-based approach?', in B.E. Woolnough (ed.) *Practical Science*, Buckingham: Open University Press.

Gott, R., Duggan, S. and Johnson, P. (1999) 'What do practising applied scientists do and what are the implications for science education?', *Journal of Research in Science and Technology Education*, **17**, pp. 97–107.

Green, N.P.O., Stout, G.W. and Taylor, D.J. (1990) *Biological Science Vols 1 and 2*, Cambridge: Cambridge University Press.

Hall, A.R. (1954) *The Scientific Revolution 1500–1800: The Formation of the Modern Scientific Attitude*, London: Longmans Green & Co.

Holman, J. (1986) *Science and Technology in Society: General Guide for Teachers*, Hatfield: ASE.

Hughes, M. (ed.) (1996) *Progression in Learning*, Clevedon: Multilingual Matters.

Hurd, P. (1998) 'New minds for a changing world', *Science Education*, **82**, pp. 407–416.

Jenkins, E. (1997) 'Towards a functional public understanding of science', in R. Levison and J. Thomas (eds) *Science Today*, London: Routledge.

Job, D. (1999) *New Directions in Geographical Fieldwork*, Cambridge: Cambridge University Press.

John, P.D. (1994) 'Academic tasks in history classrooms', *Research in Education*, **51**, pp. 11–22.

Jones, M. and Gott, R. (1998) 'Cognitive acceleration through science education: alternative perspectives', *International Journal of Science Education*, **20**, pp. 755–768.

Jones, M. and Jones, G. (1997) *Biology; Cambridge Coordinated Science*, Cambridge: Cambridge University Press.

Kant, I. (1983) *Critique of Pure Reason* (3rd edn), London: Longmans.

Keiler, L.S. and Woolnough, B.E. (2002) 'Practical work in school science: the dominance of assessment', *School Science Review*, **83**, pp. 83–88.

Keogh, B. and Naylor, S. (1993) 'Progression and continuity in science', in R. Sherrington (ed.) *The ASE Primary Science Teachers' Handbook*, Hemel Hempstead: Simon & Schuster.

Kuhn, D. (1989) 'Children and adults as intuitive scientists', *Psychological Review*, **96**, pp. 674–689.

Kyriacou, C. (1997) *Effective Teaching in Schools*, London: Stanley Thornes.

Layton, D. (1973) *Science for the People*, London: Allen & Unwin.

Leach, J. (2002) 'Teachers' views on the future of the secondary science curriculum', *School Science Review*, **83**, pp. 43–50.

Letts (2002) *Science for Secondary Teachers*, London: Letts.

Lovelock, J. (1979) *Gaia – A New Look at Life on Earth*, Oxford: Oxford University Press.

McCormack, A.J. (1992) 'Trends and issues in the science curriculum', in *Science: Curriculum Resource Handbook*, New York: Kraus International Publications.

McCulloch, G. (1997) 'Teachers and the National Curriculum in England and Wales: socio-economic frameworks', in *Teachers and the National Curriculum*, London: Cassell.

McGrath, C. (1993) 'Science, technology and society', in R. Hull (ed.) *ASE Secondary Science Teachers' Handbook*, Hemel Hempstead: Simon & Schuster Education.

Mendel, G. (1865) in R.M. Henig (2000) *A Monk and Two Peas*, London: Weidenfeld & Nicolson.

Mendeleyev, D.I. (1869) in A.R. Hall (1954) *The Scientific Revolution 1500–1800: The Formation of the Modern Scientific Attitude*, London: Longmans Green & Co.

Millar, R. (1993) 'Science education and public understanding of science', in R. Hull (ed.) *ASE Secondary Science Teachers' Handbook*, Hemel Hempstead: Simon & Schuster Education.

Millar, R. (1996) 'Towards a science curriculum for public understanding', *School Science Review*, **77**, pp. 7–18.

Millar, R., Gott, R., Luben, F. and Duggan, S. (1996) 'Children's performance of investigative tasks in science. A framework for considering progression', in M. Hughes (ed.) *Progression in Learning*, Clevedon: Multilingual Matters.

Moseley, D. and Higgins, S. (1999) *Ways Forward with ICT: Effective Pedagogy Using Information and Communications Technology for Literacy and Numeracy in Primary Schools*, Newcastle: University of Newcastle School of Education – a report for the Teacher Training Agency.

Multimedia Science School (1998) New Media Press, PO Box 441, Henley-on-Thames, Oxford, http://www.new media.co.uk

National Council for Educational Technology (NCET) (1994) *Enhancing Science with IT: Classroom Activities*, Coventry: NCET (now the British Educational Communications and Technology Agency (BECTA)).

National Curriculum Council (NCC) (1989) *Non-Statutory Guidance for Science in the National Curriculum*, York: National Curriculum Council.

National Curriculum Council (NCC) (1993) *Teaching Science at KS3 and KS4*, York: National Curriculum Council.

Naylor, S. and Keogh, B. (2000) *Concept Cartoons in Science Education*, Crewe, Cheshire: Millgate House.

Newton, D.P. (1989) *Making Science Education Relevant*, London: Kogan Page.

Newton, D.P. (2000) *Teaching For Understanding: What it is and How to do it*, London: RoutledgeFalmer.

Newton, I. (1687) 'Philosophiae naturalis principia mathematica', in A.R. Hall (1954) *The Scientific Revolution 1500–1800: The Formation of the Modern Scientific Attitude*, London: Longmans Green & Co.

Newton, L. (1997) 'Graph talk: some observations and reflections on pupils' data-logging', *School Science Review*, **79** (287) pp. 49–55.

Newton, L. and Rogers, L. (2001) *Teaching Science with ICT*, London: Continuum.

Nott, M. and Wellington, J. (1999) 'The state we're in: issues in key stage 3 and 4 science', *School Science Review*, **81**, pp. 13–18.

Office for Standards in Education (OfSTED) (2001/2002) *ICT in Schools: Effect of Government Initiatives*, http//www.ofsted.gov.uk.

Osborne, R. and Freyberg, P. (1985) *Children's Learning in Science*, London: Heinemann.

Pennell, A. and Alexander, R. (1990) *The Management of Change in the Primary School – Implementing the National Curriculum for Science and Design Technology*, London: Falmer Press.

Pollard, A. (2002a) *Reflective Teaching: Effective and Evidence-informed Professional Practice* , London: Continuum.

Pollard, A. (ed.) (2002b) *Readings for Reflective Teaching*, London: Continuum.

Ponchaud, R. (1998) 'Quality in science education', in M. Ratcliffe (ed.) *ASE Guide to Secondary Science Education*, Cheltenham: Stanley Thornes.

Popper, K. (1935) 'The logic of scientific discovery', in A.R. Hall (1954) *The Scientific Revolution 1500–1800: The Formation of the Modern Scientific Attitude*, London: Longmans Green & Co.

Qualifications and Curriculum Authority (QCA) (1996) *Science: The National Curriculum for England*, London: Qualifications and Curriculum Authority.

Qualifications and Curriculum Authority (QCA) (1999) *Science: The National Curriculum for England*, London: Qualifications and Curriculum Authority.

Qualifications and Curriculum Authority (QCA) (2000) *Science: A Scheme of Work for Key Stage 3*, London: HMSO.

Qualifications and Curriculum Authority (QCA) (2002) *Changes to Assessment 2003: Sample Materials for Key Stage 3 Science*, London: Qualifications and Curriculum Authority.

Ratcliffe, M. (1998) 'The purpose of science education', in M. Ratcliffe (ed.) *ASE Guide to Secondary Science Education*, Cheltenham: Stanley Thornes.

Ratcliffe, M. (1999) 'Evaluation of abilities in interpreting media reports of scientific research', *International Journal of Science Education*, **21**, pp. 1085–1099.

Reiss, M.J. (1998) 'Science for all', in M. Ratcliffe (ed.) *ASE Guide to Secondary Science Education*, Cheltenham: Stanley Thornes.

Roberts, M. (1991) *The Living World*, Walton-on-Thames: Nelson.

Roberts, R. (2001) 'Procedural understanding in biology: the "thinking behind the doing"', *Journal of Biological Education*, **35** (3), pp. 113–117.

Roberts, R. (2004) 'Using different types of practical within a problem-solving model of science', *School Science Review*, **85** (312), pp. 113–119.

Rogers, L.T. and Wild, P. (1994) 'The use of IT in practical science – a study in three schools', *School Science Review*, **75** (273), pp. 21–28.

Rotblat J. (1999) 'A Hippocratic oath for scientists', *Science* **286**, p. 1475.

Rumelhart, D.E. (1992) 'Towards a microstructural account of human reasoning', in S. Davis, (ed.) *Connectionism: Theory and Practice*, New York: Oxford University Press.

Schools Curriculum Authority (SCA) (1997) *Making Effective Use of Key Stage 2 Assessment at Transfer between Key Stage 2 and Key Stage 3*, London: SCA.

Scott, P. (1987) *A Constructivist View of Learning and Teaching Science* (CLISP Booklet No. 1), Leeds: University of Leeds, Centre for Studies in Science and Mathematics Education.

Shamos, M. (1995) *The Myth of Scientific Literacy*, New Brunswick: Rutgers.

Shapiro, B. (1994) *What Children Bring to Light*, New York: Teachers' College Press.

Simon, S., Brown, M., Black, P. and Blondel, E. (1996) 'Progression in learning mathematics and science', in M. Hughes (ed.) *Progression in Learning*, Clevedon: Multilingual Matters.

Social Science Research Council (SSRC) (1987) *Better Science: Making it Happen*, London: Heinemann.

Somekh, B. and Davis, N. (1998) *Using Information Technology Effectively in Teaching and Learning*, London: Routledge.

Sternberg, R.J. (1989) *The Triarchic Mind*, New York: Viking Press.

Teacher Training Agency (TTA) (1998) *Teaching: A Guide to Becoming a Teacher*, London: TTA.

Teacher Training Agency (TTA) (1999) *Using Information and Communications Technology to Meet Teaching Objectives in Science: Initial Teacher Training: Secondary: Initial Teacher Training Exemplification Materials*, London:TTA

Thomas, G. and Durant, J. (1987) 'Why should we promote the public understanding of science?', *Scientific Literacy Papers*, **1**, pp. 1–14.

Vygotsky, L.S. (1987) *Thinking and Speech*, New York: Plenum Press.

Watson, D. (ed.) (1993) *The ImpacT Report: An Evaluation of the Impact of Information Technology on Children's Achievements*, London: King's College.

Watson, R. (1997) 'ASE-King's science investigations in schools project: investigations at Key Stages 2 and 3', *Education in Science*, p. 171.

Watson, R. and Wood-Robinson, V. (1998) 'Learning to investigate', in M. Ratcliffe (ed.) *ASE Guide to Secondary Science Education*, Cheltenham: Stanley Thornes.

Wellington, J.J. (ed.) (1998) *Practical Work in School Science: Which Way Now?*, London: Routledge.

Wellington, J.J. (1985) *Children, Computers and the Curriculum*, London: Harper & Row.

White, R.T. (1988) *Learning Science*, Oxford: Basil Blackwell.

White, R.T. and Gunstone, R. (1989) 'Meta-learning and conceptual change', *International Journal of Science Education*, **11**, pp. 577–586.

Williams, L.P. (1965) *Michael Faraday: A Biography*, London: Chapman and Hall.

Wittrock, M.C. (1994) 'Generative science teaching', in P. Fensham, R.F. Gunstone and R.T. White (eds) *The Content of Science: A Constructivist Approach to its Teaching and Learning*, Brighton: Falmer Press.

Wynn, C.M. and Wiggins, A.C. (1997) *The Five Biggest Ideas in Science*, New York: John Wiley & Sons.

Index